The Other Solzhenitsyn

Other works of interest from St. Augustine's Press

Philippe Bénéton, *The Kingdom Suffereth Violence:*
The Machiavelli / Erasmus / More Correspondence

Albert Camus, *Christian Metaphysics and Neoplatonism*

Peter Augustine Lawler, *Allergic to Crazy:*
Quick Thoughts on Politics, Education, and Culture

Rémi Brague, *On the God of the Christians (& on one or two others)*

Rémi Brague, *Eccentric Culture: A Theory of Western Civilization*

Edward Feser, *The Last Superstition: A Refutation of the New Atheism*

H.S. Gerdil, *The Anti-Emile: Reflections on the Theory and Practice*
of Education against the Principles of Rousseau

Gerhard Niemeyer, *The Loss and Recovery of Truth*

James V. Schall, *The Regensburg Lecture*

James V. Schall, *The Modern Age*

Pierre Manent, *Seeing Things Politically*

Josef Kleutgen, s.j., *Pre-Modern Philosophy Defended*

Marc D. Guerra, *Liberating Logos:*
Pope Benedict XVI's September Speeches

Peter Kreeft, *Summa Philosophica*

Ellis Sandoz, *Give Me Liberty:*
Studies on Constitutionalism and Philosophy

Roger Kimball, *The Fortunes of Permanence:*
Culture and Anarchy in an Age of Amnesia

George William Rutler, *Principalities and Powers:*
Spiritual Combat 1942–1943

Stanley Rosen, *Essays in Philosophy* (2 vols., *Ancient* and *Modern*)

Roger Scruton, *The Meaning of Conservatism*

René Girard, *The Theater of Envy: William Shakespeare*

Joseph Cropsey, *On Humanities Intensive Introspection*

The Other Solzhenitsyn

Telling the Truth about a Misunderstood
Writer and Thinker

By Daniel J. Mahoney

With an appendix, *The Gift of Incarnation*
by Natalia Solzhenitsyn

St. Augustine's Press
South Bend, Indiana

Manufactured in the United States of America

2 3 4 5 6   23 22 21 20 19 18 17 16

Library of Congress Cataloging in Publication Data
Mahoney, Daniel J., 1960–
The Other Solzhenitsyn: Telling the Truth about a Misunderstood
Writer and Thinker / Daniel J. Mahoney; with an appendix by
Natalia Solzhenitsyn.
pages cm
Includes index.
ISBN 978-1-58731-613-5 (hardback; alk. paper)
1. Solzhenitsyn, Aleksandr Isaevich, 1918–2008 – Criticism and
interpretation. 2. Solzhenitsyn, Aleksandr Isaevich, 1918–2008 –
Political and social views. I. Title.
PG3488.O4Z7665 2014
891.73'44 – dc23   2014009453

∞ The paper used in this publication meets the minimum requirements of
the American National Standard for Information Sciences Permanence of
Paper for Printed Materials, ANSI Z39.481984.

ST. AUGUSTINE'S PRESS
www.staugustine.net

Table of Contents

Table of Contents

FOREWORD

No writer or thinker in recent times has been subject to more misinterpretations or even calumnies than the great Russian writer Aleksandr Solzhenitsyn. His courage and tenacity are acknowledged even by his fiercest critics. Yet the world-class novelist, historian, and moral philosopher (one uses the latter term in its most capacious sense) has largely been eclipsed by a caricature particularly widespread in the Anglophone world, that has transformed a passionate but measured and self-critical patriot into a ferocious nationalist, a thoughtful partisan of grass-roots democracy into a quasi-authoritarian, a man of faith and reason into a religious zealot.

This caricature, widely dispersed in the press, and too often taken for granted, gets in the way of a thoughtful and humane confrontation with the "other" Solzhenitsyn, the true Solzhenitsyn, who is a writer and thinker of the first rank and whose spirited defense of human liberty and dignity is never divorced from moderation. It is to the recovery of *this* Solzhenitsyn, the Solzhenitsyn occluded by tendentious press reports and misrepresentations that will not go away, that this book is dedicated.

There is also a more subtle obstacle to taking Solzhenitsyn seriously. It is often repeated even by those who admire the man and have learned from his writings. It is the tendency to dismiss Solzhenitsyn as yesterday's news, someone whose writings and insights are less than relevant in a post-totalitarian age. To begin with, the new consensus rarely shows any knowledge or appreciation of the multiple writings by Solzhenitsyn that appeared in the last twenty years of his life. In addition, *The Red Wheel,*

Solzhenitsyn's great work of dramatized history tracing the events leading up to the revolution of 1917, tends to be dismissed as a failure without its critics having more than a cursory familiarity with it. It is assumed that Solzhenitsyn is forgotten in no large part because the Anglophone world, in all its insularity, has lagged far behind Russia and France in a critical engagement or appreciation of his work. It is also assumed that the lessons of totalitarianism, of the age of ideology, have little or no relevance for the present or future of the modern world. Solzhenitsyn's profound insight that Communist totalitarianism was a radicalization of the "anthropocentric humanism" at the heart of modernity is simply ignored, if not dismissed. There is a touch of self-satisfaction about this relegation of Solzhenitsyn to a past that we can comfortably leave behind.

Even a sympathetic critic such as Anthony Daniels ("Walking in Lenin's Footsteps," *The New Criterion,* November 2013, pp. 29–31) places too much emphasis on the fact that "the highest echelon of modern youth" don't know who Solzhenitsyn is. That has everything to do with an academy that pays more attention to *poseurs* and ideological extremists such as Badiou or Žižek than it does to an authentically great man, and defender of human dignity, such as Solzhenitsyn. Daniels is much too quick in denying Solzhenitsyn's "literary immortality" if not continuing relevance. Without examining his greatest works, he opines that "in retrospect Solzhenitsyn's world-renown was caused as much by his courage and political stance as by his writing." More problematically, he asserts that "his courage and his writing were tied ... to an historical and political context that now appear as ancient to young people today as that of the Medes and Persians did to us." Daniels acknowledges that Solzhenitsyn's deepest desire was "to restore mankind's awareness that the distance between good and evil runs through every human heart." But he fears that his "work was too historically specific, perhaps, to achieve this end, or even to survive beyond the reading list of specialists."

The irony is that Daniels proceeded to write a wonderfully discerning article that draws upon Solzhenitsyn's *Lenin in Zurich* in order to capture Lenin's ideological fanaticism. He rightly characterizes him as "an intelligent but brutal and domineering monomaniac who deliberately squeezed every last vestige of finer feeling from his soul, and who resorted to abuse and denigration of others ... the moment they disagreed with him in the slightest detail." Following Solzhenitsyn, Daniels captures Lenin's unbounded contempt for his contemporaries, including the "petit bourgeois" Swiss. Solzhenitsyn remains very relevant for Anthony Daniels even as he bets on the diminishing "relevance" of Solzhenitsyn in years to come.

My book, in contrast, is a bet on the continuing relevance of Solzhenitsyn. I am convinced that the immense literary and intellectual value of *One Day in the Life of Ivan Denisovich*, *Matryona's Home* and *The Gulag Archipelago* will be recognized long into the future. (It is no accident that these are the three works of Solzhenitsyn which are required reading in Russian public schools.) I am also confident that works that are less known and appreciated in the English-speaking world, *The Red Wheel* and remarkable stories such as "Ego" and "Apricot Jam" (written late in Solzhenitsyn's life), will be read for many years to come. My judgment is a bet against the insularity of the English-speaking world and a vote of confidence in the capacity of genius and what Burke called "moral imagination" to take care of themselves by winning a hearing in the public square. My examination of the "other Solzhenitsyn" is at the service of revealing the tremendous wisdom and insight to be found in the major works of Solzhenitsyn.

This book above all explores philosophical, political, and moral themes in Solzhenitsyn's two masterworks, *The Gulag Archipelago* and *The Red Wheel*, as well as in his great "European novel" (the phrase is Georges Nivat's) *In the First Circle*. We see Solzhenitsyn as analyst of revolution, defender of the moral law, phenomenologist of ideological despotism, and advocate of "resisting evil with force." Other chapters carefully explore Solzhenitsyn's conception of patriotism, his dissection of ideological mendacity, and his controversial, but thoughtful and humane discussion of the "Jewish Question" in the Russian—and Soviet—twentieth century. Some of Solzhenitsyn's later writings, such as the "binary tales" that he wrote in the 1990s, are subject to critically appreciative analysis. And a long final chapter comments on Solzhenitsyn's July 2007 *Der Spiegel* interview, his final word to Russia and the West. He is revealed to be a man of faith and freedom, a patriot but not a nationalist, and a principled advocate of self-government for Russia and the West.

A final Appendix reproduces the beautiful Introduction ("The Gift of Incarnation") that the author's widow, Natalia Solzhenitsyn, wrote to the 2009 Russian abridgement of *The Gulag Archipelago*, a work that is now taught in Russian high schools. I am grateful to Mrs. Solzhenitsyn for giving permission to publish the translation of her text in this volume.

Chapter one appears in English for the first time in its present form. Chapters three, five, and nine appear in this book for the first time. Chapter eight is a much expanded version of a review that originally appeared in *National Review*. I am grateful to *Transactions of the Association of Russian-American Scholars in the U.S.A.*, *Rivista di politica*, *First Things*, *Academic Questions* and *Society* for permission to reprint (sometimes in significantly revised form) material that originally appeared in the pages of those journals.

No book is a solitary affair. Friendship is at the heart of the intellectual life. I am grateful to Paul Seaton and Marc Guerra for their expert help in editing this work and for their friendship over the years. Philippe Bénéton, Pierre Manent, and Giulio de Ligio are precious interlocutors whose comments and engagement in this work are much appreciated. Nalin Ranasinghe and Daniel Maher have been wonderful colleagues and interlocutors about Solzhenitsyn and a host of other matters. Alexis Klimoff and Edward E. Ericson, Jr. are friends and superb Solzhenitsyn scholars who have shared everything they know about Solzhenitsyn over the years. The book literally could not have been written without them. I am also grateful to Ignat and Stephan Solzhenitsyn who have given me steady and even enthusiastic encouragement over the years while scrupulously respecting my independence as a scholar. Carmella Murphy and Gabrielle Maher have provided important technical help. Bruce Fingerhut is that rare editor-publisher who genuinely cares about ideas and who shares my admiration for Solzhenitsyn. I am grateful to him for his dedication to the book. Last but not least, I am happy to express once again my gratitude to Ingrid Gregg and the Earhart Foundation for their generous support over the years.

Daniel J. Mahoney
Worcester, Massachusetts
December 6, 2013

Chapter 1

AN ANGUISHED LOVE OF COUNTRY:
SOLZHENITSYN'S PARADOXICAL MIDDLE PATH

Aleksandr Solzhenitsyn (1918–2008) was one of the monumental figures of the twentieth century. He was that rare writer whose work not only addressed "eternal" questions—questions about the human soul and the meaning of human existence—but whose life and writings had a truly dramatic impact on the century. The seemingly miraculous publication of *One Day in the Life of Ivan Denisovich* in the Soviet Union in November 1962, that "sliver in the throat of power" as one scholar suggestively called it,[1] catapulted this obscure former *zek* and provincial teacher on to the world stage where he would remain until his death in August of 2008. *The Gulag Archipelago*, his monumental three-volume "experiment in literary investigation" did more than any other piece of writing or political act in the twentieth century to delegitimize the Communist enterprise. Solzhenitsyn was, as the distinguished Swiss Slavist and Solzhenitsyn scholar Georges Nivat has put it, the Homer of the subterranean world inhabited by the *zeks*, a world of camps, repression and death, but also of spiritual renewal that he famously named "the gulag archipelago."[2]

1   Dariusz Tolczyk, *See No Evil: Literary Cover-ups & Discoveries of the Soviet Camp Experience* (New Haven, CN: Yale University Press, 1999), pp. 253–310.
2   Georges Nivat, *Le phénomène Soljénitsyne* (Paris: Fayard, 2009), pp. 240–41.

The Ideological Deformation of Reality

Solzhenitsyn's target in the magisterial work of that same name was above all *ideology*—the utopian illusion that human nature and society could be remade at a stroke. Ideologies such as Marxism-Leninism and National Socialism were perverse social doctrines that gave "evil-doing its long sought justification and ... the evildoer the necessary steadfastness and determination" to impose his willful designs on recalcitrant human nature. It was "thanks to *ideology*" that "the twentieth century was fated to experience evildoing on a scale calculated in the millions."[3] In his *Letter to the Soviet Leaders* (1973), Solzhenitsyn urged the Soviet leadership to repudiate the "antiquated legacy of the Progressive Doctrine that endowed you with all the millstones that are dragging you down."[4] In addition to the legacy of the camps and violence engendered by Marxist-Leninist ideology, these included collectivization, the nationalization of even small trades and services, and the "senseless and self-defeating"[5] persecution of religious believers. The repudiation of the ideological foundations of Soviet rule would allow "breathing and consciousness" to return to all those peoples, Russians included, who had been ground down by Communist totalitarianism. It would be the crucial *first step* in the recovery of a normal national and civic life.

Solzhenitsyn never lost sight of what was entailed in the ideological deformation of reality. But as Nivat has also remarked, "night" ("nuit") is never Solzhenitsyn's final word in addressing the nature and destiny of man.[6] For all his experience of the dark depths of the twentieth century, he never lost confidence in the

---

3   These memorable quotations are from the chapter on "The Bluecaps" in *The Gulag Archipelago*, vol. 1, translated by Thomas P. Whitney (New York: Harper Perennial Classics, 2007), p. 174.
4   See the section entitled "Ideology" in *Letter to the Soviet Leaders* in Aleksandr I. Solzhenitsyn, *East and West* (Harper &Row Perennial Library, 1980), p. 122.
5   *Ibid.*, p. 123.
6   Nivat, *Le Phénomène Soljénitsyne*, pp. 420–21.

primacy of the Good. Paradoxically, the camps had taught him essential truths about human nature and the human soul, as well as providing powerful impetus to his desire to expose the ideological "Lie" for the chimera that it was. In the famous words of 1 *Corinthians* 15 that Solzhenitsyn quoted at the beginning of "The Soul and Barbed Wire," the crucial middle section of *The Gulag Archipelago*, the camps had shown him a "mystery": self-knowledge and spiritual ascent were possible even amidst the degradation of Bolshevik prisons and labor camps. Solzhenitsyn, however, did not rest content with a passive or merely "spiritual" response to totalitarian repression. An ideological despotism of the Soviet type did so much damage to the moral and spiritual integrity of most ordinary human beings, it abolished the "liberty" that was commonplace even under run-of-the-mill authoritarian rule, that it was imperative to resist it. One must do so out of self-respect and in defense of the dignity of human beings who were are made in "the image and likeness of God." There is a spirited aspect to his response to ideocracy.

Recovering Truth and Memory

Solzhenitsyn the writer and fighter was led to become a historian, searching to recover the truth about the origins of the Soviet tragedy in the revolutions of 1917. More broadly, Solzhenitsyn reflected on those constructive paths that Russia might have taken that would have allowed her to escape ideological contagion; these would have combined the best of her national and cultural traditions with a regime of civic and political liberty. Solzhenitsyn first conceived what became *The Red Wheel*, his other masterwork and the central project of his life, as a young Marxist in 1936. His arrest in February 1945, and the years in prison, camp, and exile that followed, profoundly transformed the way he conceived this great multivolume historical novel and work of dramatized history. *The Red Wheel* and *The Gulag Archipelago* would henceforth form a diptych: The revolutionary upheavals that Pyotr Stolypin, the Prime Minister of Russia from 1906 until his assassination in

1911 and the last great figure of the Russian old regime, did everything to avoid, paved the way for a regime that would make ideological "counterselection," the destruction of everything bright, noble, energetic and distinctive in human nature, its animating principle. To remain faithful to those who perished during the Red Terror, in the camps, or as a result of forced collectivization, it was necessary to recover the full historical memory of Russia. In particular, Solzhenitsyn set out to expose the lie that the Bolshevik revolution (and its proximate cause, the anarchy-inducing February revolution of 1917) were "necessary" events at the service of liberty and human emancipation.

A False Consensus

However, instead of coming to terms with the remarkable riches contained in the two great "literary cathedrals" (the evocative phrase is Nivat's) that dominate the Solzhenitsynian universe, Western commentators have long been obsessed with the Russian writer's alleged penchant for authoritarianism, Slavophilism, nationalism and pan-Slavism. One American scholar writes of Solzhenitsyn's "categorical opposition to democracy"[7] despite the fact that Solzhenitsyn made the advocacy of the "democracy of small spaces" the principal political theme in his writing during the last twenty-five years of his life! Writing in the left-liberal London newspaper *The Guardian* the day after Solzhenitsyn's death, William Harrison claimed that Solzhenitsyn's "historical writing is imbued with a hankering after an idealized Tsarist era when, seemingly, everything was rosy."[8] He accused him of being an imperialist and succumbing to pan-Slavist illusions. But if one opens almost any page of Solzhenitsyn's 1994 essay *"The Russian*

---

7   Jay Bergman, *Meeting the Demands of Reason: The Life and Thought of Andrei Sakharov* (Ithaca, NY: Cornell University Press, 2009), p. 214.

8   William Harrison, "The Other Solzhenitsyn," *The Guardian*, August 4, 2008.

Question" at the End of Twentieth Century one finds Solzhenitsyn attacking the cruelties and injustice of serfdom, faulting Tsarist authorities for their blindness about the need for political liberty in Russia, and for their wasting of the nation's strength in unnecessary and counterproductive foreign adventures. Moreover, he attacks pan-Slavism, the idea that Russia had a mission to unite Slavic peoples and to come to the defense of the Orthodox wherever they were under threat, as a "wretched idea."[9]

In that essay, Solzhenitsyn unequivocally states that the Soviet Empire was both "unnecessary and "ruinous" (*RQ*, 88) for the Russian people. He reiterates a central point he had already made in his *Letter to the Soviet Leaders*: "The aims of a great empire and the moral health of the people are incompatible" (*RQ*, 88–89). If Solzhenitsyn later expressed deep forebodings for the fate of twenty-five million Russians who were left to fend for themselves in the "near abroad" without the support and solidarity of their compatriots after the break-up of the Soviet Union in 1991, his critics dishonestly see in this concern a hankering after the restoration of the Tsarist or Soviet empire. But that is a path Solzhenitsyn adamantly rejected.

In nearly every account of Solzhenitsyn, even sympathetic ones, he is presented as a "Slavophile" who romanticized the Russian past and who categorically rejected the liberal

9   Aleksandr Solzhenitsyn, *"The Russian Question" at the End of the Twentieth Century*, translated and annotated by Yermolai Solzhenitsyn (New York: Farrar, Straus and Giroux, 1995), p. 59. All subsequent quotations from this work will be cited parenthetically in the body of the text as *RQ*, followed by the page number in the 1995 English-language edition. The Russian original of this work first appeared in *Novy mir*, 1994, no. 7.

10 In *"The Russian Question"* and in the first volumes of *The Red Wheel*, especially *August 1914* and *November 1916*, Solzhenitsyn criticizes the faith that Slavophiles placed in the moral purity of the *obshchina* (also known as the *mir*) or peasant commune. In those works, he lauded the bet that Pyotr Stolypin had placed on "the path of free development for the most energetic, healthy and industrious

tradition.[10] Even those who acknowledge his status as an anti-totalitarian titan often succumb to this misplaced consensus that has developed about the great Russian writer. Some go so far as to say that "sa grandeur et ses idées appartiennent au passé," as Nicolas Weill rather crudely put it in *Le Monde* a week or two after Solzhenitsyn's death.[11] Harrison and Weill both seem to fear that readers who spend time with Solzhenitsyn will be unknowingly contaminated by a radical nationalism that is said to have informed every aspect of his historical vision. The fact that Solzhenitsyn categorically rejected such nationalism as incompatible with Christianity and true patriotism is not allowed to get in the way of a consensus that is as perverse as it is unfounded.

Even a cursory engagement with Solzhenitsyn's literary works and public statements makes clear that the critical commentary on the Russian writer is rife with misunderstandings and misrepresentations. Indeed, it is hard to think of another literary or intellectual figure of consequence whose thought has been so widely misunderstood. There are numerous factors that help explain what I have in the past not hesitated to called the "traducing" of Solzhenitsyn.[12] Anti-anti-Communism, suspicion of religion as a backward-looking or reactionary force, the assumption that patriotism is coextensive with destructive nationalism, a refusal to listen to a critique of "current modernity" (as Solzhenitsyn suggestively called it) if it does not come from the Left, and hostility to "eternal Russia" as being essentially imperialistic and despotic, undoubtedly all play a role.

But the sympathetic commentator is obliged to ask whether Solzhenitsyn himself bears *some* responsibility for these misunderstandings. The answer, we shall argue, is a qualified yes. But even

peasants." See p. 58 of *"The Russian Question"* as well as the treatment of Stolypin in chapter 65 of the augmented edition of *August 1914*.

11 Nicolas Weill, "Soljenitsyne, un 'héros inquiétant'" in *Le Monde*, August 16, 2008.
12 See Daniel J. Mahoney, "Traducing Solzhenitsyn" in *First Things*, August/September 2004, pp. 14–17.

if Solzhenitsyn had calibrated his positions with the greatest precision, his unforced melding of political moderation with a passionate if critical love of country was bound to be misunderstood by what the French Catholic poet and philosopher Charles Péguy called "the intellectual party,"[13] those who specialize in sneering at both heroes and saints and who delight in undermining liberty in the name of "liberation."

A "Lucid" Love of Country

It might be said that the intellectual party is constitutionally incapable of distinguishing, as Solzhenitsyn did, between a "clean, loving constructive (Russian) patriotism" and a "radical nationalist bent" that elevates "one's nationality above our higher spiritual plank, above our humble stance toward Heaven."[14] Solzhenitsyn lamented the absence of a strong Russian "national consciousness" even as he criticized those who reduced being Russian to a matter of blood or race or who preferred a "small-minded alliance with our Communist destroyers."[15] He was the most forceful critic of the "Red-Brown" alliance and of the National Bolshevik temptation to conflate all things Russian and Soviet and to celebrate them indiscriminately.[16] His was indeed a "lucid" love of country, as the great Russian-American Orthodox theologian Alexander Schmemann eloquently put it in a seminal article from

13 Charles Péguy, *Notre jeunesse, precede par De la raison* (Folio/Gallimard, 1993), pp. 102–3, 130. *Notre jeunesse* (*Our Youth*) was originally published in 1910.

14 See the remarkable discussion of patriotism in chapters 26 and 27 of *Russia in Collapse* (*Rossiia v obvale*, 1998). See the excerpts from that work in Edward E. Ericson, Jr. and Daniel J. Mahoney, eds., *The Solzhenitsyn Reader: New and Essential Writings, 1947–2005*, pp. 464–84, p. 475 for the quotations.

15 *Ibid.*, p. 475.

16 See the lucid discussion of National Bolshevism in John B. Dunlop, *The Faces of Contemporary Russian Nationalism* (Princeton, NJ: Princeton University Press, 1983), pp. 254–65.

the early 1970s, "a lucid, seeing love ... in which love is purified by clear vision of illusion, partiality, and blindness; in which vision is deepened and cleansed by love and enabled to see all the truth, rather than those pieces which pass for truth among idol worshipers of all types."[17]

So what precisely does Solzhenitsyn mean when he evokes the importance of patriotism and a healthy, self-critical "national consciousness"? One of his most compelling discussions of the nature of patriotism occurs in the final pages of *"The Russian Question" at the End of the Twentieth Century*, a work written in the months before his return to his native Russia in May 1994 after twenty years of forced exile. Here, Solzhenitsyn identifies nationality not with *blood* but with "a *spirit*, a *consciousness*, a person's orientation of preferences" (*RQ*, 102). All those who identify with and draw inspiration from the millennia-old Russian spirit and culture are for Solzhenitsyn *Russians*. There is nothing biological or racialist about Solzhenitsyn's understanding of what it means to belong to a people, to identify with its suffering, or to work to shape its future in directions worthy of man.

In these pages from *"The Russian Question,"* Solzhenitsyn expresses frustration that patriotic sentiment in the peripheral former republics of the Soviet Union is generally considered to be a "progressive'" force while Russian patriotism is too often identified with "chauvinism," "bellicose nationalism," and even fascism (*RQ*, 102). Solzhenitsyn in no way denies that nationalism can take immoderate and irresponsible forms. This is all the more reason why it is necessary to distinguish authentic patriotism from a radical nationalism that risks hijacking and distorting the Russian national consciousness that was in the painful process of rebirth. This consciousness had been brutally repressed by the anti-national ideology which was Marxism-Leninism and was then mutilated

17 See Alexander Schmemann, "A Lucid Love," translated by Serge Schmemann, in John B. Dunlop, Richard Haugh, and Alexis Klimoff eds., *Aleksandr Solzhenitsyn: Critical Essays and Documentary Materials*, second edition (New York: Collier Books, 1975), pp. 382–92, p. 388 for the quotation.

beyond all recognition by "Great Soviet patriotism," with its cult of the state, its uncritical support for Communist ideology, and its whitewashing of Stalin's role in leaving the USSR criminally unprepared for the Second World War and his reckless disregard for human life in the fighting of the war.

In rehabilitating a "clean, honest" patriotism, Solzhenitsyn returns to the definition of patriotism he had provided in his seminal 1973 essay "Repentance and Self-Limitation as Categories in the Life of Nations." That essay is one of three that Solzhenitsyn contributed to the Christian, patriotic, and anti-totalitarian manifesto *From Under the Rubble* (1974), a profound work of intellectual and moral recovery that anticipated all the deleterious consequences of an unthinking descent from the icy cliffs of totalitarianism.[18] The contributors to that volume aimed to show how political liberty could be judiciously and fruitfully melded with Russia's distinctive cultural and spiritual traditions. Solzhenitsyn always considered "Repentance and Self-Limitation" to be "one of his most important articles, expressing one of (his) key thoughts."[19] Writing twenty years later, Solzhenitsyn saw "no need to alter" that essay's definition of patriotism. It reads like a confession of Solzhenitsyn's political faith:

> Patriotism means unqualified and unswerving love
> for the nation, which implies not uncritical eagerness to

18 *From Under the Rubble* (*Iz pod glyb*) included essays by Solzhenitsyn and five like-minded colleagues who shared his broad vision for the future of Russia. An American edition, translated by a team led by Michael Scammell, was released by Little Brown in 1975. "Repentance and Self-Limitation" can be found on pp. 105–43 of that edition and on pp. 527–55 of *The Solzhenitsyn Reader*. See Daniel J. Mahoney, *Aleksandr Solzhenitsyn: The Ascent From Ideology* (Rowman & Littlefield, 2001), pp. 99–134, for an extended critical commentary on "Repentance and Self-Limitation."

19 Solzhenitsyn made this comment in an interview with his biographer Joseph Pearce in 1998. See Pearce, *Solzhenitsyn: A Soul in Exile* (Grand Rapids, MI: Baker Books, 2001), p. 209.

serve, not support for unjust claims, but frank assessment of its vices and sins. (quoted in *RQ*, 102)

An Exacting Patriotism

Solzhenitsyn conceded that his discussion of 400 years of Russian history in his 1994 essay "might appear monstrously pessimistic" (*RQ*, 103). That essay, and his writings more generally, are indeed filled with unequivocal criticisms of the cruelties of both the Petrine and Communist states, forceful chastisements of the Orthodox Church for its role in the persecution of Old Believers and its collaboration with a murderous atheistic state, and denunciations of the Soviet Union for the cruel massacre of the Polish military and political elite in the Katyn Forest and the refusal to aid the Warsaw uprising in the fall of 1944. These strongly worded judgments show that Solzhenitsyn did not honor this conception of patriotism in the breach. His understanding of patriotism requires both moderation or self-restraint and a willingness to repent for sins and crimes that violate the moral law and the legitimate claims of others. This exacting patriotism was both a right and obligation, one that enjoined respect for the legitimate self-affirmation of other peoples. At the same time, the Russian writer and historian demanded the same right for Russia and Russians, a people who had been subject to decades of vicious Bolshevik "counterselection," the deliberate targeting "of all that was bright, remarkable, of a higher level"[20] in human nature and the old Russian order.

In both *"The Russian Question" at the End of the Twentieth Century* and *Russia in Collapse* (1998) Solzhenitsyn firmly differentiated his model of patriotism from the faux patriots who leaned on Communism for support and those who raised "the ghosts of pan-Slavism, so baneful for Russia over the centuries, and entirely beyond our strength today" (*RQ*, 103). At the same

---

20 See chapter 30 of *Russia in Collapse* in *The Solzhenitsyn Reader*, p. 477.

time, he directed his ire at those who condemned Russia *tout court*, whose penitential impulses were indistinguishable from self-hatred and a contempt for the nation as such. In *"The Russian Question"* Solzhenitsyn cites a passage from the great Russian theologian-philosopher Sergei Bulgakov (1871–1944) which provides further essential insight into Solzhenitsyn's own self-understanding:

> Those whose hearts bled with pain for their motherland were at the same time her forthright exposers. But it is only an anguished love that gives the right for this national self-castigation; yet where it does not exist ... defamation of one's country, mockery of one's mother ... elicits feelings of disgust ... (quoted in *RQ*, 103)

Solzhenitsyn poignantly adds that he "writes here with this understanding and with this right." Everything in Solzhenitsyn's life and corpus supports this judgment.

A War on Two Fronts

Let us turn now to a capital discussion in Solzhenitsyn's memoir of his years of Western exile, *The Little Grain Between the Millstones*,[21] to see how Solzhenitsyn navigated this middle way

---

21 *Ugodilo zërnyshko promezh dvukh zhernovov (The Little Grain Landed Smack Between Two Millstones)* was published in seven installments in *Novy Mir* between 1998 and 2003. A book edition is scheduled to appear in the thirty-volume "Collected Works" of Solzhenitsyn that is in the process of being published by the Moscow publishing house "Vremia." Throughout, I have consulted the two volumes of *Le grain tombé entre les meules* published by the Parisian publisher Fayard in 1998 and 2005, respectively. See Edward E. Ericson, Jr. and Alexis Klimoff, *The Soul and Barbed Wire: An Introduction to Solzhenitsyn* (Wilmington, Delaware: ISI Books, 2008), pp. 143–46, for an excellent discussion of some of the highlights of the work as well as the significance of its proverb-inspired title.

between the anti-patriotism and self-loathing of the intellectual party (those who hated Russia much more than they disliked the Soviet Union) and the delusions of radical nationalism, with its "pagan" and racialist perversion of patriotism and with its willingness to accommodate the "lie" of Communist ideology. This intransigent double "No" to those who sever freedom from love of country and to those who recognize nothing above the self-assertion of the nation defined the theoretical and practical position of Solzhenitsyn during the last forty years of his life. This double refusal helps explain why Solzhenitsyn was equally despised by (some) secularist liberals who accused him of "extreme nationalism" and by extreme nationalists who deplored his moderation and his unremitting rejection of Communism and all its works. There is absolutely no evidence to support the "developmental" reading of Solzhenitsyn, the widely held position that the Russian writer's views somehow grew more rigid, more narrowly nationalistic and authoritarian, in the last thirty or forty years of his life. Nonetheless, Solzhenitsyn's prudential judgments evolved in light of changing circumstances, and sometimes dramatically so.

In a particularly significant chapter ("Russkaia bol'," "Russian Anguish") of *The Little Grain Between the Millstones: Sketches of Life in Exile* Solzhenitsyn shows how his views on the enemies he confronted changed dramatically through the course of the 1970s.[22] Solzhenitsyn's eyes gradually opened to the fact that he was now fighting a war on two fronts. Until the early 1970s, Solzhenitsyn had single-mindedly focused on Communism as "the absolute enemy." He had not seriously envisioned the possibility of the crumbling of a united "anti-Bolshevik front." He had focused *all* his attention on the

22 The chapter entitled "Russkaia bol'" ("Russian Anguish") appeared in *Novy Mir*, 2000, no. 9, pp. 112–53. I have consulted the French version of that chapter, "La douleur russe," in Soljénitsyne, *Esquisses d'exil: Le grain tombé entre les meules, 1979–1994* (Paris: Fayard, 2005), pp. 9–115. The quotations from that chapter in this article are all drawn from pp. 73–79 of that edition.

liberation of his country from the inhuman regime that had held it captive for over a half century. The turning point for Solzhenitsyn was the publication of *August 1914* in the West and in *samizdat* (underground self-publishing) in 1971. That novel was openly patriotic, sympathetic to religion, and bereft of any socialist sympathies or leanings. It met a ferocious response from the official Communist press as well as from the "National Bolsheviks" associated with the samizdat journal *Veche*.[23] The only kind of patriotism that was acceptable to the regime or to those whose patriotism had a crimson Soviet hue was one that genuflected before the Communist "Lie." And the "smatterers" (the *obrazovanshchina*, "la tribu instruite") as Solzhenitsyn called them, the demi-educated Soviet intelligentsia that he would lambast in *From Under the Rubble* were addicted to politically correct clichés and had no time for any kind of patriotic or religious affirmation.[24]

The hostile reception that his *Letter to the Soviet Leaders* received from left-liberals in both Russia and the West "continued to open (his) eyes." Solzhenitsyn was now convinced that the intellectual party "had set about masticating everything that bore the name of Russia." Russian emigrés and Western journalists directed their ire at the rebirth of Russian national consciousness which they associated without any nuance or qualification with extremist nationalism and anti-Semitism. Some emigré intellectuals even made clear their preference for the stability provided by a Soviet empire which was said to have largely made its peace with human nature and the international community. In their eyes, the real danger came from a resurgent

---

23 *Veche* was a patriotic *samizdat* journal with decidedly "National Bolshevik" leanings. Eleven issues were produced between 1971 and 1974 before it was ruthlessly suppressed by the Soviet regime. As John B. Dunlop comments (p. 233) in *The Faces of Contemporary Russian Nationalism*, some of its contributors believed "one could have both Lenin *and* Dostoevski as mentors."

24 See Solzhenitsyn's "The Smatterers" in *From Under the Rubble* (Boston: Little, Brown and Company, 1975), pp. 229–78.

Russian nationalism, one that was given added prestige by the moral authority of Solzhenitsyn. Solzhenitsyn's old friend Efim Etkind did not hesitate to call him a "Russian Ayatollah" and the Paris-based dissident Andrei Sinyavski inaugurated a twenty-year campaign against Solzhenitsyn's alleged indulgence of nationalism, authoritarianism, and Orthodox obscurantism.[25] It is in this atmosphere that Solzhenitsyn wrote a note to himself, dated June 28, 1979, that clarified the new situation he faced. This note is of such importance for understanding Solzhenitsyn's evaluation of the situation he confronted during the years of his Western exile that it is necessary to quote it in its entirety:

> Little by little, during the course of the years, toward 1977–1979, I perceived the true meaning of my new situation, as well as my new mission: to defend foot by foot the integrity of Russian history and the paths to the future for Russia. Added to my constant enemies, the Soviets, is the hostility of the pseudo-educated public of both the East and West, as well as, one must say it—even more powerful circles. This is why even here in America I am not truly at liberty but once again in a cage. My liberty (here) is to not fear house searches and to be able to write everything I wish and to keep it in reserve, but people even snort at publishing the *Knots* (of *The Red Wheel*).

25 Sinyavsky penned a particularly vitriolic attack on Solzhenitsyn in the *New York Review of Books* in November 1979 ("The Dangers of Solzhenitsyn's Nationalism"). In his forceful response to Etkind's playing of "the Persian trick," his insidious suggestion that Solzhenitsyn wanted new Ayatollahs and new gulags, Solzhenitsyn noted that his critics ascribe to him ideas and sentiments which he has "never expressed and never published, and which bear no resemblance to those I truly hold." See Solzhenitsyn, "I am no Russian Ayatollah" in *Encounter*, February 1980, pp. 34–35.

A New Mission

Solzhenitsyn does not use the word "mission" lightly. It is the same word he used to describe his obligation to tell the truth about those who perished in the camps or who otherwise were victims of Bolshevik repression. It is the same word he used to describe his commitment to recovering the authentic history of Russia and to chronicling how the seemingly inexorable "Red Wheel" might have been stopped in the first place. The defense of the honor or integrity of Russia, and the recovery of the vital distinction between things Russian and Soviet, so central to Solzhenitsyn's historical writings and public interventions in his later years, also stemmed from a deeply felt sense of mission. But as we have suggested, this mission was fully compatible with that lucid, non-ideological love of country which Father Alexander Schmemann so memorably articulated in the early 1970s.

Writing this chapter of *The Little Grain* in 1982, Solzhenitsyn remarks that "three years have passed and I can repeat it (the note of June 28, 1979) almost word for word." This third "mission" would inform all of the Russian writer and historian's activities to the day he died in August 2008. It took on an importance that matches his two other great missions. He became the self-appointed scourge of Russophobes, even as he continued to call on his compatriots to confront the full truth about the Soviet past, to repent for the crimes of the Communist period, and to resist all nostalgia for "Great Soviet patriotism." In the 1982 text, Solzhenitsyn declares that "to ally with the Communists, the tormentors of our country, was out of the question." His rejection of National Bolshevism was a *non possum* that set him apart from those "patriots" who did not hesitate "to turn towards the red-crimson sun," happily identifying and allying with those who during the seventy years of Bolshevik rule murdered and persecuted patriots and believers with impunity. At the same time, Solzhenitsyn categorically refused "to ally with the enemies of our country." He must take on those who blame everything on "eternal Russia" which they see as "rotten and incorrigible" to the core, "the skunk at the picnic of the world." He was, he confessed, caught between "two millstones." In light of his new situation, he strove to find new ways to maneuver. At the same time, he asked how this lamentable situation had come to be and he freely acknowledged that Russia was in no small part the victim of self-inflicted wounds.

Self-Inflicted Wounds

Solzhenitsyn always insisted that the blindness and inaction of the Russian state and state authorities in the years before the revolution had prepared the way for this near universal enmity directed against Russia. To be sure, foreign visitors to Russia had painted a false picture of a menacing, invincible "Asiatic despotism" on Russian soil. These "cock and bull stories" had contributed to and reinforced the "specter" of an alien Russia that threatened the entire civilized world. But it was the Russian authorities under Elizabeth, Catherine the Great, Paul, Alexander I, and Nicholas I who had pursued "immoderate military actions" accompanied by "stupid bravado and even mercenary motives." Solzhenitsyn also comments on the "insouciance" of Tsarist rule which for a century before the revolutions of 1917 "hovered up above in the empyrean without drawing any lessons from the *public life* that had developed in the entire civilized world." Moreover, it refused to condescend to explain its actions: "Why should it have to justify itself," Solzhenitsyn adds sarcastically. The Russian writer defends a vision of Russia that is in some important respects "apart in the domains of faith, traditions, and mode of life." But in Solzhenitsyn's view, Russia had much to learn from the political liberty of the western world, especially the accountability of public officials before the considered judgment of civil society (that "society" must, however, be mature and responsible which Russian "society" most assuredly was not in the half century before the Bolshevik Revolution). Solzhenitsyn admired the West's "historically unique stability of civic life under the rule of law—a hard-won stability which grants independence and space to every private citizen," as he put it in his 1993 Lichtenstein address.[26] Those who say that Solzhenitsyn categorically rejected democracy and the Western political tradition in the name of an utterly self-sufficient Russian tradition are imposing a "Slavophile" grid on him that is completely alien to his political reflection.

The Pathologies of the Russian Right

This mixture of self-inflicted wounds at home and egregious accusations from abroad "stuck and accumulated, like strata superimposed upon each other." When the Bolsheviks began their systematic assault on everything associated with the old Russian order, Western public opinion "remained confounded," unable to distinguish the Bolshevik destroyers of Russia from the country that lay prostrate at their feet. This confusion has continued to color Western perceptions of Russia to this day. But Solzhenitsyn does not respond to Russia's suffering or affliction by turning a blind eye to the pathologies that afflicted nationalist currents in Russia in the years before 1917 and that continue to afflict Russian nationalism to this day. He speaks of the "doltishness and inexperience" of the prerevolutionary political journalists on the right who substituted insults for reasoned arguments and who were convinced that "their little closed group possessed a monopoly on the truth." Anyone who thought differently was considered a "traitor, an enemy of Russia." They hated Stolypin, "the savior of Russia," with particular vehemence. These extreme nationalists were, and remain, an example to be avoided.

Yet "all the nationalists—the moderate as well as the extreme—were crushed by the Soviet steamroller." When Russian national consciousness began to reassert itself in the 1960s and '70s, it did so under the vigilant eye of the guardians of Soviet

26 See "We have ceased to see the Purpose," Address to the International Academy of Philosophy, Liechtenstein, September 14, 1993 in *The Solzhenitsyn Reader*, pp. 591–601, p. 599 for the quotation.

power. Too many "patriots" expressed sympathy for the authority and historical achievements of the very regime which was committed to destroying them. They praised the Soviet Union for restoring the Russia empire, justified the cruelties of collectivization in the name of the "fraternal traditions" of the Russian peasantry, and denied that ideology had anything to do with the exercise of Soviet power. "Out of weakness," Solzhenitsyn writes, Russian nationalism "condemned itself to turn into National Bolshevism." It is the National Bolsheviks, the "commie patriots" as Solzhenitsyn once called them,[27] who were in large part responsible for the word "Russian" taking on such "a turgid, debased alloy."

But Solzhenitsyn also directed his ire at those "pagan" currents of nationalism which rejected Christianity because it was said to weaken strength or virility, because of its historical and theological links to Judaism, or because they awaited a new belief coming from Asia that would reinvigorate Russian spirit and willpower (what in subsequent years became known as "Eurasianism," an anti-Christian nationalist ideology with pronounced "geopolitical" pretensions).[28] Once again Solzhenitsyn cited the wise words of Sergei Bulgakov, who had responded to comparable currents in the years before the Revolution: "A great nation cannot find a solid foundation only in the national principle." Adamantly rejecting this "denial of memory," this "new paganism" as something that would subvert Russian national consciousness, Solzhenitsyn expressed yet again his preference for a humane, constructive nationalism. Such a moderate nationalism would reject the temptation of vengeance and hatred and would aim to produce "elevated souls" who would not replicate the vices (the blaring voices, the resort to ridicule, the ideological poses) so typical of the patriotic party in the years before the Revolution.

27 Solzhenitsyn, *The Oak and the Calf: A Memoir*, translated by Harry Willetts (New York: Harper & Row, 1979), p. 245.

28 See the excellent discussion of "Eurasianism" in James Billington, *Russia in Search of Itself* (Washington, DC: Woodrow Wilson Center Press, 2004), pp. 69–94.

Orthodox Universalism: The Other Extreme

At the same time, it would avoid the other extreme of "falling into an excessive Orthodoxy which, under the pretext of universalism, renders one indifferent to the national existence of one's own people." This might be said to be Solzhenitsyn's response to Father Schmemann *avant la lettre*. In his journal entries from the 1970s and early 1980s (but which were only published posthumously in 2000),[29] the great Orthodox theologian succumbed to precisely such "an excessive Orthodoxy." He presumed that a passionate concern with the "national existence" of one's people meant that one recognized no spiritual or moral principles above the "national principle," as Bulgakov had called it. In his private journals, Schmemann continued to express admiration for the man and writer but criticized his friend Solzhenitsyn for an "idolizing obsession with Russia." As for himself, he wrote, "Russia could disappear, die, and nothing would change in my fundamental vision of the world."[30]

Schmemann imagined a universal *ecclesia* that at the deepest level was indifferent to the fate of nations. In contrast, Solzhenitsyn insisted, in the words of his *Nobel Lecture*, that "nations are the wealth of mankind, its generalized personalities, the least among them has its own unique coloration and harbors within itself a unique facet of God's design." The disappearance or leveling of nations "would impoverish us not less than if all men should become alike, with one personality and one face."[31] In response to the twin temptations of idolatrous nationalism and an apolitical, "excessive Orthodoxy," Solzhenitsyn affirmed both the precious heterogeneity of national and cultural life, and the fundamental non-relativity of moral and spiritual principles. He held Russia to the same demanding standards of "repentance and self-limitation" to which he held all great nations and peoples. At

---

29 See *The Journals of Father Alexander Schmemann, 1973–1983*, translated by Juliana Schmemann (Crestwood, New York, 2002).

30 *Ibid.*, p. 61. The entry in Father Schmemann's *Journals* is dated January 20, 1975.

31 See *The Nobel Lecture* in *The Solzhenitsyn Reader*, p. 520.

the same time, he insisted that contrition should not be confused with masochistic self-hatred. Solzhenitsyn's capacious conception of love of country had a place for self-respect and a healthy instinct of national self-preservation, while never forgetting the need for penitential impulses, properly understood.

But this middle path, this arduous effort to evade two deadly millstones, was bound to be misunderstood. As we have seen, even an early admirer of Solzhenitsyn such as Alexander Schmemann feared that Solzhenitsyn's humane and self-critical patriotism had given way to a blind defense of all things Russian. In Schmemann's view, Russia had become an idol for Solzhenitsyn, and his early "lucidity" had given way to a single-minded preoccupation with Russian history and culture that was finally incompatible with Christian universalism. We have suggested that Father Schmemann failed to understand Solzhenitsyn as he understood himself and did not take seriously the possibility that a burning love for one's motherland was compatible with humility before God and deference to a universal moral order. At the same time, it must be acknowledged that Solzhenitsyn's *tone*, his resort to spirited rhetoric in dealing with such contentious issues as the future of the Ukraine or the claim of some Russian Jews that the history of Russia is reducible to anti-Semitism, sometimes made it harder to discern the fundamental moderation of his principles and of his political and historical judgments.

The Question of Tone

There is every reason to take seriously the sincerity of Solzhenitsyn's call in his last major work, *Two Hundred Years Together,* for mutual repentance on the part of Russians and Russian Jews. That massive historical study can be understood as a demanding practical application of the principles of "repentance and self-limitation" that are at the core of Solzhenitsyn's moral and political reflection.[32] Rejecting both collective guilt

32 The two volumes of *Two Hundred Years Together* were published by the Moscow publishing house "Russkii put'" in 2001 and 2002,

and the radical individualism of modern liberal political theory, Solzhenitsyn upheld the need for both great peoples to take *responsibility* for their "renegades," those on both sides who had done so much to aid the cause of nihilistic revolution in the Soviet Union. He ends chapter 15 of volume two of *Two Hundred Years Together* with an eloquent, high-minded call for the Jewish people to answer "for the revolutionary cutthroats" who had broken with the faith of their fathers ("not to answer before other peoples, but to oneself, to one's consciousness, and before God") even as Russians "must answer—for the pogroms, for those merciless arsonist peasants, for those crazed revolutionary soldiers, for those savage sailors." "For if we release ourselves from any responsibility for the actions of our national kin, the very concept of a *people* loses any real meaning."[33] Solzhenitsyn could write with great sensitivity about the suffering of the Jewish people, especially during the Holocaust on Soviet territory.[34] At the same time, Solzhenitsyn was clearly angered by those Jewish writers and activists who could only remember Soviet persecution of the Jews, and not the "disproportionate" Jewish involvement in the new Bolshevik order in the first decades of its existence. All too often it is overlooked that in *Two Hundred Years Together* Solzhenitsyn emphatically denied that the Russian revolutions of 1905 or 1917 were the result of a Jewish "conspiracy" or machinations.[35] Belief in such a "conspiracy" is a cherished trope on the extreme Russian Right. But Solzhenitsyn's insistence in volume II of that work in demonstrating the extent of Jewish involvement with Bolshevik power in the first decades of Soviet rule was somewhat at

respectively. The two volumes have been published in French as *Deux siècles ensemble*. No edition has yet appeared in English but substantial excerpts are available in *The Solzhenitsyn Reader*.

33 See *The Solzhenitsyn Reader*, p. 505.

34 I especially have in mind chapter 21 of volume two of *Two Hundred Years Together*.

35 For an example see chapter nine of *Two Hundred Years Together* in *The Solzhenitsyn Reader*, p. 496.

cross-purposes with the generous motives informing his book. Such an emphasis, even if it was necessary to correct certain one-sided presentations of the past, was bound to give rise to new misunderstandings.

Likewise, Solzhenitsyn could write in the third volume of *The Gulag Archipelago* with remarkable generosity about the need for the Ukrainian people to decide their own destiny, however much he desired a voluntary federation between these two peoples (it must be remembered that Solzhenitsyn was Ukrainian of his mother's side). In *Rebuilding Russia* (1990), responding to the anti-Russian sentiments of Ukrainian nationalists, he speaks movingly of Russians and Ukrainians "as common victims of the communist-imposed collectivization forced upon us all by whip and bullet." These two great Slavic peoples have, he suggests, been "bonded" by "common bloody suffering."[36] Yet Solzhenitsyn's intervention in *Pravda* in April of 2008 on the question of whether the Ukrainian genocide was a Russian "genocide" directed against the Ukrainian people, in which he rightly insisted that this was an *ideological* and not an ethnic crime, was sufficiently polemical that many commentators falsely concluded that Solzhenitsyn was either denying the fact, or the monstrous and murderous character, of the Ukrainian famine.[37] Solzhenitsyn allowed a "defamation" put forward by Ukrainian nationalists to give the impression that he was a Russian nationalist of a comparable type. Once again, however, it was a matter of tone, of a certain defensive, polemical edge leading commentators to overlook the fundamental moderation of Solzhenitsyn's position.

The occasionally polemical or brusque *tone* of some of Solzhenitsyn's formulations led Western commentators to confuse

36 Solzhenitsyn, *Rebuilding Russia: Reflections and Tentative Proposals*, translated by Alexis Klimoff (New York: Farrar, Straus, and Giroux, 1991), p. 16.
37 An English-language version of Solzhenitsyn's April 4, 2008 *Pravda* piece appeared as "Ukrainian Famine Not a Genocide" in the *Boston Globe*, April 5, 2008.

his quasi-isolationist position (in 1979 Solzhenitsyn told a BBC interviewer that post-Communist Russia would need a 1,000 years of "recuperation")[38] with support for aggressive nationalism. In truth, Solzhenitsyn always emphasized the priority of "inner development" over "the ruthless squander of national strength on the pursuit of external aims of no benefit to Russia" (*RQ*, 70). To be sure, he was distressed that the Western world took advantage of the unnatural weakness of Russia during her "third Time of Troubles" as he called the massive chaos, corruption, and demographic freefall of the kleptocratic Russian 1990s. He supported, in a qualified way, the national and social restoration that occurred in Russia under Vladimir Putin in the first years of the twenty-first century. The Russian writer feared above all a repetition of the chaos that followed the February revolution of 1917 and that paved the way for seventy years of totalitarianism

For this reason, among others, Solzhenitsyn thought that Western encouragement of "color" revolutions in the former Soviet Union was completely misplaced. It was up to Russians and other peoples who had been subjected to Soviet despotism to recover what Solzhenitsyn called "civic space" and to learn how to cultivate that "independent activity and self-organization" (*RQ*, 106) that is so essential to free and civilized social life. At the same time, Solzhenitsyn lamented the absence of true democracy and self-government in contemporary Russia. He knew that Putin's Russia was no democracy and that the building of true civic institutions in his country was still very much a task for the future. Solzhenitsyn noted in *Russia in Collapse* that in his conversations with ordinary Russians after his return from his Western exile in 1994, it was always himself who spoke about the imperative of setting up *self-government*.[39] It was not something that was particularly on the minds of his compatriots.

---

38 See the conclusion of the 1979 "Interview with Aleksandr Solzhenitsyn by Janis Sapiets" in *East and West*, p. 182.
39 See chapter 1 of *Russia in Collapse* in *The Solzhenitsyn Reader*, p. 470.

A Theorist of Self-Government

In fact, as we have said, the preeminent political theme of Solzhenitsyn's during the last twenty-five years of his life was precisely the need to patiently build institutions and habits of self-government *from the bottom up*. Few people in the West think of Solzhenitsyn as a theorist of self-government but that is precisely what he became in writings such as *Rebuilding Russia* and *Russia in Collapse*. After the totalitarian experience of brutally establishing a new order *ex nihilo* Solzhenitsyn knew that democracy could not be imposed from the top, Bolshevik-style, in abstraction from the habits and traditions of a people. He looked for "organic" precedents of self-government in the Russian tradition and found them principally in in the *zemstvo*, the self-governing local and provincial councils which existed in the last fifty years of the Tsarist regime, and which were responsible for a wide range of executive functions. He did not advocate a "return to the past" but a shaping of the future in accord with the best national traditions.

Solzhenitsyn was also confident that the spirited resistance to totalitarianism on the part of some Russians (from the peasant revolt in Tambov province in 1920–1921 until the brutally repressed worker's strike in Novocherkassk in 1962 that he had made famous in the third volume of *The Gulag Archipelago*) made clear that the people of Russia were not bereft of the spirit of liberty. And as he argued in his last major interview in *Der Spiegel* (July 2007) there was much Russia could learn from the Western experience of self-government. "I have always insisted on local self-government for Russia, but I never opposed this model to Western democracy. On the contrary, I have tried to convince my fellow citizens by citing the examples of highly effective local self-government systems in Switzerland and New England, both of which I saw first-hand."[40] Solzhenitsyn kept his eyes open during

40 See Solzhenitsyn, "I Am Not Afraid of Death: An Interview" in *Der Spiegel*, July 23, 2007 and the analysis of that interview in Chapter 9 of this book.

the years of his Western exile, and not merely to criticize the weakness of the West vis-à-vis Soviet power, or to lament the decline of traditional Western culture.

Beyond Tired Polemics

As the foregoing suggests, to the day he died Solzhenitsyn remained fully committed to a "middle line" of social development, as he called it in chapter seven of *November 1916*, as well as to a moderate and humane version of Russian patriotism. Confronted by those who condemned the Russian tradition *tout court*, who despised "eternal Russia," he fiercely defended her unique spiritual and cultural traditions, even as he acknowledged her need to learn from the political achievement of the West. He resisted "Eurasianism" and "National Bolshevism" as perverse spiritual and political temptations that were blind to the truth about Communism and that would prevent the rebirth of a constructive Russian patriotism. He adamantly rejected many of the ideological positions, such as pan-Slavism, that are habitually attributed to him. Derided as an authoritarian and nationalist, he was in fact a theorist of self-government and a critic of imperial overreach. It is time to transcend the falsehoods and polemics that have surrounded Solzhenitsyn's name and open ourselves to the wisdom and moderation that informs his writings. Tired binary categories such as "Westernizer" and "Slavophile" obscure much more than they clarify Solzhenitsyn's thought and achievement.

Chapter 2

"The Active Struggle Against Evil": Reflections on a Theme in Solzhenitsyn[1]

Aleksandr Solzhenitsyn was a forceful defender of the view that free human action plays a decisive role in shaping the individual and collective destinies of human beings. He therefore famously opposed every form of historical determinism. But at the same time he understood human freedom to be an integral part of a moral order independent of any human agency, an order that men disregard at their peril. In an interview with the writer Daniel Kehlmann that first appeared in the German literary and political review *Cicero* in October 2006 and in French translation (*Le Figaro*) two months later, Solzhenitsyn clarified his views about the need for human beings to exercise their moral freedom by fighting for justice and by actively struggling against evil.[2] This interview provides a most helpful entrance to a problem that is at the center of Solzhenitsyn's moral and political reflection. To wit, how can a human being exercise his liberty, his "inner freedom," at the service of the good and in active opposition to the forces of tyranny and moral destruction?

1   An earlier version of this paper was delivered at an international conference on the occasion of 90th anniversary of Solzhenitsyn's birth, held at the Russian State Library in Moscow, December 5–6, 2008.

2   In the *Cicero* version, the interview is entitled "Wir treiben uns selbst ins Grab." The *Figaro* translation appeared in the issue of December 1, 2006 under the title "La future démocratie russe ne doit pas être un calque de l'Occident." Strangely enough, the Russian original text was published only after the writer's death, on what would have been his 90th birthday: "My tvorim svoiu istoriiu sami, sami zagoniaem sebia v iamy," *Izvestiia*, December 11, 2008.

In the course of the interview Kehlmann asks Solzhenitsyn about "one of the central themes of his work": his admiration for "simple, decent human beings" (*einfache, anständige Menschen*) who stand alone confronting chaos. Kehlmann follows up this remark by asking if "simple human decency" (*simpler menschlicher Anstand*) can be an adequate response to "absolute evil." In addition, he asks Solzhenitsyn to clarify his understanding of evil. Solzhenitsyn's lucid response goes right to the heart of the matter. He readily agrees that simple but defenseless (*bezzashchitnye*) human beings such as Matryona and Ivan Denisovich (who in their different ways embody the humanity of a pre-Bolshevik peasant Russia) inspire in him "much sympathy." But he makes clear that he feels even "greater sympathy" for those who have "revealed themselves to be combatants for justice" (*kto vystupaet bortsom za obshchuiu spravedlivost'*). He notes in this connection that he has placed great emphasis on such human beings in both *The Gulag Archipelago* and *The Red Wheel*. And he states emphatically that "simple decency" (*prostaia poriadochnost'*) is not a sufficient response to universal evil. Radical evil, in his view, is not reducible to madness or stupidity. It has, he states, "a dense nucleus or core" which has the capacity to strike out in every direction. Given its power, nothing less than "an active struggle" (*bor'ba aktivnaia*) is necessary to combat it. Solzhenitsyn adds that evil gains strength "when a great number of human hearts are touched by it" as was surely the case in a Russia overrun in the first part of the twentieth century by the demons of ideology and nihilistic revolution.

Of the manifold occasions in which the "active struggle" for justice and against evil is represented in Solzhenitsyn's writings, I turn first to two notable examples in *The Red Wheel*.

Vorotyntsev and Stolypin

These two characters stand out by virtue of their integrity, their commitment to fighting revolution with reform, and their moral courage in standing up to those whose blindness and inaction impedes the spiritual and political renewal of Russia. Colonel Georgi Vorotyntsev, the fictional hero of *The Red Wheel*, embodies the patriotic single-mindedness of those intelligent, forward-looking officers who represented Russia's best hopes for renewal amidst the devastation of war and revolution. He spent much of the war on an isolated front because he had had the temerity to speak up in the presence of the Grand Duke Nikolai Nikolaevich, the supreme commander of Russia's Imperial forces, against the vicious scapegoating of General Samsonov after the disastrous Russian defeat at the Battle of Tannenberg. The confrontation in chapter 82 of *August 1914* between the truth-telling Vorotyntsev and the timeservers on the general staff is one of the most dramatic scenes in the entire work. But as a fictional character, Vorotyntsev is unable to alter in any decisive respect the relentless (but by no means fated) unfolding of a national tragedy. We last see this great man in chapter 186 of *April 1917* where he is busy organizing officers for what would in effect become the "White" movement.[3] While the liberals and socialists associated with the Provisional Government are shown to be blind to the emerging Bolshevik threat, Vorotyntsev maintains his lucidity. He prepares for the coming battle with those who would destroy Russia and civilization. His determination to resist evil contrasts with the lethargy and lack of moral and intellectual clarity of so many of the historical actors. The great exception was Pyotr Stolypin.

Stolypin is Solzhenitsyn's beau ideal of a statesman.[4] This is a theme we will return to time and again in the course of our dis-

---

3   An English translation of Chapter 186 of *April 1917* can be found in Edward E. Ericson and Daniel J. Mahoney, eds., *The Solzhenitsyn Reader: New and Essential Writings: 1947–2005* (Wilmington, DE: ISI Books, 2006), pp. 460–63.

4   Solzhenitsyn discusses Stolypin's statesmanship and its significance for modern Russian history in the "Stolypin cycle" (chapters 8 and 60–73) of *August 1914*. See also chapter four, titled "True and False Liberalism: Stolypin and his Enemies in *August 1914*" in my book, *Aleksandr Solzhenitsyn: The Ascent From Ideology* (Lanham, MD: Rowman & Littlefield, 2001), pp. 65–97.

cussion. He was a conservative reformer who embodied the "middle line for social development" (as Solzhenitsyn called it in chapter seven of *November 1916*). For this he was hated alike by the violent revolutionary Left and by the reactionary Right. Stolypin respected Russia's post-1906 constitutional order while doing what was necessary to repress the forces of anarchy and despotism. His far-reaching agrarian reforms promised to create a new class of peasant proprietors in Russia and thus the social basis for a revitalized monarchy in that country. The well-intentioned but profoundly mediocre and ineffectual Nicholas II never truly appreciated the gift from on High which was Pyotr Stolypin. As Alexis Klimoff has pointed out, Stolypin perfectly embodied the balance that Solzhenitsyn admires and recommends between confidence in God's purposes and the determination to exercise moral will at the service of the common good.[5] And as Solzhenitsyn makes clear in chapter 69 of *August 1914*, Stolypin rejected the twin extremes of pietistic fatalism and unfounded confidence in the ability of human beings to remake society without reliance on God's justice. Brought down "at the heights of his powers" by an assassin's bullet at the age of 49, the dying Stolypin never loses confidence in the mercy or justice of God even as he laments that he will not have time to finish the work of restoring the moral and political health of Russia. The country he loves is "still rent by the rabid hostility of civil society toward the imperial power,"[6] by a blind and uncomprehending court, by nihilistic revolutionaries, and by an Emperor who does not appreciate the fragility of Stolypin's project of civic and social restoration.

5   See Alexis Klimoff, "Inevitability vs. Will: A Theme and Its Variations in Solzhenitsyn's *August 1914*" in *Transactions of the Association of Russian-American Scholars in the U.S.A.*, vol. 29 (1998), pp. 305–12, esp. 310.

6   Solzhenitsyn, *August 1914*, tr. Harry T. Willetts (New York: Farrar, Straus and Giroux, 1989), p. 646.

A Pusillanimous Monarch

If the thought and action of Vorotyntsev and Stolypin admirably brought together moderation, justice, and the moral will, the Emperor Nicholas II reveals the powerlessness of decency when it is shorn of prudence, perspicacity, and a willingness to act in an intelligent, determined, and forceful manner. From the point of view of natural moral virtue, the true "king" is Stolypin, the new "Peter" (who is far more humane than his great namesake), rather than the tragic and ineffectual Tsar.[7] Solzhenitsyn had no principled opposition to monarchy as long as it respected moral limits and the inheritance of civilization. In his *Reflections on the February Revolution*, originally completed in 1983 and published in 1995 (and again in 2007 on the occasion of the 90th anniversary of the first revolution of 1917),[8] Solzhenitsyn writes that "monarchy is a strong system on the condition that the monarch

7   On this point see especially chapter 65 of *August 1914*.
8   Solzhenitsyn wrote *his Reflections on the February Revolution* between 1980 and 1983 and originally intended its sections to appear as introductions to the four volumes of *March 1917*, the massive third "knot" of *The Red Wheel*. But fearing that the didactic character of the essay was incompatible with the form of the novel, even one that aimed to "dramatize" history, Solzhenitsyn decided against including it in *The Red Wheel*. When *Reflections on the February Revolution* finally appeared in a Russian literary review in 1995 (*Moskva*, 1995, No. 2), it passed almost unnoticed. In contrast, the republication of the work in *Rossiiskaia gazeta* on February 27, 2007 gave rise to an impassioned national debate on the February Revolution and the role it played in paving the way for the Bolshevik seizure of power in October 1917. Solzhenitsyn's readers were particularly sensitive to the parallel between the chaos unleashed by the February revolution and what Solzhenitsyn had not hesitated to call Russia's "Third Time of Troubles" that followed the collapse of the Soviet regime in 1991. I have consulted the French edition of the work, published as *Réflexions sur la revolution de Février* (Paris: Fayard, 2007). Stephan Solzhenitsyn kindly translated all the passages from the work in the body of my text from the original Russian.

is not too pusillanimous. Comport oneself as a Christian on the throne, agreed, but not to the point of forgetting one's duties, or the nation's business, in a way that blinds oneself to approaching catastrophe." Later in the same essay, Solzhenitsyn faults Nicholas for failing to take a series of steps (including sending reliable troops to crush the rebellion in Petersburg, making sure that bread was readily available, and cutting telegraph lines between Petersburg and Moscow) that might well have thwarted the revolutionary fervor before it had time to spread.

Solzhenitsyn does not mince words. This decent but "weak" monarch was too anxious to be with his family at Tsarskoe Selo and as a result "betrayed" a people and nation, the responsibility for which had been conveyed to him "by heredity, by Tradition, by God himself." "There is," Solzhenitsyn writes, "a word in Russian, *zatsarit'sia*—which means: to rule for such a long time one forgets one is ruling." That word perfectly captures Nicholas's abdication of his moral and political responsibilities. Excessively anxious to avoid bloodshed, he failed to take measures that promised to maintain order and prevent the collapse of an imperfect but civilized political order. Even if the sending of reliable troops to Petersburg risked bloodshed, Solzhenitsyn notes that this "would not have had the least resemblance with the Civil War which lasted three years on the vast expanses of Russia, with the criminal exactions of the Chekists, the epidemic of typhoid, the successive waves of crushed peasant rebellions, the Volga basin suffocated by famine—and then a half-century of the infernal gnashing of the gulag." Nicholas failed to stand up to the forces of subversion and thus played a direct role in unleashing what would become the Soviet tragedy.

Solzhenitsyn is by no means endorsing a Machiavellian political philosophy or arguing that Christian faith is ultimately incompatible with the requirements of statesmanship. But he clearly recognizes the primacy of a Christian monarch's public responsibility over familial or private considerations; the same is true of any leader charged with maintaining the common good. And in a venerable tradition of Christian political reflection, he refuses to identify the moral and Christian virtues with inaction and refusal to resist evil when it rears its head. The example of Nicholas II, at once pathetic and tragic, reveals how passivity and the abdication of responsibility can create a space for radical evil to emerge victorious in this fallen world.

Moral Freedom and Political Liberty

The theme of "the active struggle against evil" is equally in evidence in *The Gulag Archipelago* as well as in some of Solzhenitsyn's later moral and political writings. What emerges is a rich and consistent, if "dialectical," reflection (in the non-Marxist sense of the term) on the need to resist evil for the sake of the integrity of the soul and the wellbeing of the nation. An excursus on the important if secondary role of the struggle for political liberty in Solzhenitsyn's thought will provide a useful context for this discussion.

Solzhenitsyn was not an advocate or theorist of violent revolution. His preferred path for coming out "from under the rubble" of Communist totalitarianism was the self-conscious decision to "never knowingly support lies," an imperative forcefully articulated in the concluding paragraphs of the *Nobel Lecture* and in the 1974 manifesto *Live Not By Lies!*[9] In a series of writings over many decades, he made clear that "external freedom for its own sake" could never be "the goal of conscious living beings." For Solzhenitsyn, the "inner freedom of will" or "freedom of choice"[10] given to human beings at birth was the most precious gift available to us and one that was not dependent on political liberty or democratic political forms for its exercise. In a 1973

9 Both texts can be found in the aforementioned *The Solzhenitsyn Reader: New and Essential Writings: 1947–2005*.

10 See Solzhenitsyn's opening contribution ("As Breathing and Consciousness Return") to the 1974 collection *From Under the Rubble* (*Iz pod glyb*), translated by a team of translators under the direction of Michael Scammell (Boston: Little Brown and Company, 1975), p. 22.

postface to his essay "As Breathing and Consciousness Return" (from the 1974 collection *From Under the Rubble*) Solzhenitsyn goes so far as to state that "in relation to the true ends of human beings here on earth ... the state system is of secondary significance."[11] But of *secondary* importance, not of no importance whatsoever.

Solzhenitsyn's recognition of the priority of "inner freedom" to "external" or political freedom in no way entails an endorsement of passivity or "non-resistance to evil." Quite the contrary. And it should be noted that Solzhenitsyn's "Augustinian" endorsement of the priority of "the things of God" to the "things of Caesar" in a work like *From Under the Rubble* was supplemented in the last two decades of his life by a much more robust "Aristotelian" or "Tocquevillian" emphasis on the importance of self-government, especially at the local level. Self-government is not only crucial for the development of civic consciousness but for the flourishing of the full range of moral, intellectual, and civic virtues.[12] In truth, Solzhenitsyn had already articulated the tensions between—as well as the mutual dependence of—inner spiritual development and external freedom with great depth and luminosity in parts four and five of *The Gulag Archipelago*. In the 1973 postscript to "As Breathing and Consciousness Return" (an essay originally written in 1969) Solzhenitsyn states that Communist totalitarianism is humanly unbearable not primarily because "it is undemocratic, authoritarian, [and] based on physical constraint" but because in addition to these brutal physical constraints "it demands" of those who live under it "total surrender" of their souls. Solzhenitsyn famously articulated what cannot be asked of any self-respecting human being: "continuous and active participation in the general, conscious *lie*." To surrender to the lie is to lose one's soul, to abandon that inner freedom without which no man "deserve[s] to be called human." It is for this rea-

11 *Ibid.*, p. 24.
12 See my discussion of Solzhenitsyn as a theorist of "self-government" in Mahoney, *The Ascent From Ideology*, pp. 135–56.

son that Solzhenitsyn notes in the same text that "the absolute essential task is not political liberation, but the liberation of our souls from participation in the lie forced upon us."[13]

In 1973, that involved not political activism per se but rather the exercise of what Václav Havel would later call (in a Solzhenitsyn-inspired reflection dating from 1979) the self-conscious choice to exercise "the power of the powerless" by refusing to participate in the lie. But that was in a post-Stalinist Soviet Union that was already losing its ideological self-confidence. To be sure, the Soviet leaders continued to affirm and live by the ideological lie.[14] But they no longer had a burning faith in its capacity to radically transform human nature and society. The twin pillars of the regime—violence and lies—were vulnerable as never before to the liberating power of truth as well as to elementary acts of civic courage on the part of those who refused to do anything that might reinforce the remarkably brittle edifice of the lie.

The Soul of Man Under Socialism

But that was not the case in the early 1950s, a time of great unrest that culminated in camp revolts in Vorkuta, Ekibastuz, and Kengir. This was a regime that still saw itself as "the wave of the future" and that mutilated souls within and outside of the camp system. In chapter 30 of *Russia in Collapse* (published in 1998) Solzhenitsyn provides a particularly pointed encapsulation of the effects of Bolshevism on the Russian character during the "classic" period of Leninist-Stalinist totalitarianism. The regime, he states, had successfully engaged in *reverse selection*, the "deliberate destruction of all that was bright, remarkable, of a higher level." Drawing on his discussion of these same themes in part IV of *The Gulag Archipelago*,

13 The quotations in the final part of this paragraph are drawn from "As Breathing and Consciousness Return," pp. 24–25.
14 See Vaclav Havel, "The Power and the Powerless" in *Open Letters: Selected Writings, 1965–1990*, selected and edited by Paul Wilson (New York: Knopf, 1991), pp. 125–214. Havel freely acknowledges his debt to Solzhenitsyn on pp. 150, 171, and 208 of this essay.

Solzhenitsyn speaks of the "meltdown of the people's morals under the yoke of Bolshevism." Fear, secrecy, betrayal, and distrust had become ways of life. In addition, there was "a total, deafening indifference toward those who perished all around." "In place of all the good that was dying away, ingratitude, cruelty, and a thoroughly rude self-centered ambition now rose and established themselves."[15] It was in this context of the institutionalization of betrayal, mendacity, and moral indifference that Solzhenitsyn reflects on the imperative of resistance to soul-destroying despotism.

The Camp Revolts

Solzhenitsyn not only participated in the rebellion of prisoners at Ekibastuz, but took great satisfaction from the fact that the prisoners "were not the sheep we used to be" (as well as from the fact the fact that the "wolves"—the camp authorities—were fully cognizant of this new reality).[16] Under conditions of unthinkable degradation, Solzhenitsyn expressed sympathy, or at least understanding, for efforts to silence—to kill—informers or "stoolies" who were the backbone of the ubiquitous system of social control within the camps. It is easy, he writes in chapter ten ("Behind the Wire the Ground is Burning") of part five of *The Gulag Archipelago*, for those who have never gotten 25 years for nothing, or who never had to wear four number patches on their clothes, or who never had to submit to degrading searches or the indignity of the cooler, to call into question the resort to violence. Solzhenitsyn knows all the arguments and recognizes the partial truth in the "humanist" claim that by "taking up the sword, the knife, the rifle," the victims of Soviet oppression risk putting themselves "on the level of our tormentors." Yet there is

15 See chapter 30 of *Russia in Collapse* ("The Evolution of Our Character") in *The Solzhenitsyn Reader*, pp. 475–79. The quotes in this section are drawn from p. 477.

16 Solzhenitsyn, *The Gulag Archipelago*, Volume 3, tr. by Harry Willetts (New York: Harper Perennial Modern Classics, 2007), Part V, chapter 10, p. 248.

something deeply unconvincing about these objections when they abstract from the systematic assault on the bodies and souls of men to which the *zeks* were habitually subjected. "From the hole you're in, the fine words of the great humanists will sound like the chatter of the well-fed and the free."[17]

In his "Preface" to the English-language edition of the third volume of *The Gulag Archipelago*, dated November 1977, Solzhenitsyn returns to this theme.[18] There he unequivocally calls terrorism "a condemnable tool," a case of evil generating evil. But he is careful to differentiate the concentration camp "terrorism" of the 1950s from the nihilistic "left-wing revolutionary terrorism" which flourished in the West in the 1960s and 1970s. Young Western terrorists, "saturated with boundless freedom" did not hesitate "to kill innocent people for the sake of unclear purposes or in order to gain material advantages." In contrast, "Soviet camp terrorists in the fifties killed proven traitors and informers in defense of their right to breathe."

In his treatment of the camp revolts, Solzhenitsyn never endorses violent resistance as an end in itself and never disregards the moral arguments raised against the resort to methods such as the murder of stoolies. But he does not quarrel with the conclusion of the "oppressed" that "evil"—at least evil of scale and durability—"cannot be cast out by good." Solzhenitsyn welcomed the "germ of freedom" that he experienced at Ekibastuz—the *zeks'* newfound ability to speak freely and to act with self-respect—that was made possible by the decision of the politicals "to tear at their chains." He compares the "purge" of spies and eavesdroppers to "some ancient sacrificial altar" where "blood had been shed that we might be freed from the curse that hung over us." Solzhenitsyn clearly shared the exhilaration that came with recognizing that the once sheep-like politicals—victims of the authorities and the thieves alike—"could resist!"[19] If the great

17 *Ibid.*, Part V, chapter 10, p. 235.
18 *Ibid.*, xvii–xviii.
19 *Ibid.*, Part V, chapter 10, p. 248.

chapter on "The Ascent" from part IV of *The Gulag Archipelago* ("The Soul and Barbed Wire") emphasizes the luminous prospects for spiritual ascent in the camps that occurs when prisoners repudiate the idea of "survival at any price," the chapters on resistance and the camp revolts emphasize a complementary form of spiritual ascent and liberation.

It must be emphasized that Solzhenitsyn has no sympathy for a Nietzschean celebration of the "joy of the knife," of violence as a self-intoxicating end in itself. Rather, he shows how resistance to radical evil can liberate seemingly dormant noble qualities in the human soul. The chapter on "The Forty Days of Kengir"— the camp uprising that lasted from May 16, 1954 until June 26 of the same year—is undoubtedly one of the highlights of *The Gulag Archipelago* as a whole.[20] A misplaced effort to dampen the spirits of the political prisoners in this special regime camp by importing hundreds of thieves into it backfired when the politicals and thieves formed a grand alliance. Injecting the thieves into Kengir, zone #3, the seat of the camp unrest, led not to a "pacified camp" but to "the biggest mutiny in the history of *The Gulag Archipelago*."[21] Solzhenitsyn movingly describes the transformation of 8,000 men who only "yesterday" were "slaves" into free men infused with a deep sense of "fellowship."[22]

The thieves and politicals got along famously and there was no violence against women once the wall separating zone #2 (where the women were housed) and zone #3 came tumbling down (Solzhenitsyn notes that all commentators agreed that the thieves acted, perhaps for the first time, *"like decent people"*).[23] The prisoners elected a committee to conduct its negotiations with the camp authorities and for the first time in forty years genuine

---

20 See "The Forty Days of Kengir" in *The Gulag Archipelago*, Volume 3, Part V, chapter 12, pp. 285–331. The chapter on the Kengir rebellion was among the first ones that Solzhenitsyn composed when he began to work secretly on *The Gulag Archipelago* in 1958.

21 *Ibid.*, p. 290.

22 *Ibid.*, p. 297.

23 *Ibid.*, p. 306.

"self-government" appeared under Soviet rule, and in a gulag camp at that.[24] The motives of the revolt's leaders were far from transparent. The mysterious "Center" representing Ukrainian and other national groupings appeared to have inspired this massive camp revolt. The official leader of the rebels, the ex-POW Kapiton Kuznetsov, appears to have combined broad Soviet loyalties with disaffection over his imprisonment and conditions in the camp. The authorities—the "slavemasters" as Solzhenitsyn calls them[25]—could see in the rebels only rapists and plunderers. Solzhenitsyn comments acidly that it was beyond the reach of the minds of men corrupted by Communist ideology to see in the actions of the rebels any concern—however elementary or inchoate—for human justice.

The revolt was doomed from the beginning and it was naive of Kuznetsov and others to place any hope on the extenuating effect of their self-professed rectitude as Soviet citizens. As time went on the camp authorities bombarded the camp with denunciations of "gangster debauchery" and with appeals to avoid all "senseless resistance."[26] Solzhenitsyn notes that only a dozen men or so out of 8,000 mutineers responded to these appeals by fleeing the camp. This despite the fact that none of them could really have believed in ultimate victory. Solzhenitsyn suggests that the prisoners were understandably torn between a desire to save themselves "for their families' sake"[27] and the path of resistance and personal honor. Solzhenitsyn comments that "the social temperature"—the collective atmosphere—at Kengir was so high that if souls were not "transmuted" they were assuredly "purged of dross."[28] The "sordid laws" at the heart of the ideological lie—the insistence

---

24 *Ibid.*, 301. Solzhenitsyn writes that after the 8,000 prisoners at Kengir had "escaped to freedom" on the night of May 18–19, 1954 "orderlies went around the huts summoning us to the big mess hall to elect a commission for negotiations with the authorities and for self–government, as it modestly and timidly described itself."

25 *Ibid.*, p. 317.

26 *Ibid.*, p. 322.

27 *Ibid.*, p. 323.

28 *Ibid.*

that "we only live once," the palpably false claim that "being determines consciousness," the crude insistence that "every man's a coward when his neck is at stake"—"ceased to apply for that short time in that circumscribed place."[29] Against the "laws of reason and survival"[30] the prisoners had risen to a higher spiritual plane, one where freedom and dignity mattered more than self-preservation. The camp revolts gave rise to a messy form of struggle that was not bereft of spiritual ascent.

Resisting Evil With Force

In their resistance to evil—radical evil—the *zeks* rediscovered that they were beings with souls. Solzhenitsyn wryly comments that the operation of the authorities to get the prisoners to abandon honor and flee like rats that could "then be crushed" failed because "its inventors had the mentality of rats themselves."[31] To be sure, the decision to resist injustice sometimes entails the choice of unsavory means, especially under conditions of totalitarianism. But it also means a willingness to put the good of the soul above physical survival "at any price."

The Solzhenitsyn who famously asserts that suffering can sometimes be redemptive is the same Solzhenitsyn who can argue without contradiction that radical evil must be resisted for the sake of the integrity of the human soul. In his important book, *Le phénomène Soljénitsyne*, Georges Nivat claims to locate a contradiction in Solzhenitsyn's heart and mind in this regard[32] where I see a tension rooted in the structure of moral reality itself. Humility and magnanimity, redemptive suffering and "the active struggle against evil" are twin manifestations of the soul's efforts to defend itself against the dehumanizing temptation to choose "survival at any price." Solzhenitsyn finds a place for both

29 *Ibid.*
30 *Ibid.*
31 *Ibid.*
32 Georges Nivat, *Le phénomène Soljénitsyne* (Paris: Fayard, 2009), pp. 108, 196–97.

spirited self-assertion and humane self-restriction in his account of human virtues and the wellsprings of the human soul.

Under different conditions than those he encountered in the 1950s—under a less all-embracing totalitarianism—Solzhenitsyn freely recommended the path of moral revolution, of non-violent resistance to evil. But this is a matter of prudence and is utterly distinct from the moral or philosophical principle of "non-resistance to evil." In this connection, it is worth remembering that Solzhenitsyn was a great admirer of the White émigré philosopher and theoretician Ivan Il'in (also spelled Ilyin) who had admirably captured the spirit of Solzhenitsyn's reflections *avant la lettre* in his classic 1925 work *On Resisting Evil With Force*.[33] Il'in had there argued, as one scholar aptly put it, "that non-resistance to evil amounts to acceptance of evil. One has to resist evil not just to aid others, but also for the good of one's own soul."[34] It is a position virtually identical with what Solzhenitsyn would say several decades later.

For Solzhenitsyn, the human spirit—human consciousness—not material conditions, ultimately shapes the direction of the world. He repeated this affirmation over and over again in his writings. A regime and ideology that denies the soul in theory and tramples it in practice must be manfully resisted and with a clear Christian conscience. With Il'in and the memorable Father Severyan of the opening chapters of *November 1916*, Solzhenitsyn rejects any identification of Christianity with secular humanitarianism, Tolstoyan pacifism, or an evasion of moral and civic

33 See Ivan Il'in, *O soprotivlenii zlu siloiu*, ed. with a commentary by N. P. Poltoratskii (London, Ontario: Zaria, 1975). Solzhenitsyn's interest in Il'in is illustrated by references to him in *Rebuilding Russia* (New York: Farrar, Straus and Giroux, 1991), p. 12 and in the "Author's Note" preceding the English edition of *November 1916*. Concerning the latter, see the substantial article by Isabelle Faure Jaitly, "The Reflection of Il'in's Ideas on Monarchy in Solzhenitsyn's *Red Wheel*," *Transactions of the Association of Russian-American Scholars*, vol. 29 (1998), pp. 251–87.

34 Paul Robinson, "On Resistance to Evil By Force: Ivan Il'in and the Necessity of War" in the *Journal of Military Ethics* (2003), 2(2), pp. 145–59. The quote is from p. 153.

responsibilities. Solzhenitsyn is first and foremost a partisan of moral agency and responsibility.[35] Such responsibility necessarily entails a willingness to stand up to radical evil, to "actively combat it."[36]

35 In his poignant conversation with Sanya Lazhenitsyn (a disillusioned disciple of Tolstoy and a fictional representation of Solzhenitsyn's father) in chapters five and six of *November 1916*, the army chaplain Father Severyan expresses views about the differences between true Christianity and the humanitarianism and pacifism of Tolstoy that are for all intents and purposes identical with Solzhenitsyn's own convictions. See *November 1916: The Red Wheel II*, translated by Harry T. Willetts (New York: Farrar, Straus, and Giroux, 1999), especially pp. 47–54.

36 A more complete exploration of this theme would include a discussion of the 96-chapter version of *V kruge pervom*, now available in English under the title *In the First Circle*, translated by Harry Willetts, with a Foreword by Edward E. Ericson, Jr., New York: Harper Collins, 2009. In that "restored" version of Solzhenitsyn's text, the Soviet diplomat Innokenty Volodin tries to alert the American Embassy in Moscow about an imminent act of nuclear espionage on American territory. Volodin consciously betrays a regime that, as he has come to believe, is built upon violence and lies that threaten the peace of the world. See chapter 4 of this work for a discussion of the connection between Volodin's moral awakening, his recovery of conscience and natural justice, and his "active struggle" against a perverse totalitarian regime.

Chapter 3

NICHOLAS II AND THE COMING OF REVOLUTION

In *The Red Wheel* Aleksandr Solzhenitsyn defends an exacting "middle line" of political and social development against both the revolutionary left and the reactionary right.[1] As we have seen, the "middle line" is represented above all by Pyotr Stolypin, Prime Minister of Russia from 1906 to 1911. It was Stolypin who fought revolution with reform and "tried to further the development of Russia within the framework"[2] of the constitutional order established by the Manifesto of October 30, 1905. In particular, Stolypin worked to create a class of independent peasant-proprietors in Russia who would have a stake in the existing political order. In the words of the historian Geoffrey Hosking, he "hoped that the newly privatized smallholders" made possible by his reforms "would become full citizens and play their part in the establishment of a market economy, and that they would prove to be a reliable base for the monarchy and the rule of law."[3] Fearlessly confronting revolutionary terror while promoting reform, Stolypin "had hauled Russia out of the swamp of revolution"[4] and saved monarchy in the process. But his efforts were met only by ingratitude and hostility by "the intolerant extreme right."[5] As Solzhenitsyn puts it in chapter 70 of *August 1914*, the

1 Aleksandr Solzhenitsyn, *November 1916*, translated by H. T. Willetts (New York: Farrar, Straus and Giroux), p. 59.

2 Solzhenitsyn, *August 1914*, translated by H. T. Willetts (New York: Farrar, Straus and Giroux), p. 653.

3 Geoffrey Hosking, *Russia and the Russians: A History*, second edition (Cambridge, MA: Harvard University Press, 2011), p. 377.

4 Solzhenitsyn, *August 1914*, p. 653.

5 *Ibid.*

extreme right "did not want to know about reform and progress, about new ideas, and above all about concessions." It "believed in nothing but prayerful prostration before the Tsar, in petrified immobility, century and century." There is no more devastating critique of the choice for "petrified immobility"[6] as a substitute for intelligent and forceful action than the one provided by Solzhenitsyn in *The Red Wheel*.

Yet in some academic and journalistic circles, Solzhenitsyn is linked with the obdurate right that he so decisively repudiates. As we argued in chapter one, in this world of left-liberal discourse, any affirmation of patriotism, any thoughtful discussion of Russian national consciousness such as Solzhenitsyn's, is identified with the most narrow and backward-looking Russian nationalism. He is said to want to "return to some mythical past, when everything was as it should be: the tsar, the patriarch, the boyars, and the merry peasants. That is the world he longed for without understanding it an iota." (Ranko Bon, "A Letter to *The Economist*," August 12, 2008). Ignoring all evidence, Solzhenitsyn is transformed into the "personification" of "blind nationalism," and of an "immobile" past that is the enemy of the creative traditionalism he in fact represented. There is no excuse for these distortions but that they save the lazy and ideologically-inspired commentator the trouble of engaging *The Red Wheel*— and Solzhenitsyn's other major writings—on their own terms.

Far from being an advocate of immobility, or a theoretician of a reactionary utopia, Solzhenitsyn identifies the refusal to thoughtfully accommodate change as one of the causes of the revolutions of 1917. With Aristotle and Burke, Solzhenitsyn affirms that balanced reform is the best means for conserving a political order. What Russia needed in the years before the February revolution was "an untiring and active effort to reform all that was superannuated."[7] But as Solzhenitsyn argued in *Reflections on the*

---

6   *Ibid.*
7   See Solzhenitsyn, *Razmychleniia o Fevral'skoi revoliutsii*, originally written between 1980 and 1983 and published in Russia in 1995

February Revolution, after Stolypin, the monarchy lacked a program of clear and vigorous action. Both before 1906 and again after 1911 Nicholas II chose "immobility as the most commodious form of action."[8] God had sent him Stolypin, an authentically great man, who had delivered Russia and the dynasty from chaos and impending revolution. But the emperor failed to adequately support Stolypin against his enemies. He was on the verge of dismissing him when an assassination attempt was made on Stolypin at the Kiev opera in September 1911 that led to his death.

Chapter 69 of *August 1914* provides a dramatic description of Stolypin's last days. The dying man awaits a visit from an Emperor who is more keen on attending military parades than in conversing with his wounded Prime Minister. Stolypin is anxious to explain his reform program to the Tsar in order "to bequeath it to him and commit him to carrying it out." Stolypin wants no personal "reward for defeating revolution and restoring" Russia to the Emperor in "good health." Rather, he wants to do so for the Tsar's sake, "for the sake of his own future!" He knows that Nicholas does not see "what a tight corner Russia was in, even now, and what she must do to break out of it."[9]

These dying thoughts are prophetic. On the one hand, the brief period from 1906 to 1913 was in retrospect a kind of "golden age" for Russia marked by "torrid industrial development," "complete freedom for private economic activity," remarkable social mobility, an independent court system, and "a true parliament and multiparty system."[10] On the other hand, these very real achievements needed to be followed up by energetic reforms that addressed the difficult situation of the working classes and the inequality in the rights of the peasant class. Given the intense

and again in 2007. I have drawn on the French edition of the work published as *Réflexions sur la révolution de Février* (Paris: Fayard, 2007). The quotation is from p. 108.

8   *Ibid.,* p. 40.

9   Solzhenitsyn, *August 1914,* p. 645.

10 Solzhenitsyn, *"The Russian Question" at the End of the Twentieth Century* (New York: Farrar, Strauss and Giroux, 1995), p. 72.

hatred of educated "society" for the established order it was imperative to avoid a repeat of 1904–1905, when an unpopular war with Japan provided an opportunity for liberals and radicals to foment unrest and defeatism. But instead of a responsible, active, and competent administration the Russian monarchy was dominated by a lethargic class of hereditary nobles that had lost its sense of duty, was embarrassed by its hereditary privileges, and that was deficient in Russian national feeling.[11] Everywhere the educated class denounced the legitimacy of the existing order at no real cost to itself. The monarchy slept precisely at a time that it needed to combine reform with resistance to revolution. That somnolence owed much to the weakness and vacillation of Nicholas II. As we have already seen, he was a better man and better Christian than almost all his predecessors as Tsar. But he lacked the capacity to take those actions, at once firm and measured, that might have saved Russia and the dynasty.[12]

The sources of Tsar Nicholas II's abdication of political responsibility are brilliantly traced in the character sketch of the Emperor that Solzhenitsyn provided in chapter 74 of *August 1914*.[13] The chapter was originally published separately in *Vestnik Russkogo Kristianskogo Dvizheniya* in 1978 under the title "Study of a Monarch." The chapter is precisely that: a study of the first eleven years of Nicholas's reign with an addendum that addresses the crisis of July 1914 and the coming of the First World War. In *The "Russian Question" at the End of the Twentieth Century*, Solzhenitsyn stresses the point that Nicholas's reign can be divided into two equal periods of eleven years a piece. In 1905, at the end of the first eleven years, "he had nearly let all power slip from his hands, but this time Stolypin retrieved it." Solzhenitsyn tellingly adds that "at the end of the next eleven years, there was no one to repeat the feat."[14] Chapter 74 of *August 1914* follows

---

11 *Réflexions sur la révolution de Février*, p. 111.
12 *Ibid.*, pp. 37–42.
13 *August 1914*, pp. 687–784.
14 *"The Russian Question" at the End of the Twentieth Century*, p. 68.

directly upon the Stolypin cycle in that work (chapters 8 and 60 to 73) and shows how close the monarchy came to self-destructing before Stolypin came to the rescue. As Solzhenitsyn argues in chapter 65 of *August 1914*, Stolypin was the true pillar (*stolp*) of the Russian state and "became the hub of Russian life as no Tsar had ever been."[15]

But Stolypin is present in chapter 74 only by his absence. His five years at the helm of the state had already been analyzed at length in the chapters that lead up to this one and in any case they do not directly relate to the principal theme of chapter 74: the weak and vacillating character of Nicholas II and its relationship to the unfolding "Red Wheel." In the addendum to chapter 74 ("July 1914") a tormented Nicholas must decide whether to call a "general mobilization" of the armed forces even if such a decision pushes Russia to the brink of war with Austria-Hungary and Germany. "Torn by conflicting forces, near to bursting," the Emperor cannot rely on his own "tormented, vacillating mind."[16] It is at this crucial moment that he "felt the need of a single man of superior character and intelligence who could take responsibility for the decision, who could say at once, 'This way, and no other,' and act accordingly." For a fleeting moment Nicholas acknowledges that "there had been such a man—Stolypin!" And he recognizes "how sorely he needed Stolypin at that very minute."[17]

Nicholas II is a decent, God-fearing man who is utterly devoted to his family. But he is the furthest thing from a man of superior character and intelligence. He is overwhelmed by responsibilities of state and dreads meeting with his ministers. He takes solace in military parades, in inspecting regiments, and above all in the pleasure of being home with his beloved Alix and his children. This chapter makes clear that his impulse in February 1917 to flee his political responsibilities and to be with his family at Tsarskoe

15 *August 1914*, p. 582.
16 *Ibid.*, pp. 776–77.
17 *Ibid.*, p. 777.

Selo was in fact the impulse that had guided him from the beginning of his reign. He loved his wife, his girls, and the "little treasure," the heir to the throne, with a love that was heartfelt and in many ways admirable. But Nicholas felt at a loss with anyone outside of the family circle and only wished for stronger emotional ties with the Russian people. Rule was a burden for him, a burden he accepted as a cross to bear. "To be Tsar of Russia was difficult beyond endurance,"[18] he thinks to himself in chapter 74. He vacillated over every decision of state and did not know whom to listen to or trust among his advisors (although he finally deferred to Serge Witte, the most competent statesman of the pre-1905 period, as he would later defer to Stolypin). He believed himself to be an autocrat, an "anointed monarch" whose power came from God. But he had to be persuaded by his wife to remember that fact, and to try to exercise authority firmly and with the requisite self-confidence.

As the chapter shows, he was easily manipulated by his cousin Wilhelm, the German Kaiser, who was "so friendly, so affectionate, so lovey-dovey, to Nicky and Alix"[19] even as he pursued Germany's foreign policy interests with brazen self-confidence. There was indeed something theatrical about Wilhelm's display of friendship for Nicholas. This "friendship" culminated in the farcical Björkö agreement of 1905 where the two emperors signed a secret three-way treaty of friendship with France with the Kaiser telling the Tsar that France "would join later."[20] In chapter 74, we see Wilhelm encouraging the imperialist delusions of Nicholas in

18 *Ibid.*, p. 694.
19 *Ibid.*, p. 701.
20 For a discussion of the Björkö agreement, see Solzhenitsyn, *August 1914*, pp. 752–53, 765–66 and *"The Russian Question" at the End of the Twentieth Century*, pp. 68–69. For a somewhat different account of the Björkö affair that emphasizes how quickly Nicholas recovered from his initial manipulation by Wilhelm, see Hélène Carrère d'Encausse, *Nicholas II: The Interrupted Transition*, translated by George Holoch (New York: Holmes & Meier, 2000), pp. 76–78.

the Far East (informally crowning the Tsar "Emperor of the East" and "Admiral of the Pacific") while ceaselessly pursuing Germany's interests (for example, Wilhelm imposed a particularly oppressive trade agreement on Russia in 1904). Yet instead of weighing and balancing Russia's interest in keeping good relations with both France and Germany (the "time-tested arrangement of Peter I"[21] as Solzhenitsyn puts it in The "Russian Question" at the End of the Twentieth Century) the Tsar kept his father's "secret" alliance with France while placing great store in his "friendship" with Wilhelm. It is painful to see a head of state so easily manipulated in the name of an estimable private, good, friendship that has limited validity to international affairs. As Solzhenitsyn argues in Reflections on the February Revolution, for all his decency, Nicholas had far less appreciation for the "substance" of the Russian nation, for the dignity and grandeur of the state, than his innumerable predecessors as Tsar of Russia.[22]

Chapter 74 of August 1914 provides numerous illustrations of the poisonous hostility of Russian "society" to the Russian state. Solzhenitsyn makes clear that the Russo-Japanese War was the height of folly. Nicholas pursued imperial goals that were incompatible with balanced internal development. Moreover, these goals were positively dangerous in light of the unrelieved animosity that so much of educated society directed toward the state.[23] The war with Japan was "distant, unpopular" and "inexplicable" and brought forth an almost nihilistic "craving for defeat."[24] While young Japanese volunteered to join the armed forces, Russian students wrote to the Mikado expressing their hopes for a Japanese victory in the war. Solzhenitsyn does not for a minute approve this hatred for Russia that animated so much of her intellectual and professional elite. But the deeper responsibility for this moral crisis lies with the Tsar himself. He pursued a reckless Asian policy

21 "The Russian Question," p. 69.
22 Réflexions sur la révolution de Février, pp. 41–42.
23 August 1914, pp. 719–20.
24 "The Russian Question," p. 68.

that nearly led to the collapse of the monarchy. Having travelled once to the Far East, he considered himself an expert on that part of the world. He aimed to "strengthen Russia's lines of communication, her military presence, her influence in Asia, to which the Siberian land mass gave her a natural entry."[25] He took advantage of the weakness of imperial China to expand the Russian presence in Manchuria and to compete with Japanese influence in Korea. His "great plan"[26] for Russian expansion in Asia ignored the fragility of the Russian social order and underestimated the strength of a newly industrialized and self-confident Japan. It also had strategic defects. Because of tensions with Austria, Russia was forced to maintain her best troops on the western front. The Trans-Siberian railroad was not yet completed (there was a major gap at Lake Baikal) so there was no easy way to transport masses of troops to Russian positions in Manchuria.

The fall of Port Arthur and the devastating naval defeat at the Tsushima Straits on May 27–28, 1905 humiliated Russia in the eyes of the world even as they emboldened a "society" that expressed open contempt for the monarchy and demanded a radical change of regime. Nicholas's concessions, culminating in the granting of a constitution with the Manifesto of October 30, 1905, did nothing to assuage the opposition. "All restraint was abandoned and the whole press and all those who could make their voices heard began demanding immediate reform, war or no war, and a stiff dose of freedom, which might completely emasculate the state."[27] The goal of the obdurate enemies of the monarchy was indeed the emasculation of the state. But the decision to go to war, and the pursuit of a ruinous "plan" of imperial expansion gave the most irresponsible elements in society a chance to pursue their destructive designs. Solzhenitsyn is clear: Nicholas would make a similar unthinking decision for war in July 1914, a decision that might have been prevented by a far-seeing statesman

25 *August 1914*, p. 710.
26 *Ibid.*, p. 720.
27 *Ibid.*, p. 735.

such as Stolypin who appreciated the unfinished work of reform in Russia and the dangers that remained despite the considerable progress made after 1906. We know that Solzhenitsyn is convinced that Stolypin, if he had lived and returned to power, would not have taken Russia into the war. The great Russian statesman fully appreciated that Russia's internal development in peace, prosperity, and freedom, his paramount concern, could not have withstood such an assault.[28]

In *The Red Wheel*, Solzhenitsyn shows that it was indeed the war in its totality that provided the occasion for revolution. No war, and no February or October revolutions, and the almost unimaginable bloodshed, tyranny and generalized mendacity that would follow. But Nicholas, in his supreme indecision, is incapable of grasping the big picture. He is overcome by the burden of choice and still places inordinate hopes in his "friendship" with Wilhelm. He is angered that there is no plan for a "partial mobilization" against Austria alone and accepts a "general mobilization" not because he is convinced of its merits but because it will put an end to his agonizing indecision. At the end of the chapter, we see him buoyed by the surge of popular patriotic enthusiasm for the war. Nicholas does what he didn't have the courage to do in 1905: he stands on the balcony of the Winter Palace, "face-to-face with his people," convinced that his reign had begun anew.[29] But readers of *The Red Wheel* know just how deceived he is. For

---

28 Solzhenitsyn's argument is supported by Stolypin's best biographer Abraham Ascher. Acknowledging the speculative character of such judgments, Ascher is nonetheless persuaded that "given his previous insistence that Russia must avoid war, that even in 1914 Stolypin would have tried to keep Russia at peace." Stolypin's protégés such as Krivoshein, the minister of agriculture, and even some of his bitter enemies such as the arch-conservative P. N. Durnovo may well have sided with him in "pressing for the avoidance of war." See Abraham Ascher, *P. A. Stolypin: The Search for Stability in Late Imperial Russia* (Palo Alto, California: Stanford University Press, 2001), p. 394.

29 *August 1914*, p. 783.

what awaits Nicholas II is not a glorious reign but the gradual unraveling of the monarchy and the further sapping of Russia's national spirit. Society remains as irresponsible as ever, and when its representatives come to power in March 1917 they turn out to be "nullities" of the first order.[30] More mediocre than Nicholas, Prince Georgi Lvov and Aleksandr Kerensky are no match for the Lenins and Trotskys of the world.

One other point is worth stressing. In chapter 74, Solzhenitsyn emphasizes how pained Nicholas was by the loss of life in Petersburg on "Bloody Sunday," January 22, 1905. When workers under the leadership of the charismatic Father Gapon marched peacefully on the Winter Palace to present a petition to their "father" the Tsar, the unarmed crowd was met by a hail of bullets that took about two hundred lives. That event struck at the legitimacy of the Tsarist regime and haunted Nicholas thereafter. This man of peace, this "father of his people," did not want to see a repeat of "Bloody Sunday" at the end of February 1917. But as Solzhenitsyn stresses in *Reflections of the February Revolution*, the unrest in February 1917 was still limited to the capital and nine-tenths of Russia remained loyal to the monarchical principle. It was still in the Tsar's power to cut telephone and telegraphic lines, to appeal to loyal troops, to use a minimum of violence to put an end to the revolutionary contagion.[31] His desire to avoid bloodshed *at all costs* and his concern for his family ultimately led him to abdicate on behalf of himself and his son.[32] Solzhenitsyn

30 Solzhenitsyn is particularly insistent on this point in his January 1979 BBC interview with Janis Sapiets in *East and West* (New York: Harper & Row, 1980), pp. 149–52.

31 *Réflexions sur la révolution de Février*, pp. 32–36.

32 *Ibid.* pp. 34–35. In *Nicholas II: The Interrupted Transition*, the distinguished historian of Russia Hélène Carrère d'Encausse emphasizes Nicholas's patriotic motives: he wanted above all to do nothing that would hamper or undermine Russia's war efforts or her obligations to her allies. See d'Encausse, *Nicholas II*, pp. 218–34. But this sympathetic biographer also acknowledges that the decision to abdicate on behalf of his son as well as himself was an example of "the father" winning out "over the monarch." It was, she suggests, "a

does not hesitate: by doing so this "weak Tsar"[33] shamelessly abandoned the millions of his loyal subjects who remained loyal to the monarchical principle. Nicholas had no moral right to abdicate when an immense danger menaced the nation. For the sake of an illusory civic peace, he stepped down from his throne when Russia could least afford it. The immediate beneficiary of this act was not a powerless Provisional Government (the alleged representatives of "society") but the Executive Committee of the Soviet of Workers' and Soldiers' Deputies, "a band of good-for nothings, semi-intellectuals, semi-revolutionaries, who had been elected by no one."[34] And seventy years of Bolshevik despotism would follow.

To be sure, Nicholas thought of himself as an autocrat, as God's anointed. But he had never appreciated the differences, and possible tension, between private and public virtue. And he had never learned the decisiveness that is an essential element of public responsibility. For all his decency, therefore, Nicholas provides an instructive lesson in what is to be avoided. As we emphasized in the previous chapter, he is a Christian monarch who forgets essential features of Christian monarchy rightly understood. He never acknowledges much less acts upon his overriding obligation to place public responsibilities before familial and private considerations. Unlike Stolypin, he did not have the soul of a true statesman or a man born to be king.

Thus, as Edward Ericson and Alexis Klimoff have well observed in *The Soul and Barbed Wire*, Solzhenitsyn "holds the Tsar primarily responsible for Russia's descent into the revolutionary maelstrom."[35] This argument is stated most emphatically in *Reflections on the February Revolution*. But independently of

tragic decision whose consequences were grasped neither by him or by his interlocutors from the Duma." See d'Encausse, p. 228.

33 *Réflexions sur la révolution de Février*, p. 56.
34 *Ibid.*, p. 72.
35 Edward E. Ericson, Jr. & Alexis Klimoff, *The Soul and Barbed Wire: An Introduction to Solzhenitsyn* (Wilmington, DE: ISI Books, 2008), pp. 159–60.

those four summary essays, originally intended to introduce each of the four volumes in the knot, the material in *March 1917* amply demonstrates the point. The "picture of anarchy in the streets"[36] that is so vividly described in the multiple short chapters of that 3,000-page knot is coupled by an equally compelling portrait of a Tsarist regime that "was afflicted by something far more serious than mere incompetence."[37] The Tsar had indeed forgotten what it meant to be a ruler. Yet despite these harsh judgments on Nicholas's ultimate responsibility for the disaster that would overtake Russia, Solzhenitsyn never loses human sympathy for him or his family. This Tsar who had voluntarily abdicated to avoid civil war, and who had pledged support to his successors, did not deserve the terrible fate that awaited him.[38]

The expertly drawn scene on "The Abdication of Nicholas II" (chapter 349 of *March 1917*) shows a helpless and dispirited man who fears that his departure might lead to greater bloodshed in Russia. He is on the verge of "capitulation" (unbeknownst to Guchkov and Shulgin, who had been sent by the Duma to solicit an abdication, he had already signed such a document) and under immense strain makes the fateful decision to abdicate on behalf of both himself and the young Tsarevich; he cannot bear the thought of no longer having access to the heir apparent. He thus unintentionally dooms the five centuries-old Russian monarchy and the three centuries-old dynasty. All he wants is to be with his wife and family while the once fervent monarchist Guchkov fears what would happen if he were to be reunited with his "willpower."[39] "After three days and nights spent driving around in a senseless, frenetic circle" he is authorized to return to Mogilev (but not yet to Tsarskoe Selo), having "lost a crown on the way."[40] The

---

36 *Ibid.*, p. 159.
37 *Ibid.*
38 *Réflexions sur la révolution de Février*, p. 85.
39 See *The Solzhenitsyn Reader: New and Essential Writings, 1947–2005*, edited by Edward E. Ericson, Jr. and Daniel J. Mahoney (Wilmington, DE: ISI Books, 2006), p. 431.
40 *Ibid.*, p. 432.

reader sympathizes with the Tsar who maintains something of his composure, his dignity, even as he signs a crown and an empire away. Solzhenitsyn's art does justice to this moment, and to the humanity of Nicholas II, in a way that no merely historical account could do.

Solzhenitsyn's portrait of a Tsar who was too hesitant and mediocre to lead a great nation and empire at a time of crisis does not preclude attentiveness to his virtues or sympathy for his fate. As we have noted he is no more mediocre, and a good deal more virtuous, than the spineless nullities who would succeed him at the helm of what was left of the Russian state. Chapters 349 and 531 of *March 1917*, so well drawn and full of psychological and spiritual import, have even more power when they are contrasted with the equally effective "snapshot-like glimpses" of revolutionary unrest in that volume's "street scenes."[41] The contrast between a revolution that seems to happen of its own accord, anticipated by neither friend nor foe, and a weak and ineffectual Tsar whose humanity is never lost to us, gives life and force to *March 1917*.

In the aforementioned chapter 531 of *March 1917*, Solzhenitsyn shows the Tsar, at long last reunited with his family, being "produced for inspection."[42] A despairing Tsar, in a "drowsy torpor, his mouth half open, groaning" is subjected to a "new suffering and humiliation."[43] Dressed in his Household Cavalry uniform, the deposed emperor is forced to go for a stroll on the second floor of his palace, to remove his hat, and to show the representatives of the revolutionary Soviet that he is indeed living at Tsarskoe under house arrest. He notices the hatred in the eyes of the assembled commissars, a hatred that "stung and burned."[44] "This stark manifestation of pure malice"[45] is a portent of worse indignities—and measureless violence—to come.

41 Edward E. Ericson, Jr. & Alexis Klimoff, *The Soul and Barbed Wire*, p. 159.
42 *The Solzhenitsyn Reader*, pp. 438–42.
43 *Ibid.*, p. 440.
44 *Ibid.*, p. 442.
45 *Ibid.*

Conclusion

At the beginning of this chapter, I made reference to Solzhenitsyn's humane and creative traditionalism. Far from being a reactionary, Solzhenitsyn fully appreciated that a living tradition must be open to the challenges of the present and must be able to anticipate trouble in the future. Decent and humane rulers need to cultivate moderation or self-limitation and are obliged to put balanced internal development before reckless foreign adventures that sap the strength of a people. At the same time, Solzhenitsyn knew that the prudence of the statesman is incompatible with meekness or pusillanimity. A ruler who truly knows how to rule must combine moderation and spiritedness, a sense of limits and decisiveness in dealing with the enemies of civilized order. Solzhenitsyn's wonderfully crafted portraits of Nicholas II and Pyotr Stolypin are of more than historical interest. In his portrait of Stolypin we observe the qualities of heart and mind that are necessary to govern a great and free people; in his account of Nicholas II we see an "anointed" monarch bereft of those fundamental qualities of soul necessary to preserve a living national tradition amidst the unceasing dynamism of the modern world. Solzhenitsyn's reflections on statesmanship, so amply on display in *The Red Wheel*, provide an enduring contribution to historical and political understanding.

Chapter 4

THE ARTIST AS THINKER:
REFLECTIONS ON *IN THE FIRST CIRCLE*

With his passing at the age of 89 on August 3, 2008 the English-speaking world was obliged to come to terms once again with Aleksandr Isaevich Solzhenitsyn. It was time to sum up and take stock of the Russian Nobel Laureate, anti-totalitarian writer, and courageous if unnerving moral witness. The response was more abundant and on the whole more respectful than one might have anticipated. Positive judgments and appreciations generally out-weighed the criticisms and misrepresentations that had character-ized journalistic discussions of Solzhenitsyn since at least the beginning of his western exile in 1974. Still, there was something disturbingly anachronistic about the American and British com-mentary. Almost all of the obituaries and critical commentaries highlighted the 1978 Harvard Address and Solzhenitsyn's status as a "dissident" (a word he *never* used to describe himself), and they were inordinately concerned with his judgments about the Yeltsin and Putin years. And in writing about Solzhenitsyn's recent political views commentators relied more on recycled news accounts than on an examination of Solzhenitsyn's own speeches and writings. Nonetheless, most commentators understood that Solzhenitsyn had played a truly decisive role in bringing down an "evil empire" and paid tribute to *The Gulag Archipelago* as a book that told essential truths about Communism.

Solzhenitsyn's death was a solemn moment that allowed greater perspective—and thus justice—to come to sight. It was if the views and characterizations of old were too small-minded for the occasion, that of commemorating and taking measure of the life and world historical achievement of a genuinely great human being.

Still, there were egregious offenders. A lengthy obituary in *The New York Times* (August 4, 2008) was laden with factual errors and repeated every possible cliché about Solzhenitsyn's political and religious convictions. The *Times'* readers learned little to nothing about Solzhenitsyn's major literary projects over the past twenty years, a significant lacuna as we shall see. Yet even the *Times* acknowledged Solzhenitsyn's indispensable role in undermining the moral legitimacy of Soviet totalitarianism as well as his status as a "literary giant." Similarly, an otherwise respectful article in *The Economist* (August 9–15, 2008) suggested that Solzhenitsyn's fierce criticisms of the criminal oligarchy that came to the forefront in the Russian 1990s were rooted in personal pique: Solzhenitsyn, against all evidence, was said to have yearned for political power for himself!

Professional Solzhenitsyn bashers Cathy Young and Zinovy Zinik went further in the pages of *The Boston Globe* and the *Times Literary Supplement,* respectively. They argued that Solzhenitsyn's legacy was "tarnished," that he had become the theoretician of Putin-style authoritarianism, and even a quasi-fascist of sorts. Of course, such tendentious commentators never discuss Solzhenitsyn's detailed proposals for building democratic self-government in Russia from the bottom up, proposals that are at the heart of his political vision as articulated in *Rebuilding Russia* (1990), *Russia in Collapse* (1998) and the luminous speeches and addresses collected in *A Minute Per Day* (1999).

Most commentators also missed the fact that Solzhenitsyn's support for a broad "social restoration" in Russia after 2001 was not equivalent to uncritical support for the Putin regime. Solzhenitsyn openly criticized the party-dominated character of the Russian legislature, the lamentably slow development of local self-government in his homeland, the massive corruption in private and public life. He argued that the government ought to do much more to encourage entrepreneurial capitalism by supporting vigorous independent small and medium-size businesses. While he welcomed the restoration of Russian national pride or self-respect during the Putin years (while categorically repudiating imperialism or foreign adventurism) he parted from the Russian government's increasing refusal to confront the monstrous character of the Soviet past. As his wife and intellectual and literary collaborator Natalia Solzhenitsyn put it at an international conference on Solzhenitsyn at the University of Illinois in June of 2007, Solzhenitsyn believed that "the most rotten thing of all" about contemporary Russia was the failure to adequately *repent* for the crimes of Communism. "In avoiding a clear verdict of society on Communism's evil deeds, we have robbed ourselves—robbed ourselves of the essential experience of historical catharsis." The American—and Western—commentary that followed Solzhenitsyn's death in truth captured very little of the complexity or nuance of Solzhenitsyn's political judgment after his return to his native Russia in May 1994.

Even sympathetic commentators tended to miss the *high-mindedness* of Solzhenitsyn's concerns, which presupposed a breadth and depth of perspective that one can only characterize as philosophic. As the article he was working on at the time of his death attests,[1] Solzhenitsyn was particularly concerned about the estrangement of contemporary Russians from the millennia-old spiritual patrimony of the nation, a patrimony that had bequeathed to them faith in God, "a free, rich and vivid language," and "traditions of home and business life." He was not a nationalist in the narrow sense of the term but he was deeply committed to the preservation of Russian "national consciousness." And he worried about the failure of democracy—particularly the "democracy of small spaces" to take root in his beloved Russia. Once more he reiterated his conviction that local self-government of the Swiss or New England variety would be a "welcome solution" or outlet for the energy of ordinary, decent citizens.

---

1   See "Fugitives from the Family," *Rossiyskaya Gazeta*, December 11, 2008.

As this rapid survey makes clear, American critics and commentators have paid little attention to either the literary or philosophical dimensions of the Russian writer's work. One notable exception is Carlin Romano who was one of the first literary critics to engage the "new" writings of Solzhenitsyn that Edward E. Ericson, Jr. and I collected in *The Solzhenitsyn Reader: New and Essential Writings, 1947–2005*. Some of these writings, like the camp poems and the 7,000-word autobiographical narrative poem *The Trail* date from the 1940s and '50s, while others—short stories, prose poems, speeches, political reflections, and excerpts from later volumes of *The Red Wheel*—are of much more recent provenance. In a thoughtful appreciation of Solzhenitsyn that appeared in *The Philadelphia Inquirer* on August 11, 2008, Romano wrote that these writings provide a "fine antidote to ... simple-minded pigeonholing of Solzhenitsyn as the brave anticommunist who later went off the deep end." They instead reveal "an unrelenting artist ... a flexible and theologically minded philosopher ... an often daring stylist ... and a political and nationalist 'ideologue' only in the eyes of predisposed critics."

For the most part, however, Solzhenitsyn's writings that have appeared over the past two or two and half decades remain unknown in the United States, and his chef d'oeuvre, *The Red Wheel,* is far more talked about than read. The crucial volumes dedicated to the revolutionary upheavals of *March 1917* are still unavailable in English although efforts are underway to make them available by the centenary of Solzhenitsyn's birth in 2018. The contrast with France couldn't be more striking. Almost as many of Solzhenitsyn's books are available in French as in Russian, and they have been the object of more thoughtful analysis than is generally the case in the Anglophone world. An exception is the remarkably comprehensive and insightful critical survey of Solzhenitsyn's life, thought, and major writings provided by Alexis Klimoff and Edward E. Ericson, Jr. in *The Soul and Barbed Wire: An Introduction to Solzhenitsyn*. This work appeared from ISI Books in August 2008 but, alas, has been almost uniformly ignored by the critics. American critics are in the main content to

believe that they know what they need to know about
Solzhenitsyn.

The Three Pillars

So it is sometimes necessary to turn abroad for deeper treatments
and appreciations. In *Le phénomène Soljénitsyne,* published at the
beginning of 2009 by the distinguished Parisian house Arthème
Fayard, the Swiss Russianist Georges Nivat incisively analyzes
Solzhenitsyn's achievement as an innovative writer and as a penetrating moral thinker, who recovered old but enduring verities in
the age of ideology. As we have already pointed out in Chapter 1,
Nivat argues that there are two peaks, two immense "cathedrals,"
that dominate the Solzhenitsynian literary universe: *The Gulag
Archipelago* and *The Red Wheel.* The first is an absolutely unique
"experiment in literary investigation" that tells the truth about
Soviet repression after 1917 even as it profoundly follows the soul's
confrontation with "barbed wire." The multi-volume *The Red
Wheel* (coming in at no less than 6,000 pages) combines literary
innovation (the street scenes of Petersburg during the February revolution have no analogue in modern literature) with dramatized
history worthy of Thucydides. These two works differ in tone and
style but nonetheless form a diptych. There was nothing fated or
inevitable about the Russian revolutions of 1917. But through certain choices or the lack thereof—brilliantly chronicled in its
pages—the "red wheel" began to turn with something like cosmic
intensity. Its *telos,* it ultimate destination, was nothing less than
"the gulag archipelago," the massive system of Soviet repression
centered around the forced labor camp system. Solzhenitsyn establishes beyond a reasonable doubt that the gulag flowed logically
and in that sense inexorably from Lenin's self-proclaimed project
to "purge Russia of all the harmful insects," to eliminate the real
or imagined enemies of a quasi-mythological socialism. Nivat also
suggests, rightly in my view, that *In The First Circle* forms a third
peak or pillar of Solzhenitsyn's achievement. It combines masterful
artistry with a philosophical depth rarely found. It is, Nivat argues,

a great "European novel" that speaks to both the West and the East and to the broader meaning and sources of the Soviet tragedy, while never losing sight of the ultimate human questions.

The availability of *In The First Circle* in a "restored" 96-chapter version is therefore a publishing event of the first order. The book was released by Harper Collins in the fall of 2009 as part of its "Harper Perennial" series.[2] Like its 87-chapter predecessor, the restored 96-chapter version (now available for the first time in English and under its original title *V kruge pervom—In The First Circle)* beautifully captures the paradox of male friendship and philosophical disputation flourishing in this relatively privileged outpost of the gulag archipelago. In the remainder of this chapter I will comment on the novel at some length in order to provide concrete illustration of Solzhenitsyn's philosophical depth and moral insight. As much as any of Solzhenitsyn's works, *In The First Circle* reveals his greatness as an artist and thinker.

The setting of the novel is a privileged scientific research prison, *a sharashka,* on the edge of the gulag system. This is the real and metaphorical "first circle" of hell to which its Dante-inspired title refers. But the work is misread if it is reduced in a crude or mechanical way to "gulag fiction" as if Solzhenitsyn's *only* purpose was to expose the infernal operations of the Soviet system of political repression. This self-described "polyphonic" novel is above all dialogical in a manner that resembles a Platonic dialogue or a Dostoevskyan novel. It is characterized by a complex narrative structure that combines the third-person point of view with the subjectivity that belongs to a first-person narrative. Different characters alternate as the focus of a chapter or group of chapters in the book. Novelistic polyphony respects pluralism—the variety of perspectives and voices—while inviting readers to join in the search for truth.

2 *In The First Circle* translated by Harry T. Willetts, with a Foreword by Edward E. Ericson, Jr., (New York: Harper Collins, 2009) xxx + 741 pp. References to this "restored" edition of *In The First Circle* will be cited parenthetically in this chapter as *IFC* followed by the page number in the text.

At the same time, one of the main characters, the young Gleb Nerzhin, 31 years of age and five years "in the harness" (*IFC*, 41) as the action unfolds on four crucial days (December 24–27) at the end of 1949, is a faithful literary representation of the young Solzhenitsyn. Nerzhin is the spokesman for Solzhenitsyn's own deepest convictions at the time. A brief excursus on the composition of the work is crucial for understanding the distinctiveness of the version now available to the English-speaking world.

The Two Versions

Solzhenitsyn originally composed *In The First Circle* between 1955 and 1958, after spending many years in prison, labor camps, and internal exile. But it underwent an extensive process of "softening" and "hardening" before a "distorted" or self-censored version was published in the West in 1968. As Solzhenitsyn tells us in the "Author's Note" at the beginning of this version, he "restored" the original text in 1968 precisely as the distorted version was being published in the West in both English and Russian (the definitive "restored" version of the work was first published in his Vermont "Collected Works" in 1978). It should be noted that the "restoration" of *In The First Circle* was completed in the same year—1968—that Solzhenitsyn finished writing *The Gulag Archipelago*.

Nine of the chapters in the restored version are new to English-language readers and twelve are significantly altered. Among other things these new chapters clarify the intellectual *metanoia* of one of its principal characters, the Soviet diplomat Innokenty Volodin, whose dramatic phone call sets the entire plot in motion. Moreover, Harry Willetts' splendid translation, unlike the earlier translations of the 87-chapter version, captures the rhythm and idiom of the original and allows Solzhenitsyn's prose to breathe. As a result, we are now in a much better position to judge Solzhenitsyn's achievement.

The 96-chapter version of *In The First Circle* is in important respects a new work. But one should not overstate the differences between the two versions. Both versions of the novel have the same rich, variegated "polyphonic" structure. Both take place in the Marfino *sharashka* in the Moscow suburbs (thinly disguised as Marvino in the 87-chapter work) where Solzhenitsyn spent three years as a prisoner between 1947 and 1950. Both are peopled by the same principal characters. These include the aforementioned Nerzhin and Volodin, as well as Nerzhin's closest friends and principal interlocutors, Lev Rubin and Dmitri Sologdin who are based on the well-known real-life figures Lev Kopelev and Dmitri Panin. Rubin, a linguist and Germanist as well as a steadfast Communist, is torn between his humane instincts and his uncompromising commitment to revolutionary principles. Sologdin, an engineer, is a fierce opponent of the Communist regime and a self-described Christian individualist (his Christian convictions are much more pronounced in the 96-chapter version of *In The First Circle*). A host of other characters from the half-blind janitor Spiridon (whose moral good sense owes nothing to philosophical reflection) to Stalin (who grows old without friends and with death literally eating away at his soul) provides a brilliant microcosm of Soviet society from the top to the bottom. *First Circle-87* devoted four chapters to Stalin, the vampire-like nocturnal being who keeps the entire bureaucracy awake into the early hours of the morning. He is shown fantasizing about conversing with his "philosophical equals" Kant and Spinoza and of being "Emperor of the World." The "new" version includes five, not four chapters on Stalin. It follows the long-held suspicion that Stalin had been a double agent of the Tsarist secret police during his revolutionary youth, a suspicion he needs to extirpate.

In both versions, Solzhenitsyn instructively captures the tension between the "classical" and the "ideological" tyrant. The one seeks power for personal ends, the other as a means for promoting the revolutionary transformation of the world. The same Stalin who dreams of ruling the world spends part of his time writing a book on Marxism-Leninism and linguistics. The Stalin chapters powerfully renew the classical philosophical critique of the tyrant who loses his humanity, even his ability to relate to other human beings as human beings, in the course of gaining the world. Like Plato in the *Gorgias,* Solzhenitsyn suggests that it is better to suffer harm and to maintain one's moral integrity than to impose injustice on others.

Both versions of *In The First Circle* begin with a dramatic, life-altering telephone call. In *IFC-87* the talented young Soviet diplomat Innokenty Volodin calls a doctor friend to warn him that the sharing of a life-saving medical discovery with doctors from the West would be perceived by the authorities as an act of treason, rather than the humanitarian act that it is. In a totalitarian regime, the ordinary meaning of words and deeds are turned upside down. Volodin's call is recorded by the secret police and the effort to find the caller (and thus the "detective" element of the novel) begins. The scientist-prisoners in the Marfino *sharashka* are given the task of using the new science of "phonoscopy" or voice decoding to track down the person responsible for this allegedly treasonous act. There can be little ambiguity in judging the perversity of a regime that identifies elementary human decency with treason.

In the new version, the opening chapter becomes two chapters and the nature of Volodin's deed is fundamentally transformed. He surreptitiously places a call, not to a doctor friend, but to the American embassy to warn about an act of nuclear espionage that is about to occur in a radio shop in New York (this part of the plot is based on the real life case of the Soviet spy Georgy Koval). It is Christmastime in the West and the embassy is understaffed and otherwise unprepared to receive Volodin's warning. The naval attaché speaks poor Russian and is suspicious of Volodin's information. Therefore, the young Soviet diplomat's heroic and treasonous act which is based on his fear of the Soviet regime getting its hands on the atomic bomb, is seemingly for naught. As Georges Nivat has shown in an authoritative 1980 interpretive essay on Solzhenitsyn's "Different Circles," the new opening of *IFC-96* decisively transforms the meaning and import of Volodin's act. In the 96-chapter version of the novel, Volodin is moved by "active hatred of the communist regime." He consciously "betrays" the regime he represents. Solzhenitsyn thus raises the question of whether one is obliged to honor the commands of a truly perverse regime. Nivat is not wrong to compare this problematic to "the medieval disputations on the legitimacy of tyrannicide" or, one might add, to Aristotle's famous question in the *Politics* about whether the "good man" is the same as the "good citizen." As the late Delba Winthrop liked to point out, the 96-chapter version of In *The First Circle* thus begins by raising a question of *political philosophy* that became all the more pressing under conditions of totalitarianism. It should be added that the patriot Solzhenitsyn always refused to identify the Leninist-Stalinist regime with the cause of Russia or to succumb to the charms of "Great Soviet patriotism."

"But We Are Only Given One Conscience, Too"

Among the principal characters in the novel Innokenty Volodin and Gleb Nerzhin stand out because their fidelity to conscience ultimately leads them down a path that culminates in imprisonment in the gulag labor camps. Nerzhin refuses to participate in a project that will buy him time in the *sharashka* because it will ensnare innocent people and will distract him from the "passion" that has come to grip him, contemplation of the truth and the cultivation of his soul. He is recognizably the same character in the two versions of *In The First Circle*. Volodin, in contrast, is an even more interesting and weighty character in the "new" version of the work. As in the earlier version, we witness his movement from being a privileged, carefree, and cosmopolitan member of the Soviet elite to being a conscientious young man troubled by doubts about, and a growing aversion to, the regime that he had hitherto served without qualms of conscience. He is estranged from his beautiful wife Dotnara, the daughter of the public prosecutor in Moscow, who is at home with the evasion of moral responsibility that is coextensive with being a privileged child of the Soviet regime. As in the 87-chapter edition, a crucial flashback scene, chapter 60, gives us access to the inner transformation that leads to Volodin's estrangement from his wife and his decision to make the life-altering phone call.

"But We Are Given Only One Conscience, Too," is one of the most important chapters in the work as a whole. Too nervous to attend a party at the home of his in-laws a mere twenty-four hours after the fateful call, Volodin reflects on the first six years of his marriage where "no inhibitions, no obstacles" were allowed to "come between wish and fulfillment." He and his wife traveled widely and "were eager to sample every new, exotic fruit." Their motto was an Epicurean one (at least in the popular sense of that term): "We are given only one life!" (*IFC*, 435).

Volodin then reflects on the momentous change that occurred in his sixth year of marriage. He had reached a dead end. The life of endless novelty and material pleasure began to "disgust" him. His soul was ripe for self-examination. "His friends had long ago decided he was an "Epicurean," and he readily accepted the label, without really knowing what it meant." The crucial moment came when he "had the amusing idea of reading what his 'master' had in fact taught" (*IFC*, 437). Searching through the cabinets of his late mother he found not only a book of Epicurus's sayings but also a series of her letters and diaries. He had always admired, even idolized his father, a revolutionary naval officer who had been killed in 1921 repressing an independent peasant rebellion in Tambov province. He now discovered that his "bourgeois" mother had thought deeply and widely about matters—"Truth, Beauty, Goodness, the Ethical Imperative" that had no place in the "progressive" Soviet world that had shaped his soul. "Something he had lacked" —a moral anchor, a principled "point of view," was "stealing into his heart" (*IFC*, 439). His discovery of the moral law (in his mother's words, "Injustice is stronger than you ... but let it not be done through you") (*IFC*, 439) leads him to rethink the claims made on behalf of the Bolshevik revolution of 1917. His work as a "diplomat": the secret meetings, the code names, the passing on of instructions and money, began to seem sordid, distasteful, repellant. In some of the most important words of the book, Solzhenitsyn writes:

The great truth for Innokenty used to be that we are only given one life.

Now, with the new feeling that had ripened in him, he became aware of another law: that we are given only one conscience, too.

A life laid down cannot be reclaimed, nor can a ruined conscience. (*IFC*, 441)

With the full force of his art, Solzhenitsyn chronicles the "existential" recovery of those elemental moral experiences that give evidence of the moral law and that give the lie to every ideological denial of the soul's connection to goodness and truth and its responsibility before them.

A Crucial Encounter

The restored version of *In The First Circle* contains two additional flashback chapters that give us fuller access to Volodin's remarkable spiritual and political transformation. The most important flashback scene is the one provided in chapter 61, "The Uncle at Tver," which immediately follows upon Volodin's internal repudiation of "Epicureanism." Eager to know more about his mother and to connect to her past, Volodin sets out to visit her sole remaining relative, Uncle Avenir, whom he had only seen in childhood. His uncle lives in dignified poverty in Tver. Avenir is a free man who maintains his moral integrity by, as much as possible, opting out of a system that wars against the human conscience. He is a handyman, a jack-of-all-trades (supported by his wife who works as a hospital nurse). In his conversation with Innokenty he repeats a question by the nineteenth-century Russian thinker Herzen about the limits of patriotism, of loyalty to a government or regime that is intent on "destroying its own people" (*IFC*, 449). His home, little more than a patched-together hovel, is filled with camouflaged old newspapers that tell the truth about the Bolshevik revolution of 1917 and thus expose the lies about the past to which the Soviet people are daily subjected.

While Volodin's "hero" father Artem had worked to violently disperse the democratically elected Constituent Assembly in

January 1918, Avenir was among those students who had bravely protested this brutal totalitarian act. Avenir gives Volodin a civics lesson imbued with truth and moral passion. He sees the Second World War as a tragedy in which the Soviet people struggled heroically for the homeland only to be ground down by "the man with the big Moustache" (*IFC*, 451). He is convinced that the Soviet regime could never obtain the atomic bomb by itself but that it will resort to espionage and thievery to do so. The people of the Soviet Union would then lose all hope for freedom. The meeting with Avenir stiffens Volodin's resolve and cures him of any remaining ideological illusions. He is determined to make up for the sins of the father by doing what he can to prevent an odious regime from attaining the atomic bomb. The Epicureans of old eschewed politics and attempted to cultivate their private "gardens." But to do so in the context of an ideological regime that relentlessly wars on the bodies and souls of human beings is to become complicit in evil, to risk permanent spiritual corruption.

Volodin thus follows the dictates of conscience and takes a stand for his country and humanity and against the totalitarian regime he is officially committed to uphold. But after doing so he is desperately afraid of being exposed and is even more worried that his call was for naught. The thoughtless, frivolous attitude of the naval attaché on the other end of the phone suggests the decadent character of the prosperous West. In his moments of frustration, the young diplomat is not sure that the West deserves to be saved or is capable of acting on the warning he has given it. He was right to try to prevent Stalin from stealing the bomb. But will ordinary Soviets, herded together and subject to the most mendacious propaganda, truly appreciate what was at stake in his "treasonous" act?

The Decisive Metanoia

Several chapters near the end of the work chronicle Volodin's arrest, interrogation and imprisonment. These chapters mirror Solzhenitsyn's own experience after his arrest in February 1945. If

Nerzhin is Solzhenitsyn's authorial alter ego, Volodin's intellectual and spiritual transformation as described in *In The First Circle* also parallels Solzhenitsyn's intellectual and spiritual "ascent" as described in *The Gulag Archipelago* and elsewhere in his work. The newly modified conclusion of chapter 93 ("Second Wind") takes on added importance in this regard.

Volodin now recognizes that "he would have done no other. He could not have remained indifferent" (*IFC*, 710). It was Uncle Avenir's Herzen-inspired remarks about the limits of one's obligation to a truly perverse regime that turns out to have been decisive. It was the memories of his two days with Avenir that were the most significant to Volodin as he began his descent into the gulag. "No one in his life had ever been so important to him" (*IFC*, 710). The spirited wisdom of Avenir is contrasted with the "stupid" thought of Epicurus that "our feelings of satisfaction and dissatisfaction are the highest criteria of good and evil" (*IFC*, 710). Volodin—and Solzhenitsyn—appreciate the difference between vulgar and philosophical Epicureanism. But in both cases how can the mind find serenity if all is reduced to "matter in motion"? The ancient philosopher's refined, apolitical hedonism, his carefully calibrated weighing of pleasures and pain, can provide no principled ground for refusing the Tyrant's claim that his pleasure is "good." "Stalin, for instance, enjoyed killing people—so that, for him, was 'good'?" Those "who are imprisoned for the truth get no satisfaction from it—so is that evil?" (*IFC*, 710).

Epicureanism represented a dead end, a spiritual obtuseness of the first order. "The great materialist's wisdom" now "seemed like the prattle of a child" (*IFC*, 711), to the imprisoned Innokenty. He had ascended to a higher moral and spiritual plane than the one provided by a hedonistic calculus. "Good and evil were now distinct entities, visibly separated by that light gray door, those olive green walls, and that first night in prison" (*IFC*, 711). This was the decisive *metanoia,* the discovery of a moral universe, of the real divide between good and evil. Volodin eloquently articulates the heart of Solzhenitsyn's mature moral vision.

Beyond Fanaticism and Skepticism

Volodin's call to the American embassy on the 24th of December, 1949 (the Western Christmas eve) sets in motion the dramatic "detective story" within the novel. The Soviet diplomat's call is intercepted by the secret police (although the officers monitoring the embassy calls are themselves distracted by petty concerns and almost miss the call). Led by the dissident Communist Lev Rubin, the prisoners of the *sharashka* are then given the task of using the new science of phonoscopy to encrypt and then uncover the identity of the voice that has been recorded on the audiotape.

Rubin welcomes the challenge. He has been unjustly imprisoned but still wholeheartedly identifies with the cause of revolutionary socialism. He urges Nerzhin to "look at things in historical perspective" by which he means the perspective of "historical necessity," the "inevitability" that allegedly conforms "to the inherent laws of history" (*IFC*, 41). For his part, Nerzhin is a self-described skeptic but one whose skepticism is directed first and foremost at ideological fanaticism. This is even more apparent in the restored version of *In the First Circle*. Nerzhin wonders how he could have once "worshipped" Lenin whose dogmatism and fanaticism are unworthy of a decent and reflective human being (*IFC*, 42). But skepticism is not enough intellectually or morally. It is useful as a way of "silencing fanaticism" but it is at best a halfway house—it cannot give a man a reliable footing to stand on.

Edward Ericson explains in his insightful foreword to the restored edition of *In The First Circle* that the Nerzhin-Solzhenitsyn of the *sharashka is* not yet a religious believer but has been "brought to the edge of religious belief." He is in search of a principled "point of view," and is, in Solzhenitsyn's words, fully committed to the great task of "cutting" and "polishing" his soul "so as to become a human being" (*IFC*, 496).

But as the important "new" chapter 47 ("Top-Secret Conversation") makes clear, Nerzhin had already moved significantly beyond skepticism toward a much more substantial affirmation of justice, conscience, and self-limitation. Rubin pleads with him to work on the voice decoding project and warns him about the foolhardiness of "getting in the way" of the movement of History. Nerzhin cannot see what "all the great thinkers in the West," Sartre preeminently among them see, the self-evident superiority of "socialism" to "capitalism." Rubin derides him as *"Pithecanthropus erectus,"* an ape-man out of touch with the requirements of History (*IFC*, 339). But Nerzhin refuses to accept this terminology or to become imprisoned by ideological abstractions. He will have nothing to do with "blasted fanatics" (*IFC*, 340) who refuse to give human beings space to live and breathe. But now he roots his opposition to fanaticism in "moral self-limitation" and mocks the Marxist idea that justice is nothing but a "class-conditioned idea." In a beautiful *cri de coeur* he proclaims that "justice *is* the cornerstone, the foundation of the universe!... We are born with a sense of justice in our souls; we can't and don't want to live without it!" (*IFC*, 340).

Nerzhin remains committed to a life of *reflection* about human nature and the order of things, now wedded to a conception of human dignity that does justice to the moral nature of man. He is now able to affirm certain truths that further open his eyes. Nerzhin-Solzhenitsyn's *philosophical* affirmation of natural justice, of the experience of the soul that the good is not unsupported, is a precondition of his recovery of faith that is described with great luminosity in the central section of *The Gulag Archipelago*, "The Soul and Barbed Wire." Solzhenitsyn's mature thought is best described as a philosophical Christianity that never loses sight of the philosophical *metanoia* of both Volodin and Nerzhin as described in the full version of *In The First Circle*.

The Remarkable Continuities of Solzhenitsyn's Reflection

The publication of the full version of Solzhenitsyn's novel thus provides a most welcome opportunity to look beyond "the distractions of celebrity and controversy that once beclouded" the great Russian writer, as Edward Ericson puts it in his foreword to the volume. Readers will confront a subtle thinker and gifted writer who recognizes that philosophical friendship and dialogue, with its rich interplay of voices and "worldviews," is an essential element of the soul's ascent to truth. They will be better able to discern the connection between the polyphonic novel and the philosophical tradition inaugurated by Plato and Plato's Socrates. *In The First Circle* solidly establishes the continuity of Solzhenitsyn's thought with the deepest and most humane currents of classical and Christian thought.

What the restored version of *In The First Circle* also makes clear are the remarkable continuities that inform Solzhenitsyn's political and philosophical reflection from the late 1940s onward. Solzhenitsyn, a Captain in the Red Army when he was arrested in East Prussia in February 1945, was a still a Marxist of firm conviction: as Nerzhin tells Rubin in chapter 9 of *In The First Circle,* "it made me sick at heart to part with that doctrine! It was the clarion call, the ruling passion of my youth" (*IFC*, 42). But he "lost many arguments" (*IFC*, 42) in prison and the scales began to fall from his eyes. One of the new chapters in *In The First Circle* (chapter 90, "On the Back Stairway") reveals just how profound these continuities in Solzhenitsyn's thought are.

Nerzhin, who is about to be shipped off to the gulag proper, has a clandestine nighttime conversation with Illarion Gerasimovich, a *zek* engineer and optics expert who is serving his second term of incarceration. Gerasimovich has unfounded confidence in the power of a properly constituted technical or scientific elite to govern the world. He places his hope in a Revolution that will bring the true men of science to power. Nerzhin has no time of day for "the rational society"—the enemy of all reason and decency—and proclaims "To hell with revolution" (*IFC*, 666). He knows that there is no technical solution to the political problem that can bypass the need for human beings to live well with their freedom. He even expresses an admiration for the "Swiss model" of self-government which we know would become particularly dear to Solzhenitsyn's heart in the last decades of his life (*IFC*, 666). Like the mature Solzhenitsyn, Nerzhin emphatically repudiates the entire modern ideology of progress since it conflates moral and technical progress and turns a blind eye to the human capacity for evil, a capacity made worse by "beautiful" modern ideas (*IFC*, 670). There is no "backward and forward in human history," Nerzhin tells his interlocutor. Rather, history is "like an octopus, with neither back nor front" (*IFC*, 670). Gerasimovich is scandalized that a man of science, a mathematician, can raise doubts about the self-evident goodness of modern "progress." But Nerzhin refuses to cede any ground. He reminds his fellow zek that "plenty doesn't mean Progress!" (*IFC*, 670). And in a manner reminiscent of Solzhenitsyn's great 1973 essay "Repentance and Self-Limitation in the Life of Nations" and of a host of more recent texts, Nerzhin identifies true progress with self-limitation, with "a general willingness to share things in short supply."

For fifty years or more, Solzhenitsyn's life and art bore witness to his confident belief, so eloquently expressed in his *Nobel Lecture,* that art could "defeat the Lie!", that "one word of truth" could finally "outweigh the whole world." In his exchange with Gerasimovich, Nerzhin appealed to the power of the Word to shatter violence and lies, to restore Reality in all its multifaceted lucidity (*IFC*, 671–72). We fail to do justice to Solzhenitsyn's manifold contributions as writer, historian, philosopher, and moral witness if we allow ourselves to be deceived by caricatures or to be excessively preoccupied with his passing judgments about daily events in post-Communist Russia. With the publication of the restored version of In *The First Circle* we have an opportunity to rise to the challenge and to take Solzhenitsyn seriously again as an artist and thinker of the first rank.

Chapter 5

A PHENOMENOLOGY OF IDEOLOGICAL DESPOTISM: REFLECTIONS ON SOLZHENITSYN'S "OUR MUZZLED FREEDOM"

An Introduction: Theorizing Totalitarianism

There has been no shortage of debates about totalitarianism, which Hannah Arendt rightly called a "novel" form of government which first saw the light of day in the great political drama of the twentieth century.[1] Present-day historians and social scientists have tended to dispense with the notion, arguing that it lacked precision, that it could not account for change within so-called totalitarian regimes, and that it exaggerated the capacity of any tyranny to establish "total" control over the minds and bodies of its subjects.[2] Arendt herself acknowledged that the "totalitarian attempt to make men superfluous" was an "experiment" that needed "global control in order to show conclusive results."[3] In retrospect, it can be argued that she placed too much emphasis on terror in totalitarian regimes and not enough on the fundamental "lie" at the heart of the ideological enterprise. Arendt, as a result,

1   See Hannah Arendt's 1958 essay "Ideology and Terror: A Novel Form of Government" in *The Origins of Totalitarianism* (New York: Schocken Books, 2004), pp. 593–616. This essay, which is Arendt's most complete theoretical articulation of totalitarianism, was added to later editions of the work.
2   See Michael Geyer and Sheila Fitzpatrick, eds., *Beyond Totalitarianism: Stalinism and Nazism Compared* (Cambridge: Cambridge University Press, 2009).
3   Arendt, *The Origins of Totalitarianism*, p. 591.

lost interest in totalitarianism in the post-Stalin period and confused the Soviet Union after 1956 with an ordinary dictatorship or authoritarian regime. Still, there is much to learn from her writings on totalitarianism. To begin with, they have the advantage of showing that the tradition of political philosophy from Plato to Kant and Montesquieu could not adequately account for the strange novelty of totalitarianism.[4] The party-state was much more than a capricious despot—and a fearful response by individuals could not guarantee protection from ideologically-inspired arbitrariness the way it could in an ordinary despotism.[5] She sensed that the goal of a totalitarian regime was to replace the distinction between fact and fiction and truth and falsehood with a "surreality" which aimed to make thinking and morally responsible individuals "superfluous."[6] Arendt hated totalitarian mendacity but feared that human nature itself was at "stake" in the great totalitarian experiments of the twentieth century.[7] Like Orwell, her analysis, deep and profound, was marked by excessive pathos.

The French philosophical historian Alain Besançon had much greater confidence in the capacity of the "real" to resist totalitarian control and manipulation.[8] In his view, totalitarianism could not possibly succeed. It could only impose an artificial *surreality* on the "real world" rooted in human nature and an "order of things." The world of ideology was a *parasite* that depended on a host whose abolition it pronounced inevitable but whose survival was necessary to give ideology a place, a base, in the human world.

4   *Ibid.*, p. 594.
5   *Ibid.*, pp. 600, 602.
6   *Ibid.*, p. 610.
7   *Ibid.*, p. 591.
8   See Alain Besançon, *A Century of Horrors: Communism, Nazism and the Uniqueness of the Shoah* translated by Ralph C. Hancock and Nathaniel H. Hancock (Wilmington, DE: ISI Books, 2007) and Besançon, "On the Difficulty of Defining the Soviet Regime (1976)" in F. Flagg Taylor IV, ed., *The Great Lie: Classic and Recent Appraisals of Ideology and Totalitarianism* (Wilmington, DE: ISI Books, 2011), pp. 31–50.

"Ideology imposes the fiction of another already existing reality, its own. The regime is not terroristic only because it brings the ideology from potency to act, but also and especially because it claims that the ideals of the ideology already actually exist."[9] Man is supposed to live in an imaginary eschatological time, i.e., the world of socialism, but the nature and needs of real human beings still persist. The party, the upholder of the great eschatological illusion that is History and the Progressive Doctrine, is quite distinct from an Aristotelian tyrant or an oriental despot. It is nothing less than the instrument for managing the dialectic of human nature and ideological surreality. Its purpose, which it cannot admit to itself, is to maintain the perilous balance between parasite and host, between totalitarian aspiration and a residual but unacknowledged toleration of human nature. This dialectic is managed by terror but above all, and more enduringly, by the Lie. The Soviet regime was above all an *ideocracy*.[10] Contrary to many academics who wished to normalize it, to see it as merely one dictatorship among many, it depended upon a fictive "surreality" to "which it constantly tried to give reality and constancy."[11] Besançon unequivocally sided with Solzhenitsyn in the Solzhenitsyn/Sakharov debate of the 1970s about the function of ideology in the Soviet regime. As Solzhenitsyn wrote in his *Letter to the Soviet Leaders* "everything is steeped in lies and *everybody knows it*."[12]

Without ideological justification, without the world of illusions created by the ideological lie, the Soviet Union would wither away as it, in fact, did once *glasnost* lifted the curtain on the surreal world of ideology. Besançon was one of the first in the West to appreciate the full import of Solzhenitsyn's prophetic insight regarding ideology and ideological mendacity. Let us turn to a crucial chapter in *The Gulag Archipelago* to examine Solzhenitsyn's

9   Besançon, "On the Difficulty of Defining the Soviet Regime," in *The Great Lie*, p. 45.
10 *Ibid.*, p. 40.
11 *Ibid.*, p 48.
12 Solzhenitsyn, *Letter to the Soviet Leaders* in *East and West* (New York: Harper & Row Perennial Library, 1980), p. 126.

insights into the working of the ideocratic regime. His analysis gives vivid, concrete expression to many of Besançon's more theoretical insights.

The Soul and Barbed Wire

One of the most gripping—and revealing—discussions in *The Gulag Archipelago* is the account of "free" life in the Soviet Union—that is, life outside the camps—that Solzhenitsyn describes in a chapter entitled "Our Muzzled Freedom."[13] This chapter appears in the middle section of the work, the fourth section of seven, which is aptly entitled "The Soul and Barbed Wire."[14] Decidedly dialectical, this section explores the effects of Communist totalitarianism and particularly the effects Soviet prisons and camps had on the human soul. The first chapter, "The Ascent"—perhaps the most memorable chapter in *The Gulag Archipelago*, is profoundly autobiographical.[15] In it, Solzhenitsyn shares his personal experience of spiritual "ascent" in the camp. He writes movingly about his belated discovery of the line between good and evil in each human heart and of his concomitant repudiation of the "lie" that evil lies exclusively in certain suspect groups or classes whose elimination will somehow "solve" the problems that are part and parcel with the human condition. That remarkable chapter ends with the jarring exclamation "*Bless you, prison, for having been in my life!*"[16] "The

---

13 "Our Muzzled Freedom" is the third chapter of the fourth section of *The Gulag Archipelago* and appears in volume II of that work. It is literally at the *center* of *The Gulag Archipelago* as a whole. All subsequent quotations from the work will be cited parenthetically in the body of the text as *GAII*, followed by the page number in the 2007 edition released by Harper Perennial Modern Classics.

14 See *Gulag Archipelago*, Volume II, translated by Thomas P. Whitney, Foreword by Anne Applebaum (New York: Harper Perennial Classics, 2007), pp. 595–672.

15 *Ibid.*, pp. 597–617.

16 *Ibid.*, p. 617.

Ascent" suggests that *metanoia* and self-discovery are paradoxically most available under conditions of imprisonment when one has time to think and to join in real *conversation* with one's fellow inmates. This chapter also shows that the camps are less "totalitarian" than the broader Soviet society. But it would be a mistake to draw "quietist" political conclusions from the moving account of the soul's rediscovery of itself. "The Ascent" is followed by a chapter called "Or Corruption?"[17] In this chapter, Solzhenitsyn readily concedes that the vast majority of prisoners in the camps are corrupted beyond recognition. The experience of spiritual ascent is far rarer in the camps than in prison. It remains the experience of a few noble souls who are prepared to learn essential truths about human nature and the human condition. This "corrective" chapter is followed by "Our Muzzled Freedom." This chapter reveals yet another paradox: if prisons and camps allowed some space for discussion and self-discovery, the broader Soviet society was "totalitarian" in a more profound sense. It closed off the possibility of anything like a decent human life for the vast majority of Soviet citizens. Such a system must be resisted both out of self-respect and in order to make possible the eventual recovery of mutual trust and free political life in a Russia that had been colonized and brutalized by Bolshevik ideologues. "The Soul and Barbed Wire" ends with a short, arresting chapter ("Several Individual Stories") highlighting the moral decency and courage of several perennial fighters for truth and justice who had spent years in and out of the camps.[18] These living reproaches to the "Lie" demonstrate that even in the worst circumstances it is possible for at least some human beings to resist the totalitarian degradation of the soul. As our brief outline of "The Soul and Barbed Wire" suggests, in this section of *The Gulag Archipelago* Solzhenitsyn never loses sight of the highest human possibilities nor of the myriad ways in which the Bolsheviks "put the Russian character in irons and redirected it

17 *Ibid.*, pp. 618–31.
18 *Ibid.*, pp. 656–72.

to their own ends."[19] The truth about "the soul and barbed wire" is profoundly equivocal.

Solzhenitsyn knew that the Bolshevik regime was unthinkable without the gulag archipelago and the terror that accompanied it. But he always emphasized that "the universal, obligatory force-feeding with lies" was "the most agonizing aspect" of life in the USSR, worse than "material miseries," "worse than any lack of civil liberties."[20] It might be said that the Lie, the illusion of creating a radically New Man and Society which in decisive respects were beyond good and evil, takes "ontological" precedence over violence and brutality. In this sense, "free" Soviet life was in important respects more surreal and horrifying than the terrible brutalities of the gulag archipelago. And the institutionalized lie would survive "Stalinism" a full thirty years even as the gulag diminished in size and potency.

"Our Muzzled Freedom" is the closest we have to an exact description of the soul of man under ideological despotism. I would suggest that before "theorizing" the Soviet regime, it is necessary to adequately describe it. That is precisely what Solzhenitsyn does in this chapter. He provides what the philosophers call a rich and ample "phenomenological" description of ideological despotism and its effect on the Russian character and the human soul. He brings his considerable literary talent, philosophical insight, and psychological acumen to bear in describing a reality that in important respects is beyond description. As the great Russianist Martin Malia liked to point out, literary art was much more effective in describing the "phantasmagoric" reality of "really existing socialism" than social science ever could be.[21]

---

19 *The Solzhenitsyn Reader: New and Essential Writings 1947–2005,* edited by Edward E. Ericson, Jr. and Daniel J. Mahoney (Wilmington, DE: ISI Books, 2006), p. 447. The quote is from chapter 30 of 1998's *Russia in Collapse.*
20 *Letter to the Soviet Leaders* in *East and West,* p. 127.
21 See Martin Malia, *Russia Under Western Eyes: From the Bronze Horseman to the Lenin Mausoleum* (Cambridge, Harvard University Press, 1999), pp. 396–98.

Social science tends to flatten and homogenize the world it theorizes, emphasizing commonalities between "systems" where differences abound. By contrast, an "experiment in literary investigation" of the sort Solzhenitsyn presents in *The Gulag Archipelago* can describe the breaking point of the human soul without ever losing sight of the fact that it is human beings, human nature *in extremis*, that one confronts in the nether world of totalitarianism.

"Free Life" in a Totalitarian Regime

Solzhenitsyn begins "Our Muzzled Freedom" by emphasizing the sheer surreality of "free life" in the Soviet Union of the 1930s, '40s, and early '50s. It is difficult to understand "what ... freedom was like" in a country that dragged the ubiquitous gulag archipelago within itself. Solzhenitsyn draws a comparison with the tumor the size of a large man's fist that had "swelled and distorted" his stomach in the early 1950s. What was most terrifying about this cancerous tumor that had nearly taken Solzhenitsyn's life was the fact that it "exuded poisons and infected the whole body." In an analogous manner, the entirety of the Soviet Union had been "infected by the poisons of the Archipelago." Solzhenitsyn emphasizes the "loathsomeness" of the state in which Soviet citizens lived and dedicates himself to describing that loathsomeness in its "entirety." It must be explored for what it is and not covered over or normalized in a way that reinforces the ideological denial of reality. Once again, Solzhenitsyn highlights the crucial role of literature as a humanizing vehicle of truth. There was, he insists, no authentic literature in the Soviet Union in the thirties, forties, or fifties since literature could barely hint at the truth and operated in a zone of mendacity unrestrained by any moral considerations. It is works such as *One Day in the Life of Ivan Denisovich* and *The Gulag Archipelago* that finally breached the wall of the Lie and restored literature to its essential truth-telling role (all quotations in the paragraph from *GAII*, 632).

Solzhenitsyn next turns to what he calls an "enumeration" of the features of "free life" (*GAII*, 632–33) determined by its proximity to the Archipelago. His "phenomenology" of ideological despotism, his examination of the ten defining texts of Soviet life outside the gulag archipelago, reveals the momentous effects of ideocratic despotism on the Russian character and the human soul. This was no ordinary *regime*. Not only did it abolish political life, but it warred on what was most humane and valuable in the Russian past. Assaulting memory and trust, it established an immensely perverted "political" order, in fact an anti-political order that condemned *personhood* and the very possibility of moral and political responsibility and accountability. When human beings became "vassals of fear" (*GAII*, 637) they resorted to betrayal and lying on a truly colossal scale. This was a social order that abolished civic friendship and social trust and posed a deadly threat to the integrity of the human soul.

Constant Fear

The first trait of ideological despotism described by Solzhenitsyn is "constant fear" (*GAII*, 633). He emphasizes the sheer ubiquitousness of Soviet terror. "Just as there is no minute when people are not dying or being born, so there was no minute when people were not being arrested." This fear excluded no adult inhabitant of the country. Everyone was vulnerable, "whether a collective farmer or a member of the Politburo." "One careless word or gesture" could send one flying off "irrevocably into the abyss" (*GAII*, 633). But it is important to recognize that "fear" was not the "principle," the spring of action of the Soviet regime, to use Montesquieu's indispensable category.[22]

That honor was instead held by ideology, which set the Soviet machine in motion and demanded and justified the repression of real or imagined enemies of the people. Nor was the Soviet Union

---

22 See the remarkable suggestive articulation of the "nature" and "principles" of republics, monarchies, and despotisms in Books Two and Three of Montesquieu's *The Spirit of the Laws*.

an "oriental despotism" of the sort described by Montesquieu, Hegel, or Custine.[23] The victims of oriental despotism came almost exclusively from the ruling elite while Soviet repression struck every layer of what had once been a vibrant "civil society" in the final decades of Tsarist rule. Nor did oriental despotisms engage in ideological justification of their cruelties other than through an appeal to habitual religious obedience. It is true that Stalin came closer to being a despot of the type described by the classical historians and philosophers than Lenin had been (the latter was a pure fanatic in the manner of Robespierre). But Stalin's exercise of despotic control was ultimately unintelligible without ideology. He, too, was dedicated to "building socialism" and to safeguarding the singular claim of Marxism-Leninism to reinterpret and remake every aspect of the human world. And as *The Gulag Archipelago* demonstrates beyond any doubt, the Soviet system of camps and repression were coextensive with the Soviet regime itself and were not some later "Stalinist" aberration.[24] Stalin may be said to have "perfected" the system begun by Lenin with the insidious intent of "purging" the Russian land of all sorts of "harmful insects."[25] Solzhenitsyn insists that in the heyday of Soviet despotism, during its most totalitarian phase, the specter of the Archipelago haunted "everyday life." "Just as in the Archipelago beneath every trusty lay the chasm (and death) of general work, so beneath every inhabitant lay the chasm (and

23 See Besançon, "On the Difficulty of Defining the Soviet Regime" in *The Great Lie*, pp. 36–37.
24 In particular, see the opening chapter ("The Fingers of Aurora") of volume II of *The Gulag Archipelago*.
25 See Lenin's incendiary 1918 essay "How to Organize Competition" in *The Lenin Anthology*, ed. and trans. by Robert C. Tucker (New York: Norton, 1975) pp. 426–32. This essay provides a brutally frank defense of revolutionary violence and terror, one that radically dehumanizes the real and imagined opponents of Communism. Critics of Communism, in particular, and "class enemies," in general, are compared to "atrophied limbs," cancerous growths, vermin and ulcers. In the final image of the piece, they are said to be "harmful insects" who must be "purged" from the Russian land.

death) of the Archipelago" (*GAII*, 633). The country and its inhabitants "hung phantomlike above the latter's gaping maw" (*GAII*, 633). There was no such thing as non-political "everyday life." Solzhenitsyn acknowledges the primacy of ideology and rejects *avant la lettre* fashionable efforts to reinterpret Soviet phenomena in light of the alleged priority of "social history" over high politics. If the concept of totalitarianism is worth salvaging, and I think it is, it is precisely because it does justice to the crucial "ideological" dimension of Soviet experience.

Solzhenitsyn makes clear that "fear was not always the fear of arrest." He writes about the full range of "intermediate threats" including "purges, inspections, the completion of security questionnaires—routine or extraordinary ones—, dismissal from work, deprivation of residence permit," all the way up to "expulsion or exile" (*GAII*, 633). And he emphasizes that lies and deception at the service of self-preservation often caught up to people and entailed extraordinary mental dexterousness on the part of those who wished to conceal secrets from the Soviet state. The cumulative effect of these constant threats was an "aggregate fear" that "led to a correct consciousness of one's own insignificance and of the lack of any kind of *rights*" (*GAII*, 634). It should be noted that the same Solzhenitsyn who refuses to exalt human rights at the expense of human obligations sees them as absolutely essential elements of a decent and free society. Solzhenitsyn describes a phantasmagoric world where people were afraid to tell the truth to friends and family. Fear paralyzed souls and atomized society. If, according to Montesquieu, "tranquility of mind" is the very definition of liberty in a constitutional order,[26] perpetual fear marked everyday life under classic totalitarianism. "Peace of mind," Solzhenitsyn writes, "is something that Soviet citizens have never known" (*GAII*, 634). Such an order bears down with too much weight on the bodies and souls of human beings. It

26 See Book 11, chapter 6 of *The Spirit of the Laws* for a discussion of the link between modern liberty and the feeling of security or "tranquility of mind."

breaks the human spirit. It severs human ties, placing fear and mistrust where amity—civic amity—properly belongs.

One of the preconditions of the fear and mistrust was general-ized *servitude* (*GAII*, 634). Soviet citizens had no ability to change residence and no worker could quit work of his own accord. Nor could any home be sold or rented. Because of these restrictions on freedom and mobility it became "an insane piece of daring to protest in the places where you lived or worked" (*GAII*, 634). Servitude guaranteed complacence and obedience on the part of the vast majority of Soviet citizens.

Secrecy and Mistrust

Solzhenitsyn tells the "secrets of one family" (*GAII*, 635) to illus-trate how deeply the unwillingness to trust others went even among those who were intimate with each other. A husband did not tell his wife about his past as a Tsarist officer and thereby avoided arrest. Her brother was arrested and the wife of the arrested man "hid his arrest from his own *father* and *mother*—so they would not blurt it out." "She preferred letting them and everyone else think that her husband had abandoned her, and then playing that role a long time!" (*GAII*, 635). These were the secrets of one Soviet family Solzhenitsyn was told about thirty years later. "And what urban family did not have such secrets?" (*GAII*, 635).

Solzhenitsyn does not mince his words. The "universal mutual mistrust" that he describes "had the effect of deepening the mass-grave pit of slavery" (*GAII*, 635). Every effort to "speak up frankly," every "sincere protest" was treated by one's family, neighbor, or co-worker, as a "provocation." "Anyone who burst out with a sincere protest was predestined to loneliness and alien-ation" (*GAII*, 633). We are very close to what Hannah Arendt described as the "superfluousness" of the individual under condi-tions of totalitarianism. There was little or no place for fidelity to truth or spirited resistance to injustice in the broader Soviet world. In the fifth book of the *Politics* Aristotle had vividly described the efforts of the tyrant to divide, separate, and alienate his subjects.

The tyrant spent his time "guarding against anything that customarily gives rise to two things, high thoughts and trust."[27] But Aristotle could only *imagine* the "perfection" of tyranny. In practice, tyranny would need a justifying ideology to complete its work. The absolute atomization of society had merely been the dream of ancient tyrants. But the fear and mistrust that pervaded Soviet society led to "that *absolute secrecy*, absolute misinformation ... which was the *cause of causes* of everything that took place, including both the millions of arrests and the mass approval of them also" (*GAII*, 635). While the classical philosophers had described a *theoretical* possibility, the Soviets came as close to achieving the absolute atomization of society as is possible among human beings who after all are gregarious and made for life in society with one another. They achieved what had merely been the dream of ancient tyrants and the worst forebodings of the classical philosophers.

Complicity in the Web of Repression

Solzhenitsyn also describes how squealing—informing on others—"was developed to a mind-boggling extent" (*GAII*, 636). Those who spied on their friends, co-workers, and fellow citizens could only fear that they too were being spied upon. Solzhenitsyn endorses Nadezhda Mandelstam's conclusion regarding the ultimate purpose of such a large network of informants: "Beyond the purposes of weakening ties between people, there was another purpose as well. Any person who had let himself be recruited would, out of fear of public exposure, be very much interested in the continuing stability of the regime" (*GAII*, 636–37). The regime was interested in making everyone to some extent complicit in the web of totalitarian repression. As we shall see, totalitarian mendacity played the same role in transforming victims into

---

27 See Aristotle, *Politics*, Book V, Chapter 11, trans. and with an Introduction, Notes, and Glossary by Carnes Lord, Second Edition, (Chicago: University of Chicago Press, 2013), p. 161.

oppressors. Ideological despotism, as Václav Havel wrote in his seminal 1978 essay "The Power and the Powerless," is not characterized by the repression of the vast majority by the few. Rather, it creates a quasi-autonomous web of repression that is reinforced by the betrayal and lies of those who were initially victimized by it.[28]

Betrayal as a Form of Existence

Let us turn now to "betrayal as a form of existence" (*GAII*, 637), the sixth feature of "free Soviet life" that Solzhenitsyn describes and one of two (the other being "the lie as a form of existence") to which he devotes the most attention. As human beings became "vassals of fear," they concluded that "the least dangerous form of existence was constant betrayal." Solzhenitsyn describes a gradation of betrayal from the abandonment of the doomed person next to you (and the refusal to help his or her family) to the open denunciation or renunciation of alleged "enemies of the Soviet people." If a neighbor, comrade at work, and even a close friend was arrested, the safest course of action was "to turn away one's face, to shrink back." Rather than showing sympathy or solidarity, one kept silence. You knew your friend or co-worker was no "inveterate enemy of the people" but you either kept silence or added your own "condemning speech." You "had to show how hostile you were to his crimes." People rationalized these cowardly acts of betrayal by thinking of their own dear family ("what right had you not to think *about them?*") even though the arrested person left behind a wife, a mother, and children who were certainly deserving of help. But that would be to show weakness toward an *enemy* of the people and toward the wife, mother, or children of an *enemy*. After all, one had the "long education" (all quotations in this paragraph from *GAII*, 637) of one's own

28 See Václav Havel, "The Power and the Powerless" in *Open Letters: Selected Writings: 1965–1990* (New York: Knopf, 1991), pp. 125–214.

children to worry about. It should be added that throughout his writings, Solzhenitsyn emphasizes the family as a point of vulnerability used to rationalize weak and cowardly behavior.

Solzhenitsyn tells the heartbreaking story of an eight-year-old boy who managed to hide under the pedestal beneath a bust of Stalin as his arrested family was being deported from Moscow. When the little boy returned home the apartment was closed off. He then went one after another to neighbors, acquaintances, and friends of his father and mother. "Not only did no one take that small boy into their family but they refused even to let him spend the night!" (*GAII*, 639). And so the young person, with nowhere else to turn, turned himself in at an orphanage. Solzhenitsyn does not hesitate to bitterly chastise his fellow citizens. He asks them if they do not recognize their own "swinish faces" (*GAII*, 639). As he does elsewhere in *The Gulag Archipelago* to great effect, he appeals to the self-respect of Soviet citizens who are in danger of losing their souls. How can *human beings* behave this way? Can self-preservation really be the highest end or good of human existence? As *The Gulag Archipelago* makes clear, only those who have renounced self-preservation as the highest end of human existence can live well in the light of the truth.

As it turns out, the vast majority of Soviet citizens chose to live in "the *field* of betrayal." Their "best powers of reasoning were used in justification of it" (*GAII*, 639). There were untold numbers of renunciation of family members and friends, renunciations made publicly or in the press. People purchased their lives—or at least Soviet "freedom"—by betraying others in the most shameful way. But Solzhenitsyn never ends on a note of despair. Not everyone is content with being a "vassal of fear." A considerable number of Soviet citizens displayed quiet heroism at great risk to themselves. "It was safer to keep dynamite during the rule of Alexander II than it was to shelter the orphan of an enemy of the people under Stalin" (*GAII*, 641). Yet many children were taken in and saved by loving families. Secret assistance to families also occurred. Some volunteered to take the place of an arrested person's wife "in a hopeless line for three days, so that she could go in to get warm and get some sleep" (*GAII*, 641). Some brave souls even warned neighbors that an ambush was waiting for them at their apartment. Even under the worst conditions, some remained true to the imperatives of conscience, of decency and kindhearted-ness, rather than succumbing to the "class cruelty" demanded by ideology.

Solzhenitsyn rejects the idea that arrests were merely random, done only on the basis of a "lottery," or quota system. The Soviet archives have confirmed that arrests were indeed done in accor-dance with arranged quota figures. But Solzhenitsyn argues that any person who *objected publicly* was grabbed that very minute. "And it turned into a *selection on the basis of soul*, not a lottery!" The best "fell beneath the ax; were sent off to the Archipelago— and the picture of the monotonously obedient *freedom* remained unruffled" (*GAII*, 642). The purest and best, the boldest and most spirited, could not remain in that perverted society. Soviet terror was an instrument of *reverse selection* marked by the "deliberate destruction of all that was bright, remarkable, of a higher level,"[29] as Solzhenitsyn put it years later in *Russia in Collapse*. The quiet departure of noble souls marked nothing less than "the dying of the soul of the people" (*GAII*, 642).

Corruption versus Nobility

If some remained faithful to the old criteria of good and evil, oth-ers, millions upon millions, succumbed to *corruption* (*GAII*, 642–46). We have already discussed all those who became stool pigeons. While some betrayed neighbors out of fear, others, more shamelessly, did so for material gain. Still others were committed ideologues who condemned their neighbors and co-workers out of ideological considerations, as part and parcel of class warfare against the "enemies of the people." Solzhenitsyn notes that these "ordinary Soviet people" often prospered and were the last to

29 See chapter 30, "The Evolution of our Character," of *Russia in Collapse* in *The Solzhenitsyn Reader*, p. 477.

consider repentance for trampling the best and most honest underfoot during the worst period of Russian—and Soviet—history. From the thirties to the fifties, the period under consideration in this chapter, Solzhenitsyn cannot imagine a single case "of a noble person casting down, destroying, driving out a base troublemaker" (*GAII*, 644). No noble person could turn to State Security—that instrument of murder and mendacity—while the corrupt had the resources of the secret police readily at hand.

But Solzhenitsyn insists, once again, that not everyone was a prisoner of their circumstances: "Among souls who had not been brought up from childhood in the Pioneer detachments and the Komsomol cells, there were souls that retained their integrity" (*GAII*, 645). Solzhenitsyn speaks of acts of kindness by onlookers who came across trainloads of prisoners. Despite the terrible risks, there were always prospects for spiritual "transcendence." Solzhenitsyn emphasizes that we are not totally determined by our political and economic circumstances *even under the worst regime*. Not even a totalitarian regime can succeed in making individual virtue wholly superfluous.

The Lie as a Form of Existence

Let us turn now to an examination of "The Lie as a Form of Existence" (*GAII*, 646–50). We know that Solzhenitsyn believed that systematic mendacity was the defining trait of Soviet despotism and that this mendacity would persist long after the death of Stalin and the demise of the worst features of "Stalinist" rule.

"The permanent lie becomes the only safe form of existence, in the same way as betrayal. Every wag of the tongue can be overheard by someone, every facial expression observed by someone. Therefore, every word, if it does not have to be a direct lie, is nonetheless obliged not to contradict the general, common lie" (*GAII*, 646). That general, common lie is ideology itself, the Lie that socialist revolution has fundamentally transformed the nature of man and society. "A collection of ready-made phrases, of labels, a selection of ready-made lies" (*GAII*, 646) supports the claim that Communism deserves to be judged by another set of standards than the ones that have been used to judge hitherto existing societies. Conscience, justice, right and wrong—the constituent elements of the moral universe—have been displaced by "primary clichés" (*GAII*, 646). These "primary clichés" inform every book and article, and are the instruments of the general, common lie. In important respects, Soviet despotism is what Czesław Miłosz called a *logocracy*,[30] where the linguistic destruction of reality dominated the thought and action of human beings. Instead of creating a common world, a public space for free thought and action, the clichés of ideology tore men apart and denied them access to the truth about individual and collective life. Everyone lived in the Lie and reinforced it by shamelessly repeating what they knew to be absolute falsehoods. Solzhenitsyn reports that Georgi Tenno, "the committed escaper" whose heroism is highlighted in the third volume of *The Gulag Archipelago*, "recalled with shame" that a mere two weeks before his arrest "he had lectured the sailors on 'The Stalinist Constitution: The Most Democratic in the World'" (*GAII*, 647). No one was exempt from the imperative of mendacity— the lie was nothing less than a *sine qua non* for membership in Soviet society. "There is no man who has typed even one page ... without lying. There is no man who has spoken from a rostrum ... without lying. There is no man who has spoken into a microphone ... without lying" (*GAII*, 647).

I have already suggested that the ideological Lie was the defining feature of Sovietism, according to Solzhenitsyn. Terror would abate considerably in the years after 1956, although the persistence of the gulag and the memory of crimes past would act as powerful constraints on free human action. But as Solzhenitsyn makes clear in his 1974 essay "The Smatterers," from *From Under the Rubble*, the generalized lie persisted as the glue that held Soviet life together. It is in this context that Solzhenitsyn called for existential resistance to Soviet totalitarianism through the refusal to take part in the Lie. He did not call for his fellow

30 See Czesław Miłosz, *The Captive Mind* (New York: Vintage, 1990).

citizens to preach at the top of their lungs or to mutter what they think in undertones. Rather, he called on persons of integrity and conscience to refuse to say what they don't think "and that includes not whispering, not opening your mouth, not raising your hand, not casting your vote, not faking a smile, not lending your presence, not standing up, and not cheering."[31] In post-Stalinist circumstances, a deliberate strategy of non-participation in lies was "the safest and most accessible"[32] path toward freedom and the liberation of souls. It was also the most efficacious one. If tens of thousands of people took that path the country would be "purified and transformed without shots or bloodshed."[33] Yes, those who take this path may lose their jobs or educational opportunities for their children. Some courageous souls may even risk imprisonment. The path to national liberation and purification could only begin with the liberation and purification of those who refused to live the lie.

Just as Solzhenitsyn had presented a gradation of betrayals so too does he distinguish between the "forced, defensive lie" (*GAII*, 649) which is terrible enough and destructive of souls, and the "oblivious passionate lie" of the sort that so many writers distinguished themselves at. Every reader of *The Gulag Archipelago* knows that Maxim Gorky sold his soul to the Devil in order to defend the barbarities at Solovki and to sing the praises of the murderous slave labor project, the Belomor-White Sea Canal.[34] Solzhenitsyn has written a powerful binary tale, "Apricot Jam,"

---

31 Solzhenitsyn, "The Smatterers" in *From Under the Rubble*, Solzhenitsyn et. al., translated by a team under the direction of Michael Scammell (Washington, DC: Regnery Gateway, 1981), p. 276.

32 *Ibid.*, p. 277.

33 *Ibid.*

34 Solzhenitsyn, *The Gulag Archipelago*, Volume II (New York: Harper Perennial Modern Classics, 2007), pp. 60–63, 81–82, 85, 93. More than any other figure in *The Gulag Archipelago*, Gorky represents the self-enslavement of the writer, his voluntary capitulation to the ideological Lie.

which highlights a Writer as shameless purveyor of the ideological lie.[35] In "Our Muzzled Freedom" he mentions the case of Marietta Shaginyan who wrote in 1937—the most terrible year of the Great Terror—"that the epoch of socialism had transformed even criminal interrogation: the stories of interrogation showed that nowadays the persons being interrogated *willingly cooperated* with them, telling everything that was required about themselves and others" (*GAII*, 649). This claim was made as millions were being arrested and tortured, and hundreds of thousands were being shot. This is the Big Lie, one shorn of any connection to reality.

Our examination of Solzhenitsyn's account of the "Lie as a form of existence" would not be complete without a discussion of the hair-raising moral dilemmas of raising children in the country of the Lie. Children were being brought up to be Pavlik Morozovs who would betray their parents for anti-Soviet activities. Parents had to decide whether to shield their children from the truth ("so that it would be *easier* for them to live") and "then to lie forevermore in front of them" or "to tell them the truth" with "the result that they might make a slip." The latter path, the only honorable path, meant instilling in your children from the start the view that "the truth was murderous, that beyond the threshold of the house you had to lie, only lie, just like papa and mama." Solzhenitsyn arrives at a damning conclusion: "the choice was really such that you would rather not have any children" (quotations from *GAII*, 647–48). When it was most faithful to itself, from the mid-1920s to the mid-1950s, the Soviet regime fatally undermined the moral integrity of the family. Hannah Arendt argued that "natality,"[36] the entrance of new human beings into the world, challenges the totalitarian project to control every aspect of life. It is a sign of enduring hope in the human world. Yet natality depends upon a strong, semi-autonomous family to do its work. No such family existed during the heyday of Soviet totalitarianism. This is one more reason why such a regime needed to be resisted, so that

35 See my detailed analysis of *Apricot Jam* in chapter eight of this book.
36 Arendt, *The Origins of Totalitarianism*, p. 616.

human beings were not faced by impossible choices that made them complicit in immorality and the Lie.

Class Cruelty

A world dominated by fear, betrayal, and mendacity is also one devoid of kindheartedness. *Cruelty* was an inevitable byproduct of betrayal and the Lie as "forms of existence." "How could one possibly preserve one's kindness while pushing away the hands of those who were drowning?" Steeped in blood, people only became more cruel. And ideology itself "praised and instilled" *class cruelty* in the name of punishing class enemies who had no place in "socialist" society. Since kindness, pity, and mercy were ridiculed, untold numbers of Soviet citizens became "drunk on blood" (*GAII*, 650). Solzhenitsyn shows that class cruelty was an insidious instrument of the Lie and has no place in a decent political order. It is one of the means by which Ideology assaults the moral law, the timeless structure of right and wrong and good and evil, the ultimate standards for judging every political order. Russia's own post-1990 return to the civilized community of nations is above all marked by its affirmation of universal values and virtues rather than the "class categories" of an ideological regime rooted in the Lie.

Slave Psychology

Solzhenitsyn concludes "Our Muzzled Freedom" with a challenge to the self-respect of his fellow citizens. The final section, entitled "Slave Psychology," ends with a description of a certain piece of sculpture, "a plastic guard with a police dog which is straining forward to sink its teeth into someone" (*GAII*, 655). Solzhenitsyn notes that this sculpture could be found in the 1960s in Tashkent in front of the NKVD school and in Ryazan, right in the heart of the city. The Russian writer observes that his fellow Russians "do not even shudder in revulsion." Setting dogs onto people is treated as one of the "most natural things in the world" (*GAII*, 655).

Against this heritage of servitude and subjection, Solzhenitsyn appeals to the spirited side of the human soul. The "unnatural" character of the Bolshevik regime and Bolshevik ideology must be acknowledged by all. A regime that wars with its people *out of principle* is not worthy of support by human beings who care about justice and who are faithful to the moral law. As we noted earlier in this chapter, the fact that Solzhenitsyn (and others) experienced spiritual growth and enhanced knowledge about human nature and the human soul in Soviet prisons and camps is in no way an argument for political passivity and quietism. The regime of the Lie must be resisted not least to vindicate the honor and self-respect of the Russian people and the human race.

We know that the "phenomenology" of ideological despotism presented in this chapter remained important to Solzhenitsyn. He reproduced a beautiful précis of it in a memorable chapter of 1998's *Russia in Collapse* entitled "The Evolution of the Russian Character."[37] And his opposition to Communism remained absolutely undiminished despite the corruption and thievery that thrived in the Russian 1990s and the political authoritarianism (not totalitarianism) that would follow it under the tutelage of Vladimir Putin.

Conclusion: Remembering Everything

Let us conclude these reflections with some thoughts on Solzhenitsyn's views about Communist totalitarianism in the final years of his life. After returning to his native Russia in May 1994, Solzhenitsyn spoke to numerous audiences in the Russian hinterland about matters of common concern. He had surprised the world by first flying into Vladivostok rather than Moscow, the center of Russian political and intellectual life, and the choice of every other returning dissident or émigré. He stopped on his extensive train ride from Vladivostok to the Russian capital at many towns and cities along the way and engaged in lively and

37 See *The Solzhenitsyn Reader*, pp. 475–79.

sometimes contentious discussions with interlocutors who for the most part were unfamiliar with his writings. Once settled in the Moscow region, Solzhenitsyn would engage in a second extensive tour of the country in the summer and fall of 1995. During these excursions, he was sometimes confronted by those who would bitterly accuse him of nearly single-handedly destroying the "homeland," a homeland which they reflexively identified with the long-established Soviet regime. Of course, Solzhenitsyn's commitment to Russia was precisely a commitment to the "homeland"—to the "motherland"—to the Russia that endured—against an ideological regime under the Bolsheviks which "put the Russian character in irons and redirected it to their own ends."[38] Solzhenitsyn returned home to a new set of problems—to a Russia confronting imminent collapse—and he was second to none in his criticism of the new Russian kleptocracy. But as he told the Italian scholar Vittorio Strada in October 2000, this did not mean that his "opinion of the Communist regime" had "softened in the slightest."[39] And unlike many of his interlocutors, he was acutely aware of the role that the Communist *nomenklatura* had played in robbing the country blind during the misguided process of privatization. From Solzhenitsyn's point of view, nostalgia for Communism was absolutely misplaced and a sign of the desperation of many Russians during the country's "Third Time of Troubles," as he called it, as well as their ignorance of the deep recesses of the Soviet past.

As every reader of *The Gulag Archipelago* knows, Solzhenitsyn was deeply committed to paying tribute to—and recovering the memory of—the untold millions who perished under the Bolshevik yoke. This was a sacred "mission" to which he always remained faithful. But he was equally concerned with the effect of Leninist-Stalinist totalitarianism on the human soul

---

38 *Ibid.*, p, 477.
39 An English-language translation of the October 20, 2000 conversation between Vittorio Strada and Solzhenitsyn was provided to me by the author's son, Stephan Solzhenitsyn.

and what he called "the meltdown of the people's morals"[40] during the first four decades of Bolshevik rule. When confronted by Russians who remembered the Soviet Union as a "paradise" of sorts, Solzhenitsyn reminded them of the "cruelty" that was already evident in the 1920s, and the "nightmarish debut" of the 1930s where "all that we know of human relations were destroyed."[41] When he brought the evils of collectivization to the attention of these interlocutors, they would claim that this was an unfortunate byproduct of war. Yet as Solzhenitsyn pointed out to an audience at the University of Saratov in September 1995, war with the Germans would only come much later. But there had been an earlier war, a cruel and murderous ideological war inaugurated by the Soviet state against the most capable, talented, and hard-working peasants. This war had devastating human consequences. As Solzhenitsyn himself noted, many of his interlocutors were too young to remember Soviet totalitarianism in its heyday. Solzhenitsyn insisted that he in contrast remembered *everything* and would never do anything to obfuscate the truth about totalitarianism.[42] He told his audience at Saratov about a secret decree promulgated by Stalin in 1948 that obliged women—for they alone had remained in any number on the *kolkhozes*—who had not filled work norms to be deported to Siberia. Solzhenitsyn had published that revealing decree in his book series "Research on Modern Russian History" in a collection dedicated to the "Peasantry and the State." None among his listeners had heard of the decree. Some "paradise" he remarked in that pungent and sardonic tone so well known to readers of *The Gulag Archipelago*.[43]

As we have had occasion to observe, Solzhenitsyn always insisted that "violence" and "lies" were the twin pillars—the twin engines—of "really existing socialism." That diarchy of means

40 *The Solzhenitsyn Reader*, p. 477.
41 *Ibid.*
42 Solzhenitsyn, "Intervention à l'université de Saratov" in *Une minute par jour: Chroniques*, traduites du russe par Françoise Lesourd (Paris Fayard, 2007), p. 263.
43 *Ibid.*, p. 262.

and ends always needs to be kept in mind. If one concentrates inordinately on the death count associated with Bolshevism (or the rates of incarceration in the age of the gulag) one risks losing sight of the threat to the integrity of the soul that equally defined ideological despotism for Solzhenitsyn. One then forgets to ask what "freedom" was like in a fully constituted ideological regime. "What sort of country [was it] that for whole decades dragged the Archipelago inside itself?" (*GAII*, 632). This is the probing question that Solzhenitsyn asks at the beginning of "Our Muzzled Freedom." As we have suggested, this chapter is the closest thing to a complete and convincing phenomenological description of Communist despotism that one can find in the entirety of Solzhenitsyn's corpus. Of course, the main task of *The Gulag Archipelago* was not to enumerate the traits of "free life" in a system "determined by the closeness of the Archipelago" (*GAII*, 633). But Solzhenitsyn considered this task absolutely necessary for understanding the effects of totalitarian despotism on the human soul. The gulag and misnamed "free life" were part and parcel of a unitary ideological "whole." My suggestion is that "theorizing" about the Soviet experience and about ideocratic despotism more generally will benefit immensely from a close, critical engagement with this remarkable chapter.

Chapter 6

TWO CRITICS OF THE IDEOLOGICAL "LIE": RAYMOND ARON'S ENCOUNTER WITH ALEKSANDR SOLZHENITSYN

The incomparable force of Solzhenitsyn is connected with his person, to what defines his message: the unconditional refusal of the lie. It can happen that one cannot tell the truth, he repeats, but one can always refuse the lie. The Soviet regime appears to him to be perverse as such because it institutionalizes the lie: despotism calls itself liberty, the press subjugated to a party pretends to be free, and at the time of the Great Purge, Stalin proclaimed the Constitution to be the most democratic in the world. Solzhenitsyn's voice carries far and high because it does not weary of calling us back to the intrinsic perversity of totalitarianism.—Raymond Aron, *Le Figaro*, June 12, 1975.[1]

Raymond Aron and Aleksandr Solzhenitsyn are two authors who have been very important to me over the years. The first is a French philosopher turned political scientist or political sociologist who helped shape moderate and conservative opinion in France— and Europe—in the years after WWII. He showed the greatest lucidity in confronting the unique evil that is totalitarianism and

1 Raymond Aron, "Raymond Aron Dialogue Avec Alexandre Soljenitsyne," *Le Figaro*, 12 juin 1975 in Aron, *Les articles du Figaro*, tome III : *Les Crises*, 1965–1977, p. 1542.

was a model of balanced or equitable political reflection. The second, as we have seen, is a world historical figure, a writer of unsurpassed talent who dissected the Lie that is coextensive with ideology like no one else in the twentieth century. While both men were proud and principled opponents of Communist totalitarianism, at first glance they do not appear to be natural interlocutors. Aron was a secular, self-described "de-Judaized" Jew, although one who displayed no hostility to revealed religion. He was an adherent of the moderate enlightenment, preferring Montesquieu and Tocqueville to the theoretical and practical radicalism of the *philosophes* and the Jacobin tradition. He was a French patriot who carefully balanced liberal universalism with a rational and affective attachment to his *patrie*. Solzhenitsyn, too, was a patriot who did not feel obliged to lie for his country. In contrast to Aron, Solzhenitsyn combined an attachment to self-government with a sweeping condemnation of the "anthropocentricity" at the heart of enlightenment and post-Enlightenment thought.[2] Yet he, too, was a "liberal" of sorts as Aron fully appreciated. In fact, in the ten years before his death in October 1983, Aron wrote extensively, and always intelligently and sympathetically, about Solzhenitsyn. At a time when American liberals and leftists (and many Europeans, too) were turning vehemently against Solzhenitsyn—accusing him of authoritarianism and worse—Aron remained an unqualified admirer of the Russian writer.

For Aron, Solzhenitsyn was more than a political figure. The Russian *zek* represented an unconditional "spiritual" commitment to truth and liberty. Solzhenitsyn was the critic par excellence of the modern ideological "lie" that human nature and the laws of social existence could be "engineered" out of existence.

2   This theme is developed most extensively and thoughtfully in Solzhenitsyn's Harvard address of June 8, 1978. See my discussion of Solzhenitsyn's critique of "anthropocentricity" and the self-deification of man in Mahoney, *The Conservative Foundations of the Liberal Order: Defending Democracy Against Its Modern Enemies and Immoderate Friends* (Wilmington, DE: ISI Books, 2010), pp. 127–39.

Like Solzhenitsyn, Aron denied that some "super-reality" divined by ideology could replace the real world in which human beings live, breathe, and struggle. He understood that Communism had to create a fictive world ruled by ideological clichés, an *ideocracy* or *logocracy* dominated by lies, if it was to obscure the gap between social reality and the pretensions of ideology to remake human beings and society at a stroke. Aron wrote extensively about historical consciousness and endorsed a moderate version of modern "progress."[3] But fundamentally he did not believe that human nature could be changed. He adamantly refused to replace the primordial human distinction between good and evil with the pernicious ideological distinction between Progress and Reaction. He refused to subordinate human beings to ideological abstractions.

Aron was not a religious believer, at least not in any conventional sense, but he profoundly admired the spiritual witness of Solzhenitsyn. He never turned on the Russian writer or allowed their differences to undermine his admiration for him. He did not share Solzhenitsyn's religious faith, or some of his core ideas, such as the "critique of the whole body of modern civilization since the Renaissance,"[4] or his adherence to the theses of the Club of Rome (from 1973) on the immanence of ecological catastrophe and degradation.[5] He also did not share Solzhenitsyn's view from the mid-1970s that the West had lost WWIII in the years after 1945, and was then in danger of losing WWIV.[6] At the same time, he shared Solzhenitsyn's misgivings about détente especially when it

3   Raymond Aron, "For Progress," *The College: The St. John's Review* (January 1980), pp. 1–8.
4   Aron, *In Defense of Decadent Europe*, translated by Stephen Cox, with a new introduction by Daniel J. Mahoney and Brian C. Anderson (New Brunswick, NJ: Transaction Publishers, 1996), p. 256.
5   *Ibid.*
6   Raymond Aron, "Raymond Aron Dialogue Avec Alexandre Soljenitsyne," *Le Figaro*, 12 juin 1975 in Aron, *Les articles du Figaro*, tome III : *Les Crises*, 1965–1977, pp. 1539–43.

was accompanied by ideological illusions about Communism. But Aron never caricatured Solzhenitsyn or attributed to him positions that he did not hold. His treatment of the Russian writer is equitable from beginning to end.

Letter to the Soviet Leaders

Aron was one of the few commentators in the Western world to appreciate the fundamentally "libertarian" character of Solzhenitsyn's 1973 *Letter to the Soviet Leaders*. Where others wrongly attributed to it a theoretical endorsement of authoritarianism, Aron saw an admirable effort to free the people of the Soviet Union from the stranglehold of ideocracy. Aron fully appreciated the subtlety of Solzhenitsyn's *Letter*. The carefully crafted *Letter* aimed to persuade men shaped by fifty-five years of ideological despotism that it was in their interest, and in the interest of the Russian people, to begin the long descent from the "icy cliffs"[7] of totalitarianism. Aron saw that Solzhenitsyn was asking for nothing less than "ideological surrender"[8] on the part of the Soviet leaders. When he told them that they could hold on to political power as long as they jettisoned the official ideology, respected private property, allowed freedom of thought and speech, decollectivized agriculture, and stopped persecuting religious believers, many thought they had discerned a weakness for authoritarianism.[9] They did not read the *Letter* with care or with the slightest sense of the rhetoric one might use in speaking to the morally unscrupulous caretakers of an ideological despotism. In

7   Solzhenitsyn, *The Mortal Danger: How Misconceptions About Russia Imperil America*, translated by Alexis Klimoff and Michael Nicholson (New York: Harper & Row Publishers, 1980), p. 59. This image is particularly apt for thinking about the difficulties of post-communist transition in Russia.

8   Aron, *In Defense of Decadent Europe*, p. 36.

9   Solzhenitsyn addresses this misunderstanding with great lucidity in chapter 8 of *The Mortal Danger* ("What My *Letter to the Soviet Leaders* Attempted to Do"), pp. 55–62.

contrast, Aron knew that Solzhenitsyn was striking at the very foundations of the ideocratic regime. He appreciated that Solzhenitsyn was writing for the future, when a new generation of pragmatic and public-spirited leaders might be willing to make a clean break with ideocracy. As Aron astutely observed in *In Defense of Decadent Europe*, "By inviting the Soviet leaders to give up militant atheism, Solzhenitsyn is asking—and knows he is asking—for ideological surrender. The leaders would gain millions of good citizens, but not good *Soviet* citizens. There cannot be two metaphysics of salvation. Stripped of its atheism, Marxism-Leninism would lose the principle of authority on which its visionary super-reality rests and on which it relies for its judgments upon profane reality."[10] By becoming one ordinary regime among others, the Soviet regime would make its peace with profane reality and thus prepare the way for the definitive end of totalitarianism and a return of basic human liberties.

Aron also noted that Solzhenitsyn preferred "liberalization" to revolution for wholly humane reasons—in the multinational U.S.S.R. violent revolution risked tearing the nation apart, setting one nationality against another, and creating the possibilities of a new despotism.[11] But Aron saw what few readers of the *Letter* appreciated: Solzhenitsyn nowhere endorsed authoritarianism as choice-worthy in itself. Aron even compared Solzhenitsyn's choice for liberalization over revolution to Friedrich Hayek's well-known preference for liberalism over democracy.[12] Aron acknowledged Solzhenitsyn's dislike for the "lack of restraint, the exhibitionism, and the vulgarity of Western electoral warfare"[13] but he never confused that dislike for a systematic condemnation of political liberty.

In his critique of Marxist "prophetism" in the opening pages of *In Defense of Decadent Europe*, Aron draws on the *Letter's*

10 Aron, *In Defense of Decadent Europe*, p. 36.
11 *Ibid.*, pp. 255–56.
12 *Ibid.*, p. 255.
13 *Ibid.*, p. 256.

denunciation of a "decrepit" and "hopelessly antiquated doctrine,"[14] Marxism-Leninism, one which does not begin to speak to the needs of modern men and women. In Aron's view, Solzhenitsyn's *Letter* had powerfully exposed the bankruptcy of "two pseudoscientific myths: Marxism (the destruction of capitalism by its internal contradictions) and Marxism-Leninism (the transformation of society—or even *la condition humaine*—by the abolishment of private ownership of the means of production."[15] Solzhenitsyn pointed out that "even during its best decades ... [Ideology] was totally mistaken in its predictions and was never a science." It was terribly mistaken when it forecast that the "proletariat"—a mythical or ideological category in itself—would be endlessly oppressed in capitalist society. It "missed the point when it asserted that the prosperity of the European countries depended on their colonies." Its prediction that the state would "wither away" under the auspices of Communism "was sheer delusion, ignorance of human nature."[16]

In the great debate between Solzhenitsyn and his fellow dissident Andrei Sakharov over "the function of ideology"[17] Aron sided with Solzhenitsyn. Solzhenitsyn had argued in the *Letter* that it was the "same antiquated legacy of the Progressive Doctrine" that endowed the Soviet leadership "with all the millstones" that were dragging them—and the country—down. Solzhenitsyn argued for the systematic de-ideologization of the Soviet state and subtly showed how ideological tyranny and ideological skepticism coexisted in the Soviet Union of the 1970s. Ideology did nothing but "sap the strength of the Soviet people." It "clogs up the whole life of society—minds, tongues, radio and press—with lies, lies, lies." Solzhenitsyn brilliantly highlighted the paradox at the center of decayed Sovietism: "everything was steeped in lies and *everybody knows it*."[18]

14 *Ibid.*, p. 22.
15 *Ibid.*
16 Solzhenitsyn cited in *Ibid.*, pp. 22–23.
17 *Ibid.*, pp. 33–40.
18 Solzhenitsyn as cited by Aron in *Ibid.*, p. 35.

The distinguished Soviet physicist and human rights activist Andrei Sakharov shared Solzhenitsyn's opposition to Communist ideology—to the institutionalized lie—but believed that ideology was merely a cover for the cynical self-interest of the Soviet leadership. Aron believed that Solzhenitsyn had a much more profound grasp of the coexistence of faith and skepticism in the minds and hearts of the Soviet leadership and *homo sovieticus* more broadly. Marxism-Leninism was much more than a superficial and cynical cover for despotism of a traditional sort. It had created a web of mendacity about the past, the present, the future, and the human condition itself, that was the key to unraveling the Soviet enigma. The *Letter to the Soviet Leaders* was for Aron the clearest and most penetrating analysis of the mixture of violence and lies that defined ideological despotism. Aron was sensitive to Solzhenitsyn's "art of writing"— his seemingly modest "pragmatic" advice to the old men of the Politburo to abandon ideology even as they held on to power masked his genuinely radical intentions—and his fundamentally "libertarian" aims as a writer and thinker. At the end of part 1 of *In Defense of Decadent Europe* ("Europe Mystified by Marxism-Leninism") Aron attacks the conformism of intellectuals who had already begun to murmur about Solzhenitsyn's conservatism and his suspicious attachment to Old Russia and to the religion of his forebears. Citing the distinguished political theorist Claude Lefort, a man of the anti-totalitarian Left who admired Solzhenitsyn, Aron comments on the "anti-authoritarianism" evident in Solzhenitsyn's writings such as *The Gulag Archipelago*.[19] Reading the *Letter* in continuity with the broader anti-totalitarian vision of Solzhenitsyn, Aron rightly saw in it the same love of liberty and intense but moderate and humane patriotism that informed Solzhenitsyn's other writings. Aron's reception of the 1973 *Letter* still stands out for its lucidity and for its rare willingness to understand Solzhenitsyn on his own terms.

19 *Ibid.*, pp. 74–75.

A Parisian Encounter

I will now turn to three articles from 1975, 1976, and 1980 respectively, that reveal the extent of Aron's admiration for and agreement with Solzhenitsyn. The first is a beautiful text on "Solzhenitsyn's Message"[20] that appeared in the Parisian *Le Figaro* on April 18, 1975, two days after Solzhenitsyn had appeared on Bernard Pivot's *Apostrophes* program with the ex-communist Pierre Daix, the conservative-minded essayist and novelist (and *Figaro* contributor) Jean d'Ormesson, and Jean Daniel, the editor-in-chief of the left-of-center newsmagazine *Le nouvel observateur*. Aron notes in his *Mémoires* that the personality of the *zek* had touched him deeply: "coming from another world," he found in Solzhenitsyn "an extraordinary man, whose like would be difficult to find anywhere in the world."[21] Aron comments that neither Daix nor d'Ormesson had made much of an impression that evening precisely because neither had tried to. But Daniel adopted a confrontational stance toward Solzhenitsyn, comparing his own "fights against French or American imperialism to the struggle Solzhenitsyn carried out against the Kremlin."[22] Daniel also lamented the absence of a representative of the French Communist party on the *Apostrophes* panel, thus reinforcing his ideological fidelity to his Communist "comrades." Aron concedes in his *Mémoires* that he was irritated and even embarrassed by Daniel's performance. But he denied, quite rightly in my view, that he had exceeded "the bounds of legitimate controversy" as Daniel would suggest a few years later in his book *L'Ere des ruptures*. In that work, Daniel suggested that Aron had "abandoned reasoned argument and waxed indignant, with uncharacteristic violence, because I had not bowed before

20 Aron, "Le message de Soljenitsyne" in *Le Figaro*, 18 avril 1975.
21 Aron, *Memoirs: Fifty Years of Political Reflection*, translated by George Holoch, Foreword by Henry Kissinger (New York: Holmes & Meier, 1990), pp. 380–81.
22 *Ibid.*, p. 381.

an exceptional man."[23] An examination of Aron's column tells another story.

Aron begins by saying that if Dostoevsky had come back from the *House of the Dead*, from his years in a Tsarist prison camp, no one would have "proposed a tsarist bureaucrat or a lackey of this bureaucracy as an interlocutor." But by "regretting" the absence of a French Communist on the *Apostrophes* panel, Daniel had "condemned himself to a thankless role." He had reduced Solzhenitsyn to the status of a mere politician or political partisan. Aron did not deny that Solzhenitsyn's "intentions, works, and life constitute political realities possessing all the weight of suffering and genius." But Daniel had failed to see that Solzhenitsyn's convictions ultimately "transcend politics because they animate an exceptional personality, because in the last analysis they are spiritual." Eschewing every reductive or materialist explanation, Aron saw at work in Solzhenitsyn nothing less than a spiritual "faith in liberty and an unconditional devotion to the truth." "By asking the author of *Cancer Ward* to express opinions on the events of the day, the editor-in chief of *Le nouvel observateur* lowered the dialogue to the level of ordinary political debates."

Aron also denied that anyone in the West was fighting the *same battle* as Solzhenitsyn. No one on the Right or Left in the West had taken "the long journey through the concentration camp world and drawn from these same trials the invincible strength to resist the infernal machine." Aron did not regret writing books and articles on Algerian independence. But he could not compare his struggles and sacrifices with the author of *One Day in the Life of Ivan Denisovich*. When Daniel put himself on the same plane as Solzhenitsyn, he falsified reality and failed to recognize the terrible uniqueness of totalitarianism. Such moral equivalence was possible only among those who benefited from the unfettered freedom of the Western world and mistook that freedom for oppression.

Aron did not deny that Solzhenitsyn's judgments about current events (for example, his views about Vietnam, Portugal, or

23 *Ibid.*, p. 382.

Chile) were open to challenge. "Salazar's regime has left a population that is half illiterate; the Chilean generals use and abuse repression and torture... The Communists of North Vietnam will at least end the war." But Solzhenitsyn is right about the essential point. He challenges the "lie" that allows ideologues in the West to excuse the "huge Gulags" of the totalitarian East while expressing indignation about the smaller ones in right-wing dictatorships. He reminds us of the immutable truth that "camps remain camps whether they are brown or red." Solzhenitsyn challenges the self-satisfaction of "progressive" intellectuals who found reasons to excuse the "good camps" that were sanctified by the socialist cause. For decades, they saw in the homeland of the gulag archipelago the most "humane" political order in the world.

Aron's column ends by contrasting Jean Daniel's obsession with the "unity of the Left" with the moral grandeur of Solzhenitsyn. Solzhenitsyn's greatness crushes, overwhelms, all who confront it. Moreover, Aron observes that the millions of Frenchmen who viewed *Apostrophes* could not help but hear a "message of charity, faith and hope," a message that was also illumined in Solzhenitsyn's face and eyes. Aron, the unbeliever, freely acknowledged the *theological virtues* that were displayed by Solzhenitsyn. What the reader confronts is not an Aron overcome by indignation but rather one who faithfully describes spiritual greatness as it appears before him. The capacity to admire is a capacity that tends to wither in a democratic age. Aron's column of April 18, 1975 is impressive not only for its lucidity about Solzhenitsyn's message, one that is ultimately more spiritual than political, but for its ability to describe "greatness of soul" in an age that denies the soul's power or very existence. It is my surmise that Aron reproduced the column on "Solzhenitsyn's Message" verbatim in his *Mémoires* to convey the "phénomène Soljenitsyne" as he first encountered it rather than to simply score points with a French intellectual still in the grips of the "myth of the Left." In his *Mémoires*, Aron notes that Daniel could see in the North Vietnamese only a David fighting the goliath of American imperialism. Solzhenitsyn, in contrast, "saw in Vietnam in addition a new communism and new Gulags, and he was right."[24] Solzhenitsyn was the witness from the East who testified to the power of the ideological Lie to distort the ability of intellectuals to see the world clearly.

Solzhenitsyn and Sartre

A year after the publication of "Solzhenitsyn's Message" Aron published a powerful reflection ("Solzhenitsyn and European Leftism"[25]) on the encounter between Solzhenitsyn and the figure the Russian writer disparagingly calls in *The Oak and the Calf* the "ruler of minds" in the West, Jean-Paul Sartre. Written for a festschrift for his friend Manès Sperber, the Austrian-born anti-Communist novelist and essayist, this piece is Aron's most insightful tribute to Solzhenitsyn and arguably his most scathing critique of Jean-Paul Sartre.

Aron begins by noting that Solzhenitsyn had refused to meet the "Sartres" when they were guests of honor of the Writer's Union in the Soviet Union in the mid-1960s and requested a meeting with him. In *The Oak and the Calf*, Solzhenitsyn wonders "whether Sartre discerned in my refusal the depth of our aversion to him."[26] Later on, Simon de Beauvoir could only speculate that Sartre knew Solzhenitsyn better than Solzhenitsyn knew Sartre, a claim that Aron adamantly rejects. Sartre, the itinerant philosopher who led the life of a student loafer, could not possibly begin to understand or appreciate the moral witness of Solzhenitsyn.

---

24 *Ibid.*
25 Aron's article "Alexander Solzhenitsyn and European 'Leftism'" first appeared in English in *Survey* 100/101 (Summer/Autumn 1976), pp. 233–41 and has been reprinted in F. Flagg Taylor IV, ed., *The Great Lie: Classic and Recent Reappraisals of Ideology and Totalitarianism* (Wilmington, DE: ISI Books, 2011), pp. 366–76. The French original appeared as "Soljenitsyne et Sartre" in *Commentaire*, hiver 1993–1994,Vol. 16, numéro 64, pp. 687–92. I will cite the text in *The Great Lie* throughout.
26 Solzhenitsyn as cited by Aron in *The Great Lie*, p. 367.

Nor could Sartre and Beauvoir, "litterateurs" who put their works on the same level as people, begin "to understand Solzhenitsyn's rebuff."[27] "As a personality Sartre embodies everything which Solzhenitsyn loathes: the rejection of moral guidelines, the refusal to accept the age-old distinction between good and evil, the sacrifice of men's lives and the justification of crimes by appeals to an indefinite future ('indefinite' in all its senses), in short, the evil of ideology—a kind of evil which in Sartre's case takes on a pure form—indirect, delegated evil."[28] For Sartre, "Marxism is the unsurpassable philosophy of our era," a dogmatic and even "stupid"[29] affirmation that allowed him to justify the unjustifiable. Sartre defended the Soviet Union during the darkest days of Stalinism before heading off to Cuba to befriend Castro in the early years of the Cuban revolution. His heart and head always leaped to the Left. In Aron's pungent formulation, the Sartres "justify Evil by justifying the justification of it."[30]

The "Sartres" were not dogmatic Marxists so much as "philosophers of ideological thinking"[31] who embodied the unthinking "Leftism" that Solzhenitsyn pilloried in his major writings. For them, "anti-Communists are blackguards"[32] and the only people who have the right to criticize Marxism "are those who become involved in the movement." To attack Soviet concentration camps or repression is to side with the camp of the "rightists," to doom oneself to the cause of reaction. Sartre, the "philosopher of freedom," had committed himself to a "categorical imperative of Revolt" which was all too often coextensive with the "categorical imperative of violence." In a work such as the *Critique of Dialectical Reason*, Sartre justified violence in the name of human emancipation and as a liberating end in itself.

Solzhenitsyn, in contrast, made no subtle distinction between

27 *Ibid.*, p. 368.
28 *Ibid.*, p. 374.
29 *Ibid.*, pp. 368–69.
30 *Ibid.*, p. 370.
31 *Ibid.*
32 *Ibid.*

Marxism and Marxism-Leninism. Marxism was "quite simply the doctrine in whose name the Bolsheviks seized power, destroyed first political parties, then the peasantry, set up concentration camps and murdered millions upon millions of ordinary citizens."[33] For Solzhenitsyn, far from being the "unsurpassable philosophy of our era" Marxism was the "root of all ill, the source of falsehood,"[34] the principle that justified and thus amplified terror and tyranny, making them "necessary" instruments for the transformation of human beings and the world. It is Marxist ideology that "gives the criminal a clear conscience." In Solzhenitsyn's memorable phrase from the first volume of *The Gulag Archipelago*, "thanks to ideology the twentieth century was fated to experience evildoing on a scale calculated in the millions." Solzhenitsyn did not deny that other doctrines besides Marxism (e.g., nationalism, colonialism, even the political use and abuse of Christianity) could provide ideological fodder for tyranny. But Marxism has a special place in the catalogue of ideological evil because the "quantitative" difference brought about by its extermination of tens of millions marks a "qualitative" change in the nature of despotism itself.[35] Marxism is ideology *par excellence*. "Evil needs an ideology before it can operate in the millions"[36] and Marxism-Leninism provides the social theory which, in Solzhenitsyn's words, "gives evildoing its long-sought justification."

Aron suggests that if they had ended up meeting, the dialogue between Solzhenitsyn and Sartre would have amounted to nothing. Solzhenitsyn rightly emphasized the intrinsic perversity and mendacity of Communist totalitarianism. Compared to Lenin's or Stalin's (or even Brezhnev's) Soviet Union, Franco's Spain was a liberal order where men could breathe freely and speak their minds. Sartre, in contrast, continued to identify "progressive" forms of despotism with liberation, emancipation. In the conclusion of his

33 *Ibid.*, p. 369.
34 *Ibid.*
35 *Ibid.*, p. 370.
36 *Ibid.*

essay, Aron unapologetically sides with Solzhenitsyn. He endorses his "message" which can be summarized in "two fundamental sentences": "there is something worse than poverty and repression— and that something is the Lie; the lesson this century teaches us is to recognize the deadly snare of ideology, the illusion that men and societies can be transformed at a stroke."[37]

Aron understood that compulsory lying defined the Soviet regime in its Stalinist and post-Stalinist forms. The myriad lies that were demanded in the workplace, schools, press, and what passed for public life—the demand that one say what one knew not to be true—was rooted in a more fundamental "ontological" or "metaphysical" Lie—"the illusion that men and societies can be transformed at a stroke." This was the Big Lie that gave rise to the suffocating tyranny of ideological clichés, to what Solzhenitsyn called in "Our Muzzled Freedom" "the lie as a form of existence." Soviet ideocracy was a soul-numbing despotism that was far more insidious and inhuman than a mere authoritarian order with its restrictions on political liberty and human rights. Even more than violence, the Lie was the principle that set in motion the totalitarian regime. This is why Solzhenitsyn insisted that "non-participation in lies"[38]—the refusal to spout official slogans, repeat mendacities, or denounce colleagues—was the *sine qua non* for both self-respect and for the return of something resembling normal civic life. Only when the flower of the nation had jettisoned the Lie could "breathing and consciousness return."[39] Solzhenitsyn

---

37 *Ibid.*, p. 376.

38 See Solzhenitsyn's beautiful and profound dissection of the "Lie" in his 1974 text "Live Not by Lies!" The text can be found in *The Solzhenitsyn Reader: New and Essential Writings, 1947–2005* (Wilmington, DE: ISI Books, 2006), pp. 556–60.

39 See Solzhenitsyn, "As Breathing and Consciousness Return" in Solzhenitsyn et. al., *From Under the Rubble*, translated by Michael Scammell and a team of translators (Boston: Little Brown & Company, 1975), pp. 3–25. In this text Solzhenitsyn insists that "the absolutely essential task is not political liberation, but the liberation of our souls from participation in the lie forced upon us."

fought less for democracy, which he hoped would come in due time, than for an end to ideocratic despotism which not only oppressed men's bodies but demanded of them their souls as well.

Writing in 1976, Aron identifies with the "vast silent mass" who side with Solzhenitsyn (and his friend Manès Sperber) against unrepentant ideologues in the academy and mass media. They do so by recognizing that mankind has no future except by rejecting "ideological knavery" and respecting "moral laws."[40] Against the categorical imperative of violence, against the nihilism inherent in both radical voluntarism (existentialism) and radical determinism (Marxism-Leninism), Aron asserts freedom within nature and a moral law which provides a compass for thinking and acting man. Something after all has come from the dialogue between the Russian *zek* and the French existentialist *cum* Marxist. One might say that Aron's own liberalism has been given greater moral depth by his sympathetic encounter with the Russian *zek* and by his adamant repudiation of the quasi-nihilism of his youthful friend from the *École normale supérieure*. In the encounter that he has sketched between Sartre and Solzhenitsyn, the Russian "dissident" and the European leftist, Aron finds wisdom.

Misconceptions About Russia

Aron's last major treatment of Solzhenitsyn occurred in a column he wrote for *L'Express*, dated May 17–23, 1980.[41] The column was occasioned by the French publication of Solzhenitsyn's *L'Erreur de l'occident*, a lengthy essay that had originally been published in *Foreign Affairs* under the title "Misconceptions about Russia Are a Threat to America."[42] In this thoughtful and

40 Aron in *The Great Lie*, p. 376.
41 Raymond Aron, *"L'Erreur de l'Occident"* in *De Giscard à Mitterand, 1977–1983*, Préface de Jean–Claude Casanova (Paris: Editions de Fallois, 2005), pp. 420–21.
42 See note #7 for information on the book version of this article. The French text appeared in 1980 as *L'Erreur de l'Occident* and was reis-

spirited essay, Solzhenitsyn argued that even many who opposed Communism did not appreciate the extent of its hostility to mankind as a whole. He argued that "there exist no 'better' variants of Communism" and "that it is incapable of growing 'kinder,' that it cannot survive as an ideology without using terror, and that, consequently, to coexist with Communism on the same planet is impossible."[43] The bulk of the essay was directed against a "second and equally prevalent mistake" that assumed "an indissoluble link between the universal disease of Communism and the country where it first seized control—Russia."[44]

It is the second point that Aron takes up in his column. Like Solzhenitsyn, he challenges the "spontaneous explanation of Sovietism by the Russian past." Both Aron and Solzhenitsyn insist on the "specificity of Communism," an ideological movement and political order that are "unprecedented in human history." Aron endorses Solzhenitsyn's suggestive claim that as long as Communism was admired in the West, "it was preferred as the unquestionable dawn of a new era; as soon as it was condemned, people hastened to explain it by the traditional servility of the Russians." General de Gaulle may have been right that *in the long run* "ideologies pass but nations remain." But he was wrong to see in Stalin merely a new Tsar who loved Russia in his own way. And he failed to appreciate the extent to which the body and soul of historic Russia had been mutilated beyond recognition by Communist ideology. Aron does not deny "a certain continuity between tsarist Russia and the Soviet Union: administrative forms persist, old traditions have not suddenly disappeared." But on the crucial question, he sided with Solzhenitsyn: Bolshevik despotism was not an epiphenomenal expression of "eternal Russia." One saw the "repetition of the specific traits of totalitarianism in all the countries conquered by a Marxist-Leninist party." Stalin, a

sued by Éditions Grasset in 2006 with a fine introduction by Claude Durand that takes aim at contemporary forms of "Russophobia."
43 Solzhenitsyn, *The Mortal Danger*, p. 2.
44 *Ibid.*

Georgian, was no more an expression of eternal Russia than Pol Pot was an expression of eternal Cambodia.

Aron also endorsed Solzhenitsyn's rejection of certain "fictions current in the West." Compared to the Soviet regime, the Tsarist regime was indeed comparatively liberal. There were no camps, political prisoners were small in number and prisoners were well treated. Universities "enjoyed an intellectual freedom comparable to those of Western universities." The *Okhrana*, the Tsarist secret police, was an amateur organization compared to the *Cheka-GPU-KGB* established by the Bolsheviks in 1917. Most importantly, "the enslavement of thought to the truth of state, of civil society in its entirety to the decrees of an omnipresent power, represents neither an extrapolation nor a perfecting of the prerevolutionary regime." Aron insists that such an enslavement of the human spirit belongs to the twentieth century and "constitutes its cancer, its permanent threat." It cannot plausibly be blamed on the Russian old regime.

Like Solzhenitsyn, Aron believed that the Soviet leaders found legitimacy in the ideology they professed. Ideology was the anchor of Soviet life and it and it alone vouched for the truth of the "super-reality" supposedly inaugurated by the October revolution. The sheer recalcitrance of human nature and society made terror and lies inevitable. Only through them could the party-state "fictively reconcile ... words and reality." Aron did not deny that the Soviet Union was a modern industrial society that needed to "integrate individuals into organizations." As Aron laconically observes, "Sovietism is born of the conjunction of a party resolved to acquire total power and the tendency to bureaucratization which is typical of technical civilization." But neither bureaucratic theory nor the concept of industrial society provided the key for understanding an ideological despotism of the Soviet sort. That secret lay in the dialectic of reality and ideological super-reality that defined the drama of Soviet life from its creation in 1917 until its self-destruction at the end of the 1980s. Near the end of his column, Aron endorsed Solzhenitsyn's judgment that Communism was everywhere "anti-national" and that the function of ideology was to "kill the national body in which it develops." There was no *essential* connection between the Russian old regime and the Soviet Union, between the Russian nation and ideocratic despotism.

Aron's—and Solzhenitsyn's—approach allows one to understand the restoration of a non-ideological Russian state after 1991 as the victory of the national "body" over the ideological cancer which had dominated and sickened it for so long. Of course, post-Communist Russia is far from a developed democracy and some important residues and habits of Sovietism persist. But the basic liberties that existed in Russia before the October 1917 revolution have all been restored. Thought is no longer enslaved to the truth of the state. Rather than lamenting the eternal servility of Russians, Westerners ought to welcome the return of Russia to a relatively normal form of national and political life. We should not be surprised that it is taking considerable time for Russia to descend fully from the "icy cliffs" of totalitarianism. Soviet despotism was no ordinary dictatorship. In a negative way, the Soviet regime succeeded in creating a *homo sovieticus* whose habits of servility are indeed incompatible with the enterprise, initiatives and self-government characteristic of a free society.

In the final paragraph of his *L'Express* piece, Aron reports on an instructive exchange about Solzhenitsyn he had recently had with an Irish academic. In a presentation on Soviet foreign policy he had delivered to the Royal Academy of Ireland, Aron had invoked the debate between Solzhenitsyn and Sakharov and had sided with Solzhenitsyn. His respondent, a "charming" Irish professor of Gaelic, had summarily dismissed the testimony of Solzhenitsyn, coming as it had from an "Old Believer." The Irish professor was also adamant that ideology was "cynically employed" by the Soviet leaders and was of no fundamental importance. But it was precisely the jettisoning of that ideology that transformed the USSR into Russia and that offers hope for the future. However cynically employed, ideology was indeed *the* key to Soviet legitimacy as both Solzhenitsyn and Aron always argued. One is also struck by Aron's refusal to caricature

Solzhenitsyn along the lines of the Irish professor. He does not dismiss or mock Solzhenitsyn's deeply felt Christian convictions nor does he confuse his patriotic attachments with a virulent form of nationalism. From beginning to end, Aron saw in Solzhenitsyn the scourge of ideological despotism, the advocate of a more humane future for Russia and the West. There is nothing in Solzhenitsyn's life or thought after 1980 that in any way demands a refinement of Aron's judgments about the Russian writer.

Two Spiritual Families?

What accounts for the remarkable affinities between the French political thinker, a liberal rooted in the secular traditions of the West, and the Russian writer who fought totalitarianism in the name of human dignity and the best spiritual traditions of his native Russia? Whatever their ultimate spiritual differences, Aron and Solzhenitsyn shared a common devotion to truth and liberty as well as a shared hatred of the ideological lie. Moreover, there are remarkable similarities between the "philosophy of history" affirmed by both men. In *The Red Wheel*, beginning with *August 1914*, Solzhenitsyn attacked historical fatalism whether in the form of Marxist determinism or Tolstoyan fatalism.[45] "*The Red Wheel*," the churning force of destructive revolution, only became "inevitable" due to the moral abdication of those responsible for Russia's fate. As we have emphasized throughout this work, Solzhenitsyn always defended the free will of human beings and saw it splendidly at work in a noble statesman such as Pyotr Stolypin, Prime Minister of Russia from 1906 to 1911, who heroically tried to steer a "middle line of social development" in the years before his assassination in September 1911. For Solzhenitsyn, human beings are never without choices and should

45 See Alexis Klimoff, "Inevitability vs. Will: A Theme and its Variations in Solzhenitsyn's *August 1914*," in *Transactions of the Association of Russian-American Scholars in the U.S.A.* vol. 29, 1998, pp. 305–12.

never resign themselves to evil in the name of an alleged historical inevitability.

Aron, too, refused to bow before what he called "pseudo-fatality" and was a tireless critic of the "idolatry of History."[46] His philosophy of history emphasized both the limits or constraints of choice and the margins of liberty available to human beings. This agnostic paradoxically acknowledged a transcendent space above human action and the human will and experienced "horror" before the ideological breakdown of the distinction between the "sacred and the profane."[47] He was appalled by "progressive" Christians who succumbed to "secular religion" and who placed all their hopes in an unfolding Historical Process.[48] These politicized Christians had lost faith in spiritual imperatives that give dignity to man and as a result confused "one class and the Messiah," "one regime and the kingdom of God."[49] With no other criterion than the truth of History or the pretenses of an ideological party, the militant, whether Marxist, existentialist, or Christian progressive, had succumbed to nihilism. Aron refused to reduce man to revolutionary political action or to subordinate the individual to the alleged requirements of History since both paths deprived men of "the means of rejecting the unacceptable."[50] For Aron, "ethics judges politics as much as politics judges ethics." As he eloquently stated in the concluding words of his English-language "Introduction" to *Marxism and the Existentialists* (1969), "the worst error would be to fail to recognize the dialectic which determines our condition and to totally surrender to nihilism or fanaticism, either by denying all spiritual imperatives or by trusting blindly in an alleged determinism of history."[51]

46 See Aron, *The Opium of the Intellectuals* (New York: Doubleday, 1957) and Aron, *Marxism and the Existentialists* (New York: Simon and Schuster, 1969), p. 13.
47 Aron, *Marxism and the Existentialists*, p. 15.
48 *Ibid.*
49 *Ibid.*
50 *Ibid.*, p. 16.
51 *Ibid.*

These analyses confirm that Aron and Solzhenitsyn did not belong to completely different spiritual families after all. Both took aim at the dual specters of nihilism and fanaticism that haunted modern civilization. Both were sensitive to the "crisis" of modern civilization, to the decline of civic spirit when free peoples were confronted by the totalitarian challenge.[52] Both eloquently and forcefully affirmed the free will and moral responsibility of human beings. Both refused to explain away natural justice as so many modern intellectuals are prone to do.[53] In Aron's engagement with Solzhenitsyn, one witnesses a rare form of intellectual and spiritual communion, a spiritual encounter that is worthy of our admiration and that still has much to teach us today.

52 See Aron's analysis of the "crisis of civilization" in the penultimate chapter of *In Defense of Decadent Europe*, pp. 224–51. Aron's "active pessimism" became more pronounced in the years after 1968.

53 Pierre Manent tellingly observes that Aron was a natural Aristotelian who accepted the morality "immanent" in human life. Aron was never tempted to jettison natural justice in the name of a radical skepticism or a radical historicism that denied the experiences at the foundation of our sense of right and wrong, truth and falsehood. See Manent, *Le regard politique: Entretiens avec Benedicte Delorme-Montini* (Paris: Flammarion, 2010), p. 54.

Chapter 7

SOLZHENITSYN, RUSSIA, AND THE JEWS REVISITED

Volume two of Solzhenitsyn's monumental study of Russian-Jewish relations, *Dvesti Let Vmeste* (*Two Hundred Years Together*) appeared in bookstores in the writer's native Russia in the final days of 2002 (with a print run of 100,000 copies according to its publisher).* Both volumes of *Two Hundred Years Together* were runaway bestsellers in Russia and gave rise to a large and varied critical response, ranging from the friendly to the respectful to the aggressively hostile. The first volume of *Two Hundred* treated the encounter between Russians and Jews from 1772 (when 100,000 Jews were allowed to enter the Russian empire) right up until the eve of the revolutionary conflagrations of 1917.

The second volume picks up the story and covers the period from the revolutions of 1917 until the exodus of hundreds of thousands of Jews for Israel and the West that started in the early 1970s. Solzhenitsyn begins his book with a remarkable excursus on what it means to be a Jew (it is fascinating to watch the great Russian writer thoughtfully engage the likes of Hannah Arendt, Gershom Sholem, and Amos Oz). Only then does he turn to a

---

* I have consulted both the Russian edition *Dvesti let' Vmeste*, Chast' II published by Russki put' in 2002 and the French edition *Deux siècles ensemble* (1917–1972), tome deux, *Juifs et Russes pendant la période soviétique*, translated from the Russian by Anne Kichilov, Georges Philippenko, and Nikita Struve, published by Editions Fayard in 2003. My thanks to Stephan Solzhenitsyn for checking and correcting the major quotations in this chapter.

detailed examination of Russian-Jewish relations during almost the full length of the Soviet period. The first volume aimed first and foremost "to report" events and was marked by a restrained and even scholarly tone; the second volume describes events that Solzhenitsyn either knew first-hand or has spent decades investigating and writing about in works such as *The Gulag Archipelago* and *The Red Wheel*. It is the more literary of the two volumes and is graced by a lively and invigorating prose.

Both the first and second volumes of *Two Hundred* have now appeared in French and German translation but no English-language edition of either volume is in sight, although excerpts have appeared in *The Solzhenitsyn Reader*. The French reception of the two volumes of the work has on the whole been quite respectful, while as we have said, the Russian reception was decidedly more heated. Here in the United States, despite the appearance of intelligent treatments of the first volume of the work in such diverse forums as *The New Yorker*, the *TLS*, *The New Republic*, and *Society*, publishers have so far shied away from publishing one of Solzhenitsyn's last major works. Whatever their motives, this is a lacuna that should be corrected.

From Belligerence to Understanding

With a few notable exceptions, critics of *Two Hundred Years Together* have failed to come to terms with the larger intellectual and deeper moral concerns that inform Solzhenitsyn's historical analysis of Russian and Jewish relations during the period of Soviet rule. Some critics have been so preoccupied with unearthing evidence of Solzhenitsyn's purported anti-Semitism that they have barely noticed the principled personal and national commitment to "repentance and self-limitation" that informs every page of his analysis. Solzhenitsyn, in fact, explicitly eschews a partisan or nationalistic analysis of Russia's "Jewish question," yet many critics persist on the false assumption that Russian nationalism, and one of a particularly virulent character, is his "only star and compass." Throughout the book, Solzhenitsyn carefully chronicles the deeds and misdeeds of Russians and Russian Jews alike, and pleads for mutual understanding and repentance on the part of both parties.

But hostile critics suspect the worst and do their best to find it. They approach his book not in the conscientious, open-minded spirit that the book's author requests but rather in the spirit of a zealous prosecutor presenting his closing arguments to a jury (a classic example is that of a French leftist reviewer in *La quinzaine littéraire* who first attacked volume I of *Two Hundred* for its "badly controlled anti-Semitism" and then took volume II to task for its clever concealment of its anti-Semitic animus!). Despite the acrimony likely to be occasioned by his foray into treacherous waters, Solzhenitsyn remains committed to "sincere and benevolent" mutual understanding between Russians and Jews. But he has few illusions in this regard. Near the end of the work Solzhenitsyn states that, "even the most mild movements toward remembrance, repentance, and impartiality elicit a harsh reproach from the guardians of extreme nationalism—both Russian and Jewish." The heated and sometimes unhinged critical reaction to the publication of the two volumes of "200" provides ample evidence to support Solzhenitsyn's forebodings.

Why, then, did the Russian Nobel Laureate risk derision and even something of his reputation in order to dedicate many years of his life to a thoroughgoing exploration and examination of Russian-Jewish relations? The only reasonable response is that Solzhenitsyn is genuinely committed to shedding some healing light on this seemingly intractable problem, one that has been exacerbated by the ill will, animosity, and mutual suspicion of the parties. To his credit, Solzhenitsyn never allows mean-spirited or ideologically inspired criticism to deter him from his task. In the twilight of his life, he embarked on *Two Hundred Years Together* with the sincere hope that his study might contribute to finding "mutually accessible and benevolent paths along which Russian-Jewish relations may proceed."

By and large, Solzhenitsyn's work has not been initially well received by the Russian Jewish community, not to mention the left liberal intellectual establishment. The response of Russian Jewish intellectuals has been defensive, to say the least. Some have accused Solzhenitsyn of bias, others of outright anti-Semitism. A few particularly perfervid critics, such as Semyon Reznik, have accused Solzhenitsyn of being an ideologist of murderous anti-Semitism, an apologist for the Black Hundreds and the pogroms. Very few on either the Russian or Jewish side have responded affirmatively to Solzhenitsyn's call for mutual understanding and repentance.

But there have been exceptions. Solzhenitsyn himself has been heartened by the "extremely valuable article" on volume one of *Two Hundred Years* that Alexander Eterman has published in the Russo-Israeli journal *Vremya iskat'*. He admires Eterman's article in much the same way he earlier admired the penetrating scholarship of Jewish authors such as Mikhail Agursky, Mikhail Heller, and Dora Sturman who did so much to expose the Communist Lie and to promote Russian-Jewish reconciliation. These authors are imbued with deep respect for Russian culture as well as for the intellectual and spiritual traditions of the Jewish people. Solzhenitsyn continues to be confident that others in the Jewish community will respond positively to his call for respectful dialogue once the passions of the moment subside. One can only hope that Solzhenitsyn turns out to be as prescient in this regard as he was in his almost preternatural anticipation of the collapse of the Soviet Union.

Partisan or ideological deafness is not the only cause of the difficulty in actually hearing what Solzhenitsyn has to say. *National Review* editor Jay Nordlinger has rightly observed that Solzhenitsyn is far from attentive to the "sensitivities" of modern readers. Solzhenitsyn rarely shies away from controversial questions or sugarcoats uncomfortable truths. This is a mark of his greatness but also a source of misunderstandings. Solzhenitsyn's voice is much more measured than his critics suggest, but perhaps not as politic as truly prudent self-regard would dictate. He speaks frankly and takes for granted the spiritual and intellectual maturity of his interlocutors. He does honor to his readers, but this privilege also includes certain demands. In any event, one must see that his freedom from political correctness in no way has its source in antipathy to the Jews or to any other spiritually great people.

As readers of his *Nobel Lecture* know, Solzhenitsyn believes that nations play an indispensable role in God's design for humanity. He fears that the effacement or erosion of the full variety of nations would impoverish the human race and result in the "entropy of the human spirit." He greatly admires the State of Israel and believes that the creation of the Jewish state was a singular moment in the recognition of the dignity and freedom of the much-reviled and long-persecuted Jewish people. He doesn't hesitate to criticize individual Jews when warranted but never the Jewish people as such. As Solzhenitsyn put it in an important interview that appeared in the *Moscow News* on the occasion of the publication of volume two of *Two Hundred Years*, "I do not pass judgment on a nation as a whole. I always distinguish between different strata of Jews ... those who rushed headlong into the Revolution ... [and those who] tried to hold back themselves and the young, and uphold the tradition ... I do not think that I pass judgment on a nation as a whole. I believe that it is not up to humans to make such judgments on a high spiritual level."

Solzhenitsyn is convinced that the passing of summary judgments on a people as whole is "wrong on a responsible, spiritual level." Solzhenitsyn is careful, then, to make the requisite distinctions and to avoid any suggestion much less accusation of collective guilt. He does, however, call on both Russian and Jews to assume collective moral "responsibility" for the behavior and choices of their "renegade" brethren in the twentieth century as a component and requirement of genuine national belonging and self-respect (these renegades include those Russians who confused love of country with hatred of the Jews as well as those Russians and Jews who rejected the spiritual traditions of their fathers and rushed headlong into the nihilism of ideological revolution). But Solzhenitsyn explicitly opposes attributions of collective guilt. Guilt is an individual phenomenon, responsibility can be a collective one.

In this respect, Solzhenitsyn denies that speaking frankly is the same thing as speaking "belligerently." This distinction is crucial for understanding the rhetorical character of *Two Hundred Years Together*. Otherwise, readers will fruitlessly search for competing philo-Semitic and "anti-Semitic" passages in the book, keeping scorecards and confusing honest criticism with hostility and bias. In a powerful and moving *cri de coeur* that appears at the conclusion of chapter 25, Solzhenitsyn calls for Russians and Jews to renounce once and for all the terribly "distort(ed)" view that "to speak frankly means to speak as enemies." He tells the reader that while he calls things by their name, he does "not feel even for a moment" that his words "carry hostility toward Jews." Once again, Solzhenitsyn reiterates the moral aim of his book, an aim that he had first annunciated in the Author's Preface to the work as a whole: "we must both *understand each other, we must learn to put ourselves in their situation and to enter into the feelings of the other.* By this book I want to extend a hand of mutual understanding for both our futures."

Solzhenitsyn argues that this mutual comprehension must be truly "reciprocal." Russian patriotism and national consciousness should not be dismissed *a priori* as a perceived justification for imperialism and anti-Semitism. Solzhenitsyn is particularly critical of those Jewish publicists who condemn Russian patriotism *tout court*, or who conflate Soviet despotism with Russia's pre-revolutionary national traditions. He is prickly in responding to the refusal of some Jewish intellectuals to even imagine the possibility of a "pure Russian patriotism that is not guilty before anyone." Solzhenitsyn insists that Russians, no more than Jews cannot be condemned "as a whole." The path of self-limiting and ethical patriotism is in principle open to every people. Russians must forever reject the temptation of anti-Semitism and Jews must learn to distinguish between the sins of the Russian people and their rich and humanizing spiritual and cultural traditions.

Solzhenitsyn is convinced that the Russian and Jewish peoples are bound together by a "mysterious Design," a destiny that must not be forgotten now that so many Russian Jews have chosen the path of emigration or citizenship in Israel. To him, "it seems obvious that the truth of our common past is for us, Jews as well as Russians, *morally necessary.*" Solzhenitsyn thus rejects the path of enmity in the name of mutual understanding, repentance, and reconciliation. The ties that bind Russians and Jews are more than merely "historical" ones. Solzhenitsyn is able to understand "the Other" precisely because he recognizes that the nation provides access to the Universal, that "the intimate union of the national and the universal" is "the most necessary (and most fruitful quality for the centuries to come)."

Solzhenitsyn's own patriotism is devoid of all racialism or "messianic national exclusiveness." Human beings do not have to choose between patriotic attachments to their people or nation and the recognition of universal moral imperatives and of common humanity. Solzhenitsyn never simply privileges Russians above other nations or peoples (even if he loves his people with a special fraternal love) because he knows it is idolatrous to confuse a particular nation with the Universal as such. But he also understands that it is paradoxically through taking responsibility for our own nation that we are given access to the universal articulations of our humanity.

We are obliged, then, to love our country as one precious manifestation of God's multi-faceted plan for humankind. As we have already stressed in chapter 1, Solzhenitsyn's generous conception of patriotism is the furthest thing from "blood and soil" nationalism. It has absolutely no room for chauvinism and anti-Semitism. And it wisely rejects a soulless cosmopolitanism that denies the legitimacy of a humane patriotism that requires us to take responsibility for our people and to account for their manifold faults and limitations.

Rejecting the Temptation to Blame

In the opening chapters of volume two, Solzhenitsyn unequivocally repudiates the Judeophobia common to extreme rightist and nationalist circles in Russia. And he denies just as vigorously the absurd view that the nineteenth-century Russian revolutionary movement, the February revolution of 1917 that overthrew the Tsarist order, or the October Revolution that brought Lenin and the Bolsheviks to power, were the product of a Jewish "conspiracy" to enslave or destroy Russia. In volume one of *Two Hundred Years*, he had already addressed and repudiated similar claims made in reference to the nineteenth-century Russian revolutionary movement and the revolutionary upheavals of 1905. His views on this matter could not be any clearer. But this has not prevented wire services from disseminating absolutely fictitious reports about warnings of a Jewish "conspiracy" against Russia that Solzhenitsyn is alleged to have issued in a television appearance in 1998. Nor has it deterred Solzhenitsyn's more fevered critics from regurgitating these shameless misrepresentations.

In the opening chapters of volume two, Solzhenitsyn in particular examines the role of the Jews in the February and October revolutions, and in the administration and consolidation of Bolshevik control during and after the Civil War of 1918–1921. As we have said, Solzhenitsyn categorically refuses to blame Jews for a revolutionary calamity that was in decisive respects the result of decisions made by Russians themselves. Such scapegoating, he argues, does a profound injustice to the Jewish people and deflects Russians from coming to terms with their own sins and omissions.

Solzhenitsyn is severely critical of a February "revolution" that culminated in a weak and ineffective "pseudo-democracy," undermined the robust civil society that had begun to flourish in the last half century of the Tsarist regime, and ultimately paved the way for the twentieth century's first experiment in totalitarianism. Nonetheless, Solzhenitsyn approves of the efforts of the short-lived Russian democracy to grant full citizenship to Russia's Jews and he acknowledges that these measures were long overdue. But Solzhenitsyn's analysis amply demonstrates that if Jews were major beneficiaries of the February revolution, they were in no way its instigators or architects. In a particularly revealing passage, Solzhenitsyn summarizes his conclusions about the causes of the Russian revolution, causes that are abundantly detailed in the multivolume *The Red Wheel*:

> We {Russians} were the authors of this shipwreck: our anointed Tsar, the court circles, the feckless high-ranking generals, the mind-numbed administrators; and, with them, their opponents: the elite intelligentsia, the Octobrists, the Zemstvo leaders, the constitutional democrats {Kadets}, the revolutionary democrats, the socialists, and the revolutionaries; and with them also the errant elements of reservists shamefully penned up in the barracks of Petrograd. That is what led to ruin. Among the intelligentsia, there were, to be sure, many Jews, but that gives no basis to identify the revolution as "Jewish."

In pursuing his researches for *The Red Wheel*, Solzhenitsyn repeatedly encountered episodes, speeches, and writings that specifically addressed the "Jewish question." He thus faced a difficult choice about how prominently to display these themes in his day-by-day narration in *March 1917* and *April 1917* of the unfolding revolutionary drama. In the end, he made a deliberate decision not to interrupt the narrative of events with excurses on the Jewish question. He understandably feared that what might appear to be an inordinate emphasis on the Jewish question in a work investigating the sources and causes of the Russian revolutions of 1917 would feed into the deluded conspiratorial thinking of anti-Semites, of those extremists whose first inclination was to "blame everything on the Jews."

Solzhenitsyn did not want to deflect his readers' attention from "the real" or "principal causes" of the February and October revolutions and from the examination of conscience that is so crucial to the recovery of healthy Russian national consciousness. If Solzhenitsyn had placed too much emphasis on things Jewish he may have unintentionally contributed to that "easy and piquant temptation" of reducing a complex historical tragedy to the supposed machinations of a duplicitous Jewish minority. *Two Hundred Years Together* utterly rejects this pernicious temptation without succumbing to another more understandable one: that of pretending that there was never any "Jewish question" that needs to be confronted by the scrupulous historian and the engaged citizen. Solzhenitsyn has chosen a third path that poses challenges all its own. His *via media* is a spiritually demanding one that requires balanced judgment, personal discernment, and a capacity to make appropriate distinctions. At a most basic level, it is necessary to avoid summary judgments about peoples "as a whole."

Renegades and Revolutionaries

Solzhenitsyn is quite emphatic: The February revolution was welcomed by Russian and Ukrainian Jews but was not made by them. Nor did Jews play a particularly large role in the Bolshevik seizure of power in October of 1917. Those Jews such as Leon Trotsky who did play a major role in that event were committed revolutionaries, "de-Judaized" Jews who had limitless contempt for the traditions and faith of their fathers. No, the Jews had no special responsibility for the calamity of Bolshevism or the larger tragedy of Com-munist totalitarianism. It was first and foremost the stupidity of Russian elites and the immaturity of the Russian people that sealed the fate of the Russian nation in the revolutionary year 1917. "It is generally a fair rebuke: how could an entire people, 170 million strong, be driven into Bolshevism by a small Jewish minority?"

Solzhenitsyn argues that the Bolshevik revolution was a decidedly *internationalist* phenomenon, propelled by ideologues who had broken with the culture, faith, and traditions of their fathers, both Jewish and Russian. These revolutionaries respected no moral limits and had an insane confidence in the ability of Revolution to transform human nature and society. The leaders and foot soldiers of the Leninist enterprise, whether Russian or non-Russian, were self-conscious "renegades" committed to an unprecedented assault on the established political order as well as on the very pediments of civilized life.

Lenin was the renegade par excellence, a Russian inspired by boundless contempt for his country, a revolutionary who detested everything associated with the Orthodox religion and the moral heritage of the civilized world. Solzhenitsyn thus clearly affirms that the particular Russians and Jews who unleashed the furies of revolutionary violence had repudiated the rich moral inheritance passed on to them by their forebears. But a people is still obliged to take responsibility for its renegades if it wishes to come to terms with its past and "build a worthy, dignified life." Without the willingness to take responsibility for the actions of our compatriots, we risk undermining the integrity of the *nation* as a moral community rooted in collective memory and a shared sense of historical destiny.

Initially, Russia's Jews were wary of the Bolsheviks and feared that a new revolutionary conflagration would overturn the significant gains that had been achieved by them as a result of the February revolution. But the young secularized generation, cut loose from the sober wisdom of the past, placed far too many hopes in assimilation, "progress," and revolution. They concluded, with tragic consequence, that anything would be better than a return to the Russian old regime, a social and political order that had imposed crippling disabilities on the Jews and was far from vigilant in protecting them against pogroms and other eruptions of anti-Semitic violence. After initially standing aloof from the Communists in 1917, the younger generation "quickly changed mount on the fly and just as confidently launched itself into the Bolshevik gallop." They made their peace with the "renegades" in their midst. Far too many of them came to identify the fortunes of the Jewish people with the success of the Bolshevik enterprise.

Solzhenitsyn never tires of reiterating that Jews were not the principal force behind the Soviet revolution and have no special responsibility for the misfortunes that would come to afflict Russia in the terrible twentieth century. At the same time, it is wrong to overlook the fact that a remarkably disproportionate number of Jews held positions of responsibility in the middle and upper echelons of the party and secret police apparatus throughout the 1920s and 1930s. Nothing is served by ignoring this fact.

To do so means abandoning this issue to the anti-Semites who will appropriate it for their own hateful purposes. Moreover, there can be no healing of wounds without a willingness to confront the unsavory realities of the past. Solzhenitsyn is particularly insistent on this point. As he writes in his Preface to *Two Hundred Years*, "I have never conceded anyone's right to conceal events that occurred. I cannot call for an accord based on unjust witness to the past." Unpleasant facts must be confronted forthrightly without losing a sense of historical and moral proportion.

Drawing on the research of the distinguished historian of Russia Bruce Lincoln, Solzhenitsyn points out that at the height of the "Red Terror," over three quarters of those who served in the Kiev Cheka were of Jewish origin. Similar evidence of a disproportionate Jewish presence in the Party and secret police can be cited for many other parts of Russia and the Ukraine. As a result, large segments of the Russian public came to identify the "Red Terror" with the Jews, a summary identification that would do untold damage to Russian-Jewish relations. The view "that Chekists and Jews were practically the same thing" was widely accredited in the ranks of both the anti-Communist Whites as well as the Reds. This thoroughly unnatural linkage of Jewishness with a militantly anti-religious and anti-national ideology was reinforced by the crude anti-Semitic propaganda that flourished in White territories during the Civil War. But there is no escaping this fact: the *principal* cause of this unfortunate identification of Bolshevism and Judaism was the monstrous behavior of Jewish Chekists themselves.

Of course, many Jews were understandably dismayed by this identification of Jew and Bolshevik in the popular mind. In this regard, Solzhenitsyn expresses his profound admiration for Jewish intellectuals such as D. O. Linsky, Iosif Bikerman, and Daniil Pasmanik who repeatedly reminded Russians and Jews alike that Bolshevism was utterly incompatible with the moral law, the Jewish tradition, and the freedom and the dignity of human beings. This admirable circle of Russian Jewish patriots forthrightly sided with the White forces during the Civil War. In their

1924 collaboration, *Russia and the Jews*, these anti-Communist Russian Jews desperately tried to persuade their co-religionists in the West and in the émigré community that Communism posed an immense danger to the whole of humanity as well as to the moral integrity of the Jewish people. Solzhenitsyn cherishes their witness and in *Two Hundred Years Together* pays it the appropriate homage. But the contributors to *Russia and the Jews* were savagely attacked by left-wing Jewish opinion in the Western world. Progressive-minded Jews were still fighting old battles and taking aim at familiar targets. They saw no enemies to the Left and were not yet prepared to pass critical judgment on the young Bolshevik "experiment."

But the hostility of "progressive" opinion was only one of the obstacles faced by anti-Communist Jews. With a few honorable exceptions, Russian Whites foolishly rebuffed Jewish support in a struggle that ought to have rallied all decent and freedom-loving people. Some of the most fascinating pages in the second volume of *Two Hundred Years* deal precisely with the almost criminal stupidity of the White forces in failing to welcome the support of anti-Communist Jews in the common struggle against Bolshevik despotism. To be sure, White generals such as Denikin were honorable men who had no anti-Semitic proclivities and did not wish to see anti-Jewish violence in areas under their control. But they did not do enough to stop such violence or to raise their voices against the virulent anti-Semitic propaganda that flourished in White army circles.

Solzhenitsyn endorses the judgment of Winston Churchill: the anti-Semitic violence tolerated or carried out by White forces during the Russian Civil War fatally undermined the ability of men such as Churchill to rally international support for the White cause. As importantly for the prospects of a free Russia, it drove non-communist Jews into the arms of the Bolsheviks. The failure of the White leadership to welcome anti-Communist Jews into its ranks or to stave off violence against the Jewish minority "overshadowed, erased what would have been the chief benefit of a White victory: a reasonable evolution of the Russian state." These harsh truths about the negligence and sins of Russian "patriots" must also be confronted in any honest reckoning with the Russian twentieth century.

The Fortunes of Soviet Jewry

Jews were not only conspicuous among the original supporters of the Bolshevik regime, they would in time rank among its principal victims. Stalin turned on the Jews with ferocious intensity in the years after World War II. During the final eight years of his rule, Jews were subjected to "weighty ordeals." When he died in 1953, Stalin was in the process of orchestrating an unprecedented campaign of repression against the Jews. These were dark times indeed for Soviet Jews. Solzhenitsyn chronicles the changing fortunes of Soviet Jewry with sympathy and sensitivity. And he doesn't fail to draw attention to the disproportionate role played by Jews in the dissident movement of the 1960s and '70s.

Although Jews by then made up less than 1% of the Soviet population, they were without doubt the heart and soul of Soviet dissidence. They provided it with much of its remarkable moral energy and sense of purpose. Solzhenitsyn notes the contribution of Soviet Jews to the anti-Communist cause with gratitude and respect. In particular, he expresses his deep admiration for the civic courage and moral witness of the Jewish dissident Aleksandr Ginzburg. Ginzburg played a particularly impressive role in exposing the show trials of the Brezhnev period. He would later administer the Russian Social Fund on Solzhenitsyn's behalf (this fund, created from the worldwide royalties earned by *The Gulag Archipelago*, was established to provide financial support to the families of Soviet political prisoners). Solzhenitsyn also provides a moving description of the seven heroic demonstrators in Red Square (four of whom were Jewish) who saved the honor of the Russian people by protesting the shameless invasion of Czechoslovakia in August 1968.

Solzhenitsyn's thorough examination of the historical record establishes that Jews played a "disproportionate" role both in consolidating Soviet control in the 1920s and then in undermining Communist ideology in the final decades of that increasingly sclerotic regime. Truth and balance are not enough, however: some critics have faulted Solzhenitsyn for what they perceive as an excessive zeal in counting Jewish patronymics and pseudonyms among the members of the party and Cheka apparatus in the early years of the Soviet regime. And without a doubt his detailed attention to this matter will disturb many Western readers who are hesitant to make judgments about anyone or anything.

But Solzhenitsyn's aim, as we have already seen, is assuredly not to expose the "Jewish" character of the revolution or the Bolshevik regime, but rather to challenge a widely held notion that Jews were always persecuted in Russia and thus equally distant from both the Czarist and Bolshevik regimes. The sheer act of drawing attention to the "disproportionate" Jewish presence in the repressive apparatus of the Leninist state is prima facie evidence of anti-Semitism according to some of Solzhenitsyn's critics. But those who believe this never really challenge the accuracy of the *facts* to which Solzhenitsyn draws our attention. In this regard, it is worth noting that the *refuznik* turned Israeli statesman Natan Sharansky has arrived at remarkably similar conclusions to Solzhenitsyn's and surely with no anti-Semitic intent! In an article about the upsurge of anti-Semitism in the contemporary world Sharansky addresses the complex relationship of Jews to Communist theory and practice:

> As is well known, quite a few Jews, hoping to emancipate humanity and to "normalize" their own condition in the process, hitched their fates to this ideology and the movements associated with it. After the Bolshevik revolution, these Jews were proved to be to among the most devoted servants of the regime ...
>
> As it happens, although Jews were disproportionately represented in the ranks of the early Bolsheviks, the majority of Russian Jews were far from being Bolsheviks, or even Bolshevik sympathizers. More

importantly, Jews would also, in time, come to play a disproportionate role in Communism's demise. (Natan Sharansky, "Hating The Jews," *Commentary*, November 2003, pp. 31–32).

Repentance and Responsibility

In Solzhenitsyn's view, Russians and Jews must both come to terms with their complicity with the Communist regime and stop blaming others for all of their misfortunes and discontents. The Cheka carried out ruthless warfare against whole strata of Russian society. The clergy, merchants, aristocrats, "kulaks," and independent intellectuals were all targeted as "enemies of the people" and "class enemies"; they were arrested or executed for who they were more than anything they had done. In perpetrating these crimes both Russians and Russian Jews are to blame.

At the conclusion of chapter 15 ("On the Side of the Bolsheviks") of his book, Solzhenitsyn speaks difficult truths about the necessity for mutual repentance on the part of both communities. He insists that there can be no escape from the moral obligation to honestly and openly confront the collaboration of whole segments of Russian and Jewish society with an essentially totalitarian and terroristic regime. There are perfectly comprehensible reasons, Solzhenitsyn makes clear, why Jews, suspicious of White intentions during the Civil War, embraced the cause of Bolshevism. But Jews need to move beyond a merely defensive mode of justification in regard to their co-religionists who served as "revolutionary assassins" under the Leninist regime. And the same can be said for those Russian nationalists who blame everyone except the Russian people for the criminal misdeeds of the Soviet regime.

Both Russians and Jews must move beyond mutual reproaches that serve to shield each community from taking full responsibility for its own faults and limitations. He implores both communities to adopt a morally elevated response to the question of Russian-Jewish relations. Each must freely confront its sins and by doing so take responsibility for its moral life and historical destiny. The imitable model for such a liberating confrontation with the past can be found in the decision by the Federal Republic of Germany, however hesitantly at first, to atone for the horrific crimes against humanity and the Jewish people that had been committed by the National Socialists in the name of the German nation. The fact that Hitler's regime in no way spoke for decent-minded Germans did not mitigate the responsibility of democratic Germany to repent for this ignominious episode in German national life.

In my view, this analogy is somewhat inexact since the National Socialists murdered, however perversely, in the name of the German *nation* while Russian and Jewish Bolsheviks heaped scorn on traditional morality and committed their crimes in the name of an aggressively anti-religious and anti-national ideology. Jewish Chekists did not terrorize their victims in the name of Judaism any more than Lenin carried out his brutal repressions in the name of Russia and Orthodoxy. Still, Solzhenitsyn makes a compelling case that repentance is an essential component of the moral health and self-knowledge of a self-respecting people. And he adds that here "is not a question of answering to other peoples, but before oneself, before one's consciousness, and before God."

Solzhenitsyn's Moral Challenge

Solzhenitsyn's critics are so preoccupied with indicting the writer for alleged anti-Semitism that they fail to recognize the preeminently *moral* character of his call for repentance and self-limitation. They politicize his discussions, and misconstrue beyond recognition a morally elevated intervention on behalf of impartial historical judgment and mutual repentance. His critics simply take for granted that Solzhenitsyn is a romantic apologist for some "Holy Russia" of his imagination, utterly blind to the imperfections of the pre-Revolutionary Russian state and society. We have already shown just how false this misrepresentation of the Russian writer is.

If Solzhenitsyn is imbued with a deep love of country, he must, so the reasoning goes, whitewash the Russian past and apologize for its manifold imperfections and injustices. These are the same critics who condemn *The Red Wheel* for being a colossal literary failure without showing any evidence of having read it. It is precisely in that sprawling work that Solzhenitsyn presents a devastating indictment of an old regime devoid of the most elementary instinct for what was necessary to meet the challenges of an emerging modernity. Political actors on both sides of the state-society divide—courtiers and Tsarist ministers, liberal politicians and radical intellectuals—were mesmerized by the bewitching temptations of reactionary inertia and revolutionary impatience. In Solzhenitsyn's judgment, it was the combined irresponsibility of the Left and Right, of reactionaries and revolutionaries, which finally sealed Russia's fate in 1917. Few understood the demanding requirements of a moderation that had the courage to stand up manfully to the extremes.

If anything, Solzhenitsyn is consistently harder in his judgments about the Russian side than he is in his criticisms of the Jewish one. There is therefore nothing one-sided about his call for repentance and a full and an honest accounting of the Russian national past. Russians, he tells us, must "answer—for the pogroms, for those merciless arsonist peasants, for those crazed revolutionary soldiers, for those savage sailors." Repentance is a *sine qua non* of humane and self-limiting patriotism, an indispensable component of authentic national greatness. Of course, some will fault Solzhenitsyn for this very evenhandedness in analyzing the contributions and the sins of Russians and Jews. They will see in his purported impartiality a particularly subtle and therefore invidious anti-Semitism, a moral equivalence that places victims and perpetrators on the same plane.

But this judgment cannot withstand confrontation with Solzhenitsyn's text. The writer rightly rejects the moral absurdity that says because some Jews cast their fate with the totalitarian cause, the pogroms and "vexing" discrimination experienced by Jews under the old regime were somehow morally acceptable. As he persuasively argued in volume I of *Two Hundred Years*, it was precisely the failure of the old regime to adopt a rational response to the Jewish question that contributed mightily to reinforcing the revolutionary propensities of many secularized and assimilated Jews.

Likewise, Solzhenitsyn refuses a perverse logic that argues that the unacceptable presence of anti-Semitism under the old regime somehow relativizes the monstrous crimes carried out by Chekists after 1917, whatever their national or ethnic origin. Solzhenitsyn has too much respect for the Jewish people to patronize them or to consign them to the permanent status of historical victims. A fair-minded critic can only conclude that there is nothing anti-Semitic or nationalistic about Solzhenitsyn's partisanship for "repentance and self-limitation." The polemics responding to Solzhenitsyn's calls for mutual repentance on the part of Russians and Jews say much more about the intellectual confusions and spiritual immaturity of some of his interlocutors than it does about any partiality or insensitivity on the Russian writer's part.

The Holocaust

Solzhenitsyn fully appreciates that no discussion of Russia's "Jewish Question" can ignore the terrible war against Soviet Jewry that was conducted by the Nazis after their invasion of the Soviet Union in June 1941. In chapter 21 ("During the War With Germany"), Solzhenitsyn provides a somber, detailed description of the Holocaust that unfolded on Soviet territory between 1941 and 1944. He also pays tribute to the important contribution that Russian Jews made to the defense of the homeland in the common struggle against the Nazi enemy. On the latter point, he presents original, previously unpublished research refuting commonly heard accusations about an alleged lack of Jewish participation in the war effort.

Solzhenitsyn does justice to the singularity of the Holocaust, to the sheer monstrousness of the war against the Jewish people, without ever minimizing the evils that were Gulag and collectivization. He recognizes that even if "Stalin's regime was no better than Hitler's," Soviet Jews could not afford to see things this way. "At a time of war these monsters couldn't be equal" in the eyes of Soviet Jews since they were faced with nothing less than "the most terrible enemy in the whole of Jewish history."

In a dignified and somber tone, Solzhenitsyn narrates the truly "mind-boggling" facts regarding the extermination of Soviet Jews in the western zone of the Soviet Union. He provides a particularly moving description of the horrifying "hecatomb" of death and destruction wrought by the Nazis at Babi Yar. In just two days at the end of September 1941, 33,771 Jews were executed and piled in the ravine at Babi Yar on the outskirts of Kiev. By the end of the war 100,000 bodies would lie rotting in this mass grave. The extent of such physical carnage must give rise to a moral response and Solzhenitsyn does not fail to reflect on the deeper significance of this event: "The mass shootings at Babi Yar have become a symbol in world history. They horrify us precisely because of the cold calculation, the rigorous organization that is a characteristic of our twentieth century." This heartbreaking crime is much more than another example of man's inhumanity to man. Solzhenitsyn reminds us that such willful destruction and organized calculation is one product of our modern, progressive, and "humanistic" civilization. In contrast, "during the 'dark' Middle Ages people didn't kill except when swept up in a fit of fury or in the rage of battle."

As we have already noted, Solzhenitsyn refuses to set the sufferings of Russians and Jews against each other. The "totality of suffering" experienced by both Russians and Jews at the hands of the Communist and National Socialist regimes is "so great, the weight of the lessons inflicted by History so unsupportable, the anguish for the future so gnawing" that it is imperative that such suffering give rise to mutual empathy, understanding, and reflection on the part of Russians and Jews. At the service of such a goal, Chapter 21 ends with an examination of a series of Jewish thinkers who have reflected on the deeper meaning of the Holocaust and its place in God's Providential design for man. Solzhenitsyn approaches this matter delicately, respectfully. He never tells Jews what philosophical or theological interpretation they ought to give the terrible experience of the Holocaust. A few

Jewish thinkers, such as Dan Levine in the pages of the Russo-Israeli journal "22", have seen in the Holocaust an "element of punishment for certain sins" such as Jewish involvement in the Communist movement. Solzhenitsyn notes that the vast majority of Jewish thinkers dismiss such reflections as "insulting" or even "blasphemous." For his part, Solzhenitsyn would welcome "similar self-criticism," so "noble, so magnanimous" *on the Russian side.* He believes that any spiritually sensitive perception of the Russian experience in the twentieth century must "see, there, too" an element of chastisement or "punishment from on High."

Solzhenitsyn's openness to a "Providential" reading of Communist and Nazi terror as punishment in a deeper and higher spiritual sense may well be "offensive" to certain secular sensibilities. Religious believers will see in it an effort to come to terms with the "mystery of evil" and the weighty requirements of moral responsibility. But this much must be made clear: Solzhenitsyn's openness to a "Providential" reading of the Russian twentieth century in no way undermines his moral recognition of Gulag and the Holocaust as abhorrent manifestations of radical evil. Such Evil must be called by its name and fiercely resisted by decent and civilized human beings. And, as Solzhenitsyn's example indicates, radical evil ultimately gives rise to ultimate, theological issues and perspectives.

The reader cannot help but be struck by the thoughtful, dignified, and empathetic character of Solzhenitsyn's treatment of the Holocaust on Soviet territory. He expresses profound empathy for the Jewish people in their time of greatest affliction. And he ably conveys the inescapably sacred or theological dimension of this tragedy. "The Holocaust is not for nothing written with a capital H. It is an enormous event that touches an immemorial people."

Solzhenitsyn's Non Possum

It is with some regret that we turn from these heights and depths to renewed examination of some of the polemics surrounding Solzhenitsyn's treatment of "the Jewish question." Solzhenitsyn takes particular umbrage at any suggestion that a writer should present the past as it "should be" and not how it actually was. The confusion of reality with the dictates of ideology or "political correctness" was at the heart of the "socialist realist" distortion of Russian literature during the Communist period and Solzhenitsyn will have no part of it. He is understandably taken back by any suggestion that the conscientious writer is "capable of forgetting or of remaking the past." To be sure, the Jewish figures in Solzhenitsyn's belletristic and historical writings are drawn with the same scrupulous concern for historical accuracy and a faithful and humane rendering of character and motive that informs his portrayal of all the individuals in his writings. But Solzhenitsyn's refusal to apply a double standard to Jewish and non-Jewish characters is apparently unacceptable to those who are in the business of searching for signs of anti-Semitism in his work. These critics have a penchant for counting "good" and "bad" Jews in Solzhenitsyn's writings. They reduce everything to a tendentious mathematical calculus that distorts both the nature of art and the search for historical truth.

In chapter 20 of *Two Hundred Years Together* ("In the Gulag Camps"), Solzhenitsyn vigorously responds to these politically correct demands for a hypersensitive rendering of every Jewish character and theme in his writings. The Russian writer makes perfectly clear that he refuses to play by the rules of this game. He will speak the truth as he understands it even if doing so raises the ire of the guardians of political correctness. Solzhenitsyn is particularly frank in this chapter, forthrightly addressing issues that even a sympathetic reader might have hoped that he would have the prudence to sidestep. It is one thing to censor oneself in response to the demands of ideological purity, it is another matter altogether to highlight matters that in all likelihood will be seized upon by careless readers and hostile critics. The danger is that the polemics that then ensue will distract readers from confronting what is truly significant in one's argument. We have already seen this destructive pattern at work in some of the initial Russian responses to *Two Hundred Years Together*. Instead of addressing the major themes and factual arguments of the book,

Solzhenitsyn's hostile critics concentrate on a half dozen passages that they find particularly "offensive."

One such representative passage will suffice for our purposes. In response to the claims made by some Jewish authors that Jews faced a particularly onerous situation in the Gulag, Solzhenitsyn volunteers his impression (and he freely admits that it is only a "generalization" based on his own experience and knowledge) that Jews tended to benefit disproportionately from cushy "trustie" positions in the camps. He notes that Jews, to their credit, tended to look out for their own. This is a factual claim, open to dispute. And it is clear from the context that it is put forward with no anti-Semitic intent. But certain critics have jumped on this assertion as if they had finally found the smoking gun that they had long been looking for, the definitive proof of Solzhenitsyn's hostility to the Jews. These same critics almost uniformly ignore Solzhenitsyn's accompanying tribute to those Jews that he personally knew, not a few in number, who bravely refused the opportunity to work in trustie positions. These men risked early death by choosing to labor at backbreaking "general work" rather than accepting special positions or privileges within the camps. Jews such as Vladimir Efroimson and Yakov Grodzensky were among the noblest souls that Solzhenitsyn had the privilege of encountering during his years in the camps. Such men loyally shared "the common fate" even though they could have opted for the relatively easier way out. As a result of their profound sense of moral obligation, they were subjected to sarcasm and ridicule from all sides. These Jewish prisoners were the noblest embodiments of the "path of self-limitation," the only path capable of "saving humanity" according to Solzhenitsyn. Solzhenitsyn writes that he "never loses sight of such examples," but rather: "all my hope rests in them." That is high praise, indeed the highest praise. A faithful rendering of the past must do full justice to those who make their people and humanity proud, who through their choice of self-limitation vindicate the honor of the human race.

One must certainly admire Solzhenitsyn for his frankness, for his intransigent refusal to bend or distort the truth, even as one wishes that he showed more sensitivity to the delicate problem of presenting controversial or difficult truths to a public that is not always ready to receive them. Chapter 20 moves back and forth from moments of undeniable intellectual and moral elevation to thunderous polemics against Solzhenitsyn's more irresponsible critics. Solzhenitsyn thunders with legitimate indignation against those who go hunting for non-existent anti-Semitism, who wish to censor uncomfortable historical facts, or who misdirect their indignation against the author of *The Gulag Archipelago* (for reproducing photographs from a famous Soviet publication of the eight principal figures in charge of the infamous White Sea-Belomor Canal slave labor project—all but one of them happened to be Jews) rather than at the ideology that led to such criminal misdeeds in the first place. As we have amply demonstrated, anger is by no means the dominant tone in this book—far from it. But Solzhenitsyn cannot help but express his exasperation with those who create wholly unjustified obstacles to genuine, reciprocal understanding between Russians and Jews.

The second volume of *Two Hundred Years Together* is energized by this invigorating oscillation between balanced factual reporting and high-minded appeals to impartial judgment and mutual repentance, on the one hand, and a tenacious refusal to kowtow before the guardians of political correctness, on the other. But the thoughtful reader must avoid taking his bearings from the distracting polemics that have too often swirled around the book. Solzhenitsyn's work conveys profound respect for the spiritual greatness of the Jewish people. His eloquent and powerful witness to the terrible crimes committed in the name of totalitarian ideologies of the Left and the Right is an indispensable contribution to our understanding of the twentieth century. In light of these considerations, it is necessary to turn our attention away from fruitless polemics toward a thoughtful engagement with the appeal to "repentance and self-limitation" that frames and informs every page of Solzhenitsyn's remarkable book. The greatest Russian writer of the age has set forth a challenge to morally serious readers who wish to move beyond the debilitating animosities of the past and to promote mutual understanding between Russians and Jews.

We have seen that *Two Hundred Years Together* articulates a thoughtful, morally elevated, and eloquent defense of national repentance and collective moral responsibility that is incompatible with every form of chauvinism and hate-filled nationalism. Moreover, Solzhenitsyn is a Russian patriot who genuinely aspires to impartial historical judgment. Solzhenitsyn would be the first to admit that he has not attained the perfect equilibrium between universality and particularity, between what is required to defend the honor of his own people and what is required to do justice to the rightful claims of the Jews. Such a perfect reconciliation of universality and particularity lies beyond the reach of any single writer or thinker (or of any mere mortal for that matter). Solzhenitsyn is undeniably moved by the passions of the patriot but never by the hatreds of the anti-Semite. That truth must never be forgotten. Of course, readers may well find something to quarrel with in this long and passionate work. But this should not get in the way of a fulsome appreciation of Solzhenitsyn's achievement. *Two Hundred Years Together* is a remarkable work of scholarship and moral reflection that deserves our attention and respect. It is a model of humane historical inquiry that never loses sight of the questions that truly matter. For these reasons and more, it richly merits publication in the English-speaking world. We, too, must show some courage in standing up to the guardians of ideological correctness.

Chapter 8

THE BINARY TALES:
THE SOUL OF MAN IN THE SOVIET—AND
RUSSIAN—TWENTIETH CENTURY

Unlike readers in France, where almost all of Solzhenitsyn's writings are available, and generally commented on in a thoughtful and balanced way, Anglophones have yet to read the central volumes of *The Red Wheel* dealing with the February revolution of 1917, *Two Hundred Years Together*, or even the volume of memoirs, *The Little Grain*, that deals with Solzhenitsyn's 20 years of Western exile (1974–1994), 18 of them spent in the United States.

Anglophone readers and commentators are least familiar with Solzhenitsyn's life and writing after his return to Russia in May 1994. That period is covered in a memoir sure to fascinate, *Another Time, Another Burden*, a volume that will appear in the coming years in the 30-volume edition of Solzhenitsyn's *Collected Works*. Happily, with the publication of Solzhenitsyn's "binary tales" collected as *Apricot Jam and Other Stories* (eight in all, with one additional story),[1] American readers now have access to his work in one of the principal experimental genres he turned to after the completion of his chef d'oeuvre *The Red Wheel* and his return to Russia.

As a writer, Solzhenitsyn defended a "healthy conservatism,"[2]

---

1   Aleksandr Solzhenitsyn, *Apricot Jam and Other Stories*, translated by Kenneth Lantz and Stephan Solzhenitsyn (Berkeley, CA: Counterpoint, 2011). All quotations from this work will be cited internally as *AJ* followed by the page number in the text.
2   Solzhenitsyn, "Playing Upon the Strings of Emptiness: In Acceptance of the National Arts Club Medal of Honor for Literature" (January

as he called it in his 1993 address to the National Arts Club. It aimed to be "equally sensitive to the old and the new, to venerable and worthy traditions, and to the freedom to explore, without which no future can ever be born."[3] These binary or two-part stories, *dvuchastnyi rasskaz* in Russian, remain faithful to that two-fold imperative. Written between 1993 and 1999 and originally published in the distinguished Russian literary journal *Novy Mir*, they reveal Solzhenitsyn's propensity for literary experimentation even as he defended traditional understandings of humanity's moral and political obligations. Alexis Klimoff, the doyen of North American Solzhenitsyn scholarship, has succinctly defined the genre at work in these stories: "Texts of this type consist of two distinct (always numbered) parts that are related thematically in some manner, all the while exhibiting a significant shift that permits the two parts to be juxtaposed. This shift can be a gap in time, a switch of narrative mode, or even a change of fundamental subject."[4]

These beautifully crafted stories are written in a taut yet elegant style. They are full of historical, moral, and political significance and wisdom without in any way being preachy or didactic. They unobtrusively allow the stories and narratives themselves to convey the message. They reveal Solzhenitsyn as a writer of great force and finesse, and are of interest both as literary works and as testaments to the state of the soul of man in the tragic Soviet and Russian twentieth centuries: assaulted by ideology yet capable of reasserting itself.

The most riveting of these tales is "Ego," a dramatic account of rebellion and betrayal during the Tambov uprising of 1920–1921. Tambov had always captured Solzhenitsyn's imagination: It made clear that Russians had not accepted totalitarianism sitting

19, 1993) in *The Solzhenitsyn Reader: New and Essential Writings, 1947–2005* (Wilmington, DE: ISI Books, 2006), p. 586.

3   *Ibid.*

4   Edward E. Ericson, Jr. and Alexis Klimoff, *The Soul and Barbed Wired: An Introduction to Solzhenitsyn* (Wilmington, DE: ISI Books, 2006), p. 168.

down. As he movingly wrote in his 1993 address in France on the Vendée uprising:

> We had no Thermidor, but to our spiritual credit, we did have our Vendée, in fact more than one. These were the large peasant uprisings: Tambov (1920-21), western Siberia (1921). We know of the following episode: Crowds of peasants in handmade shoes, armed with clubs and pitchforks, converged on Tambov, summoned by church bells in the surrounding villages—and were cut down by machine gun fire. For eleven months the Tambov uprising held out, despite the effort to crush it with armored trucks, and airplanes, as well as by taking families of the rebels hostage.[5]

This is the poignant story that Solzhenitsyn tells in "Ego." The protagonist is Pavel Vasilyevich Ektov (nicknamed "Ego"), a populist democrat and leader of the cooperative movement who becomes a major figure in the Tambov uprising. Tambov was, indeed, Russia's Vendée (with the difference that no significant role was played by the Orthodox clergy), as Solzhenitsyn twice mentions in the text. Ektov eventually betrays the rebel cause after he is captured and must choose between the life of his wife and his young daughter and fidelity to a cause that, he rationalizes, is bound to fail in the long run. Ektov does not wish to betray these "honest men," (*AJ*, 53) as he calls his fellow rebels, and he is acutely aware that the family, "Man's eternal joy," is also "his eternal weak spot." (*AJ*, 35)

The Tambov uprising also plays a role in "Times of Crisis," a compelling account of Marshal Zhukov's life, and the distrust that his military successes gave rise to in Stalin, Khrushchev, and other party leaders. Zhukov began his career and his meteoric rise in the military command in Tambov as an energetic participant in the

---

5   Solzhenitsyn, "A Reflection on the Vendeé Uprising" in *The Solzhenitsyn Reader*, p. 604.

Soviet repression of the uprising. He remained a lifetime, loyal Communist despite the injustices that he experienced at the hands of a regime that distrusted anything resembling true human merit. It is sad to see an aging Zhukov writing memoirs which are manipulated beyond recognition by party apparatchiks.

The opening story in the collection, "Apricot Jam," is among the very best things Solzhenitsyn wrote in the last twenty years of his life. It powerfully juxtaposes the suffering of a dispossessed peasant who has nowhere to turn with the life of a privileged writer who is not without talent but who lies with impunity and has sold his soul to a criminal regime. The first part of the story consists of a letter that the "son of a kulak" writes to a famous Writer (identified only as such) from a hospital bed in Kharkov, begging for a food parcel or some other display of pity or kindness. The letter is written in exceedingly idiosyncratic peasant prose. The kulak, exhausted and emaciated from hard labor, looks back longingly to the apricot tree that stood in the family orchard before their land (with its four horses and three cows) was taken from them. That tree that had borne such succulent fruit was chopped down by the authorities, who demanded that the family reveal where they had hidden all their goods; "kulaks" after all were supposed to be far richer than this family of modest means appeared to be. Solzhenitsyn artfully conveys the cruelties that accompanied the war against peasants whose only crime was to be more industrious or slightly more prosperous than some of their neighbors. This desperate young man, a "class enemy" whose family has been deported to the tundra and taiga and who is literally alone in the world, reaches out for sympathy and understanding.

The second part of the binary tale takes place at the dacha of the Writer. While unidentified, he is clearly Alexei N. Tolstoy, a writer and essayist who had fled Soviet Russia only to return and make his peace with the Bolshevik regime. Like the more famous Maxim Gorky, he had become a shameless defender of the Soviet regime, "churning out newspaper articles, each one of them filled with lies." (*AJ*, 10) He is meeting with a professor of cinema studies who instructs him on how to write a screenplay. His neighbor ("the Critic"), an equally obsequious apologist for Soviet tyranny, has dropped in for an afternoon visit. The three of them drink tea and eat translucent apricot jam. The Writer confesses that for a long time he had lacked an adequate feel for the Russian language as spoken by ordinary Russians. Only by studying legal transcripts of prisoners from the seventeenth century being flogged and stretched on the rack had he discovered "the language Russians have been speaking for a thousand years," (*AJ*, 19) a language as colorful as the apricot jam that the three men are enjoying. The Writer approaches the subject clinically—coldly—with no apparent sympathy for the human beings who are undergoing torture. The story ends with the Writer mentioning the letter from the son of the kulak that had recently arrived in the mail. The Writer excitedly remarks that the letter's language didn't "follow today's rules" and had "compelling combinations and use of grammatical cases." (*AJ*, 20) The Critic understandably asks if the Writer is planning to respond to this evocative letter. The Writer, devoid of human sympathy and wholly caught up in the web of ideological lies, replies that he has nothing to say to this man. "The point isn't the answer. The point is in discovering a language." (*AJ*, 20)

If Solzhenitsyn himself shares the Writer's appreciation of the richness and sheer variety of ordinary Russian speech, he never severs that concern for language from a recognition of the ethical imperative underlying the writer's vocation. The Writer, in contrast, is a soulless aesthete whose genuflection before the ideological Lie is based on a more fundamental cynicism and contempt for humanity. The reader cannot help but shudder at such inhumanity and such effortless complicity with totalitarian mendacity. One learns more about the *spiritual* atmosphere of the Soviet 1920s and '30s from Solzhenitsyn's tales than from many historical and archival studies combined.

Other stories in this volume that are set in the 1920s and '30s continue this searching exploration of the soul of man under "really existing socialism." "Nastenka" (a diminutive of

Anastasia) tells the story of two young women by that name whose lives are radically transformed by the Soviet revolution and the new order that it ushers in. Father Filaret, an Orthodox priest of obvious integrity, raised Nastenka and provided her with paternal guidance and a firm moral compass. She loved going to Church and had deep affection for her grandfather. Everything changed with the inauguration of the new Bolshevik order. Nastenka and her aunts Hanna and Frosya do everything possible to distance themselves from a dreaded "enemy of the people." They do their best to hide their past and to accommodate themselves to Soviet realities. Nastenka joins the Komsomol, the Communist party youth, and undergoes a series of degrading sexual assaults, one more horrific than the other, as she works as a librarian for the party. Her aunts are less than successful in their efforts to escape from their social origins despite their willingness to abandon poor Father Filaret. For his part, Father Filaret is sent to Solovki ("the most terrible word in the language after 'GPU'") (*AJ*, 87) where he eventually perishes. The first part of "Nastenka" is a heart-rending account of the "virtual destruction of the personhood"[6] of Nastenka, a lost soul who finds solace in increasingly random and impersonal sexual encounters. She and her illegitimate son are eventually "rescued" by a Red Army officer and Civil War hero, who provides them with a life of safety and relative prosperity in Moscow. She thus becomes part of the establishment that was responsible for her dehumanization in the first place.

The second Nastenka was born in Moscow and attended a classical high school where her beloved teacher Maria Feofanova, soon to be dismissed by Bolshevik overlords, introduced her to the best Russian literature. At sixteen she and her family moved to Rostov. She enrolled in a Faculty of Literature where ideology reigned supreme. The authors she loves are dismissed as prisoners of a feudal or bourgeois past, writers on the wrong side of the uncompromising class divide, and Nastenka has no grounds for saying no to

6   Ericson and Klimoff, *The Soul and Barbed Wire*, p. 169.

this systematic mutilation of literature. Her boyfriend Shurik repeats every brutal ideological cliché and Nastenka is impressed by his brilliance rather than by his fanaticism. Her love of classic literature remains but she has no tools for defending it or pointing out the nihilism of the new mode of thinking. She eventually becomes a teacher, one who is truly devoted to her students. But she must teach a desiccated, propagandistic curriculum that is the furthest thing from real literature or pedagogy. She is compromised yet holds on to a spiritual anchor—classic Russian literature—that prevents her from becoming a full-fledged ideologue. Unlike the first Nastenka, she refuses to completely break with the world before the Revolution. She thus has some tools for the recovery of the things of the soul and for maintaining contact with reality.

"The New Generation" tells the story of an engineering professor, Anatoly Pavlovich Vozdvizhensky, who has shown kindness to a "proletarian" student, Konoplyov—a beneficiary of Soviet "affirmative action"—who was flummoxed while taking his "materials" exam. Out of basic human sympathy and a desire to go along, the professor passes him, despite the fact that the student had clearly flunked the exam. The decent if apolitical engineering professor even encourages his daughter to join the Komsomol, since it is necessary to make one's peace with the new order, if one is to have any kind of future. But as the 1920s move on, people begin to disappear, and soon *they* come for the engineering professor himself. His Chekist interrogator turns out to be his former student, the beneficiary of his act of kindness. His student turned interrogator knows that Anatoly Pavlovich has committed no crime: "I know very well that you weren't involved in wrecking. But even you have to understand that *from here* no one leaves with an acquittal. It's either a bullet in the back of the neck or a term in the camps." (*AJ*, 71)

The interrogator demands that the professor supply him with information on others, at the minimum implicating them by reporting an anti-Soviet mood among his fellow engineers. Otherwise, his possessions and apartment will be confiscated and his daughter, the most precious thing in his life, will be expelled from school as a "class alien." Vozdvizhensky does not wish to "dishonor himself, his very soul." (*AJ*, 73) Pushed to the very limits, he breaks into sobs. Solzhenitsyn's laconic ending—"A week later he was set free" (*AJ*, 73)—jars the reader. It conveys just how difficult it was to avoid complicity with evil under a fully developed totalitarian regime. In contrast to the Writer, the engineering professor is neither a cynic nor an ideologist. His act of kindness—which was also an accommodation to the "new order"—is "repaid" but in a perverse, ideological manner. He is freed but is forced to dishonor his own soul by becoming a carrier of the Lie. In the end, the choice between family and justice was too much for this weak if decent man to bear. Rather than condemning him, the reader more fully appreciates the monstrosity of a regime that places good if fallible men in such a soul-destroying position.

These stories include powerful recollections of World War II battles (*Adlig Schwennkitten*, and *Zhelyabuga Village*) and moving accounts of the sufferings of ordinary Russians during the calamitous Russian 1990s. These two themes are expertly brought together in the riveting 1998 story *Zhelyabuga Village*. The first part of this binary tale presents a dramatic account of Solzhenitsyn's sound-ranging unit as it confronted German forces near Zhelyabuga during the great offensive of 1943. One sees Solzhenitsyn's battery desperately trying to pinpoint the precise location of enemy forces under conditions that were not particularly conducive to doing so. They have set themselves up in a basement where they share space with a group of civilians who are trying to escape enemy fire. Solzhenitsyn conveys the chaos of war, but also the friendship and male camaraderie among the officers and soldiers. One sees good men who are lost as well as the hope that all this suffering will give rise to something better after the war. The first part of the story ends with the political officer, the representative of the Communist party, promising a "*fine* life" (*AJ*, 213) for ordinary Russians, such as the peasants who live in Zhelyabuga, after the war.

The second part of the story chronicles the return of Solzhenitsyn and his friend and colleague Vitya Ovsyannikov (a retired lieutenant colonel) to Zhelyabuga fifty-two years later as part of an event to celebrate the fiftieth anniversary of the end of the Second World War. The village barely exists with only a few run-down huts and emaciated animals in evidence. Solzhenitsyn and Vita meet a couple of "grannies"—old and decrepit beyond their years—one of whom had been a beauty that Solzhenitsyn had met in the basement fifty-two years before. Everything—and everyone—has been neglected. The few villagers who remain cry out for help to local and regional officials who will do what they can but who have absolutely no intention of disturbing "Moscow." Solzhenitsyn's and his friend Ovsyannikov's hearts ache for the suffering of these Russian peasants. At one point, Solzhenitsyn comments on how naïve he had been during the war, going on as he did about "world revolution." But Vitya who "knew the countryside—from the bottom up," (AJ, 222) and that included the terrible suffering of the peasantry during collectiviza-tion—knew better. And in 1995, a "democratic" Russia continued to neglect its people, continued to treat its people as raw material in an ill-defined social experiment.

As this story shows, Solzhenitsyn is the anti-totalitarian par excellence. He cannot stomach a "reform" process that was car-ried out in a heavy-handed, all-too-Bolshevik spirit. But the focus in these stories remains on the human soul and the choices that are available to conscientious human beings even in the most difficult circumstances. At the end of "Fracture Points," we see a promis-ing young student of physics turned banker in the rough-and-tum-ble 1990s lamenting the turn he had made away from an honest path. "Perhaps he shouldn't have given in to temptation," he thinks to himself. "He could see a light, far off in the distance, and it was growing dimmer. Yet a faint light persisted." (AJ, 340) These stories make clear that Solzhenitsyn never lost his confi-dence in the power of the "light" to point human beings in the direction of truly humane paths of individual and collective devel-opment. He never lost hope in his beloved Russia or in the capac-ity of human beings to renew the human adventure in accord with realities of the spirit.

Chapter 9

FREEDOM, FAITH AND THE MORAL FOUNDATIONS OF SELF-GOVERNMENT: SOLZHENITSYN'S FINAL WORD TO RUSSIA AND THE WEST

The last interview with Solzhenitsyn was conducted by the German newsweekly *Der Spiegel* in July 2007 and published on July 23, 2007, about one year before his death.[1] It is a beautiful summing up of his life and thought, as well as of the views and commitments animating the final period of his life that began with his return to his native Russia in May 1994. A close reading of the interview will allow us to assess where Solzhenitsyn stood at the end of his life. He was indeed old and frail, yet in possession of all his mental powers, with his characteristic intellectual and spiritual acuity.

The interview begins with the *Spiegel* interviewers finding Solzhenitsyn at work. The interviewers comment that even at eighty-eight, Solzhenitsyn "still feels the need to work even though [his] health doesn't allow him to walk around [his] house" (*DDD*,

---

1   I am citing the authorized English-language translation of the *Der Spiegel* interview that was corrected and approved by the Solzhenitsyn family. It can be found under the title "I am Not Afraid of Death: An Interview" on the *Der Spiegel* website. The interview also appeared in the third (enlarged) edition of Aleksandr Solzhenitsyn, *Détente, Democracy and Dictatorship*, Introduction by Daniel J. Mahoney, Prefaces and Postscript by Irving Louis Horowitz and Arthur Schlesinger, Jr. (New Brunswick, NJ: Transaction Publishers, 2009), pp. 95–107. That edition of the interview will be cited internally in the text as *DDD*, followed by the page number in the Transaction edition.

75). That is quite true: When he died in 2008, as Lioudmila Saraskina points out in her splendid biography of Solzhenitsyn, he died with his dignity fully intact.[2] There was no decline into senescence or loss of talent or self-awareness. For that one can only be grateful to Providence.

In answer to a question about the source of his strength, Solzhenitsyn replies that he always had "inner drive," and that he always "devoted himself gladly to work—to work and to the struggle" (DDD, 95). One of the premier Solzhenitsyn scholars in the Western world, Georges Nivat, the author of the extraordinarily insightful volume entitled Le phénomène Soljénitsyne, characterized Solzhenitsyn as, above all, a writer and a fighter (in French, lutteur).[3] Writing was indeed inseparable from struggle for Solzhenitsyn. It entailed struggle in the camps. It entailed a hidden struggle in the fifties as an underground writer. It entailed struggle in the sixties and early seventies as the now world-famous author was hounded by the totalitarian state. It entailed struggle during his twenty years of exile in the West as he wrote his magnum opus The Red Wheel and had to deal with his detractors among the third wave of Russian émigrés, as well as his "cultured despisers" among Western leftists and liberals. That term is indispensable for understanding the public role of Solzhenitsyn, writer-combatant.

A Life Rooted in Conscience

Solzhenitsyn notes that in the camps he would sometimes write on stone walls or on scraps of papers, then he would memorize their contents and destroy the scraps. (DDD, 95). These were horrible writing conditions. And yet in answer to a question about his arrest in February 1945, Solzhenitsyn says that at some deep level

2 Lioudmila Saraskina, Alexandre Soljénitsyne, translated by Marilyne Fellous (Paris: Fayard, 2010), pp. 929–36.
3 George Nivat, Le phénomène Solzhénitsyn (Paris: Fayard, 2009), pp. 187–204. The writer, of course, always accompanied the fighter.

he always remained "optimistic" and "held to and was guided by my views" (*DDD*, 96). He thus emphasizes continuity amidst discontinuity. From other accounts, we know that there was a fundamental transformation of Solzhenitsyn's views after his arrest in February 1945. Here, though, he affirms some underlying continuity. He explains that he always sincerely believed in what he did and "never acted against [his] conscience" (*DDD*, 96). In fact, it was precisely this conscientiousness, this rootedness in the convictions of conscience, that allowed for his intellectual, moral, and spiritual transformation during his time in prisons and camps.

Here a brief excursus on Solzhenitsyn's intellectual and moral development is in order. At the time of his arrest in February 1945, he still saw himself as a Marxist-Leninist. To be sure, he was a somewhat dissident Marxist-Leninist, one who had written letters critical of Stalin to his best friend. As we have seen, by the end of 1949, though, the time depicted in his great philosophical novel *In the First Circle*, Solzhenitsyn, like the character Gleb Nerzhin, his alter ego in the novel, was a philosophical skeptic who, nonetheless, affirmed justice and conscience as the "cornerstone" of the universe. (His skepticism was primarily directed against ideological fanaticism.) By 1952, Solzhenitsyn had taken things a step further and in a great prison poem entitled "Acathistus" (the song of praise), he reaffirmed his faith in the living God. "Oh great God! I believe now anew! Though denied, You were always with me...."[4] The affirmation of justice and conscience, of an immutable moral order, and belief in a providential God would define Solzhenitsyn's basic convictions for the rest of his life. At the end of this chapter I will return to the question of Solzhenitsyn's religious faith, and the role of faith and reason in his moral reflection during the last sixty years of his life.

---

4   Solzhenitsyn, "Acathistus" in Edward E. Ericson, Jr. and Daniel J. Mahoney, *The Solzhenitsyn Reader: New and Essential Writings, 1947–2005* (Wilmington, DE: ISI Books, 2006), p. 21. This prayer is of unusual beauty and lucidity._

A State Prize

The *Der Spiegel* interviewers next turn to questions concerning Solzhenitsyn's relationship to the Russian political order from the 1980s onward. These questions are motivated by a certain perplexity over Solzhenitsyn's markedly negative judgments about Boris Yeltsin, the figure nearly universally viewed as a democrat throughout the Western world, and his more positive (although not wholly uncritical) evaluation of his successor Vladimir Putin, a figure who is close to being universally despised in the Western world. The interviewers asked Solzhenitsyn why he turned down awards from Gorbachev and Yeltsin, while accepting a state prize from Putin in the summer of 2007. Solzhenitsyn replies that when he was first offered a prize under Gorbachev, the U.S.S.R.—whose moral and political legitimacy he never accepted—still existed. Moreover, he could not accept a prize for *The Gulag Archipelago*, "a book written in the blood of millions" (*DDD*, 96).

The second prize was offered to Solzhenitsyn in 1998 while Yeltsin was president of the Russian Federation, at "the country's low point, with people in misery" (*DDD*, 96). That was the year Solzhenitsyn published his powerful *Russia in Collapse*, which clearly distanced him from both the Yeltsin regime and its Communist critics. The Solzhenitsyn of the 1990s was defined by many things: his continuing anti-Communism, his deep-seated opposition to the pseudo-democracy, or kleptocracy, that had arisen under Yeltsin, and his uncompromising opposition to what was called the Red-Brown coalition, a toxic brew of nationalism and Bolshevism that Solzhenitsyn deemed deeply destructive of the prospects for political and spiritual recovery in Russia.[5] In the interview Solzhenitsyn says that he was "unable to receive an award from a government that had led Russia into such dire straits" (*DDD*, 96). A reading of *Russia in Collapse* makes clear that Solzhenitsyn thought that the Yeltsin regime was criminally

5   See the excerpts from *Russia in Collapse* in *The Solzhenitsyn Reader*, pp. 467–84.

culpable, that it had degenerated into a corrupt and corrupting kleptocracy that had extricated Russia from Communism in the worst way imaginable. It had betrayed the promise of post-Communist reform. Perhaps most damningly, the Yeltsin regime had mirrored Bolshevism by putting an abstraction—"reform," the introduction of a market economy, or at least a "market ideology"—above the well-being of ordinary people. It was marked by the same sort of refusal as Communism to take into account the needs, the interests, and the well-being of *real* human beings.

Solzhenitsyn then observes that the third prize, the State Prize, was not awarded by President Putin personally, but by a committee of top experts, all of whom were "authorities in their respected disciplines" (*DDD*, 97). He also highlights his own remarks on accepting the prize. He had expressed the hope that the "bitter Russian experience," which "I have been studying and describing all my life, will be for us a lesson that keeps us from new disastrous breakdowns" (*DDD*, 97). Unlike some in Putin's coalition who wanted to relativize the Communist past, Solzhenitsyn continued to emphasize the "bitter" but instructive character of the Soviet experience. Solzhenitsyn had fought all his life for the defeat of the Communist juggernaut and he continued to welcome that defeat, despite his conviction that the process had been deeply flawed. In numerous writings and interviews from 1990 onward, he referred to Russia's "third time of troubles" that had begun with the breakdown of the Communist system. Solzhenitsyn believed that the disorder that followed—the corruption, the kleptocracy, the criminality of the 1990s—rivaled two other terrible times for Russia. These were the period between the death of Tsar Feodor Ivanovich in 1598 and the establishment of the Romanov dynasty in 1613—a period marked by famine, civic unrest, foreign invasions and usurpers and imposters to the throne—and the second, even more terrible "time of troubles" inaugurated by Lenin's seizure of power in 1917. In all three nothing less than the existence of the Russian nation was at stake.

Solzhenitsyn also put Putin's relationship to the KGB in some perspective. He noted that Putin was not an interrogator or head of a camp, something that would be absolutely unacceptable to

Solzhenitsyn, but rather an officer in the intelligence services. He draws a parallel between President George H. W. Bush who was the head of the CIA before becoming President of the United States (*DDD*, 97). Natalia Dmitrievna Solzhenitsyn, the writer's wife, made the same point in an interview that *Russian Life* conducted with her in 2008. She said that what would have been absolutely unacceptable to Solzhenitsyn would have been any connection of Putin to the camps.[6] The fact that Putin had served as an intelligence officer in East Germany in the dying days of the Soviet regime, before becoming an advisor to Anatolii Sobchak, the anti-communist mayor of St. Petersburg, did not, in the Solzhenitsyns' view, disqualify him from participation in the political life of post-communist Russia.

The Prospects for Repentance

The exchange about the various prizes that were offered to Solzhenitsyn and the perplexity of the *Spiegel* interviewers concerning Solzhenitsyn's relationship with Putin is followed by a question about Solzhenitsyn's call for Russians to repent for "the millions of victims of the gulag and communist terror." The interviewers asked, "Was this call really heard?" (*DDD*, 97). Solzhenitsyn immediately responds by stating that "I have grown used to the fact that, throughout the world, public repentance is the most unacceptable option for the modern politician" (*DDD*, 97). As we have emphasized throughout this work, Solzhenitsyn had long been an advocate of what he called "repentance and self-limitation," repentance and moderation, as essential elements of decent politics and of morally serious action in the contemporary world. His 1973 essay "Repentance and Self-Limitation in the Life of Nations" in the collection *From Under the Rubble*[7] must be

---

6   Interview with Natalya Solzhenitsyn, "The Life and Legacy of Aleksandr Isayevich Solzhenitsyn" in *Russian Life* (September/ October 2008), p. 32.

7   See *The Solzhenitsyn Reader*, pp. 527–55.

seen as one of his most important statements. Without repentance there is no road forward for the Russian people. At the same time, his response suggests a recognition that his call had not been heard or heeded due to the psychological difficulty he noted.

At the same time, it would be a mistake to say that Solzhenitsyn gave up on his call for repentance and self-limitation. He remained deeply committed to these imperatives while being realistic about the likelihood of public repentance any time in the near future. The interviewers inquire about Putin's remark saying that the "collapse of the Soviet Union was the largest geo-political disaster of the twentieth century," and also bring up a remark of Putin about the danger of "masochistic brooding" over the Communist past (*DDD*, 97). The quotation from Putin about the largest geo-political disaster of the twentieth century was taken out of context, however, as it usually is in the West. In that same statement Putin had stated that the Soviet Union was a totalitarian regime that deserved to die. But he had added that the *way* in which the Soviet Union broke up, with the loss of millions of Russians in the near abroad, was a profound "geopolitical disaster." In fact, therefore, Putin suggested something far less than the nostalgia for totalitarianism that is typically ascribed to him by journalists who wish to emphasize continuities between post-Communist Russia and the Soviet Union, as well as Putin's "KGB" credentials.

Solzhenitsyn's response to these questions is quite revealing. He immediately brings up what he calls "growing concern all over the world" as to how the United States "will handle its new role as the world's only superpower" (*DDD*, 97). When asked a question about coming to terms with the Soviet past and the place of public repentance, Solzhenitsyn brings up American foreign policy. That seems perplexing unless we take into consideration the significant changes in Solzhenitsyn's views about U.S. foreign policy from the 1970s to the 1990s. In the 1970s, as he told Janis Sapiets in a January 1979 interview with the BBC (in the indispensable anthology *East and West*), he was worried that the United States and the Western democracies were giving away country after country.[8] He was concerned with the *weakness* of the West. One of his best-known collections of speeches and writings from the 1970s is entitled *Warning to the West*. By the early 1990s, though, Solzhenitsyn was worried about a new assertiveness on the part of the United States. In an interview in *Forbes* magazine with Paul Klebnikov in February 1994 (this was Solzhenitsyn's last interview with anyone in the United States before his return to Russia in May of that year), he had noted the lack of sympathy with which the United States approached the problems of the new Russia, its tendency to side with Ukrainian nationalists against Russia, and the failure to appreciate the desperate state of the twenty-five million Russians in the near abroad.[9] Solzhenitsyn was struck by the fact that the West, and especially the United States, had responded to its victory in the Cold War by taking advantage of the weakness of Russia. Solzhenitsyn had always pleaded with the United States and the Western democracies to see the Russian people as their allies in the common struggle against Bolshevik despotism.

That concern about American assertiveness in the 1990s made Solzhenitsyn appear, sometimes, to be a pan-Slavist. For example, he expressed great sympathy for the suffering of the Serbian people in 1998–1999. However, as Solzhenitsyn made abundantly clear in the interview with Klebnikov, as well as in *Russia in Collapse*, where he attacks the pathologies of Russian nationalism, he has never been a pan-Slavist. He never advocated an imperial role for Russia. He told Janis Sapiets at the end of the interview in *East and West* that he saw Russia's future as many years of "recuperation," a word he repeated and emphasized. Let us quote that passage. Sapiets asked him, "How do you see Russia's

8   Solzhenitsyn, "Interview with the BBC, February 1979" in *East and West* (New York: Harper Perennial Library, 1980), pp. 174–75.
9   The interview of Solzhenitsyn with Klebnikov, originally published in the February 9, 1994 issue of *Forbes* was posted on the Forbes webpage on August 5, 2005, two days after the Russian writer's death. See http://www.forbes.com/2008/08/05/solzhenitsyn–forbes–interview–oped–cx_pm_0804russia.html.

future?" and Solzhenitsyn responded, "I see it in recuperation. Renounce all mad fantasies of foreign conquest and begin the peaceful long, long, long period of *recuperation*."[10] Once again, we find Solzhenitsyn committed to the principle of self-limitation and its concomitant repentance, both in individual life and in the collective life of peoples. In this context, he was disturbed that the United States had broken the promise that there would be no expansion of NATO after the reunification of Germany in 1990. NATO expanded eastward so much that by the final years of Solzhenitsyn's life the United States was open to both Ukrainian and Georgian membership in the North Atlantic Treaty Organization. This seemingly inexorable movement to the east was deeply unsettling to Solzhenitsyn. It suggested that the Western democracies still saw Russia as an enemy, despite the collapse of the Soviet Union. In one 2006 interview with the *Moscow News*, he even spoke ominously about the "encirclement" of Russia.[11]

In this vein, Solzhenitsyn goes on to say: "As for 'brooding over the past,' alas, that conflation of 'Soviet' and 'Russia' against which I spoke so often in the 1970s has not passed away either in the West, or in the ex-Socialist countries, or in the former Soviet Republics" (*DDD*, 97–98). The remark, again, is significant when put in proper context. We know that from the 1970s onward, most famously in his 1980 essay *The Mortal Danger: How Misconceptions about Russia Imperil America*, Solzhenitsyn had argued that it was a terrible mistake to conflate or identify the Soviet Union and Russia.[12] Russia was the first and main victim of Communist totalitarianism. In the *Der Spiegel* interview, Solzhenitsyn notes three places where that conflation of things Soviet and Russian persists. It persists in Russia, especially in

10 *East and West*, p. 182.
11 The 2006 interview with the *Moscow News* is widely available in English on the internet.
12 Solzhenitsyn, *The Mortal Danger: How Misconceptions About Russia Imperil America*, translated by Michael Nicholson and Alexis Klimoff (New York: Harper Colophon, 1981).

leading political circles. Solzhenitsyn did not think that Putin was somebody particularly nostalgic for the Communist past. But Putin nonetheless had a tendency to bring Russia and the Soviet Union together, to treat them as two moments of a unitary national experience. This identification or conflation persists in the West as well. Conservatives, much to their credit, had been anti-Communist. They rightly fought to defend the West and Western civilization against Communist totalitarianism. And yet, for the most part, these anti-Communists remained anti-Russian after the end of the Cold War. They saw Russia as the real or potential enemy of the West. Solzhenitsyn also notes that this conflation of the Soviet Union and Russia persisted in the ex-Socialist countries and in the former Soviet republics, so much so that, as Solzhenitsyn puts it, Moscow became a "convenient target." It was still seen as Communist or Soviet at heart. Solzhenitsyn dares to hope that this "unhealthy phase" will soon be over, that all the peoples who have lived through Communism will understand that it was Communism that was to blame for the "bitter pages of their history" (*DDD*, 98). And he says in no uncertain terms that one should not ascribe the "evil deeds of individual leaders or political regimes to an innate fault of the Russian people" (*DDD*, 98); Communism could survive only "by imposing a bloody terror" (*DDD*, 98). The victims of this terror should not be confused with its perpetrators.

Unlike so many other critics of Communist terror, Solzhenitsyn had never overemphasized the Great Terror, the massive Stalinist terror campaign of the 1930s. His target was Communism, not "Stalinism." He drew attention to *Leninist* roots of Communist terror, the millions of people who perished during the Civil War, War Communism, and the period of the early 1920s. For him, beginning from its founding moment, the Communist regime was a criminal conspiracy against the Russian people. The crimes of Communism were not, as some argued then and now, the result of some later Stalinist aberration. The Soviet regime was intrinsically perverse and Russians must never make their peace with it by accepting it as some kind of legitimate political order. Solzhenitsyn reiterates his call for public repentance. "Only the voluntary and conscious acceptance by a people of its guilt can ensure the healing of a nation." But he adds, "[u]nremitting reproaches from outside, on the other hand, are counterproductive" (*DDD*, 98).

What one ultimately sees in the response to this set of questions about public repentance for the death and suffering of the millions of victims of the gulag and Communist terror, is a balanced emphasis on both repentance and self-respect. Russians need to acknowledge their guilt as a precondition for the healing of the nation. And they have to find their own path to repentance. But Solzhenitsyn also knows that Russians were victims, and so he emphasizes the need for a proper balance of repentance and self-respect. This emphasis on balance and moderation mirrors a larger theme, and tension, in Solzhenitsyn's own thought between magnanimity and humility, a theme we have emphasized in this book. Solzhenitsyn is a proud patriot, but he is also a patriot who emphasizes the necessity for guilt, repentance, and a sense of responsibility. That balance is essential to Solzhenitsyn's view of the world, and to focus on one side to the detriment of the other is to distort his vision.

An Archival Revolution

In the next part of the interview, *Der Spiegel* asks Solzhenitsyn about the availability of the archives that reveal the totalitarian nature of the Soviet regime. There is a widespread view in the West that the archives have simply closed under Putin or that they have become more or less inaccessible. There is not a serious effort, it is thought, to come to terms with Communism in Russia today. Solzhenitsyn's response is lengthy and informative. He praises some of the historians of the Soviet regime who have worked in the archives since the late 1980s and who did so much to reveal the criminal character of the Soviet regime. He mentions two in particular: Dmitri Volkogonov, the former Communist general and historian who became an anti-Communist as a result of his work on biographies of Lenin, Stalin, and Trotsky; and Alexander Yakovlev, one of the architects of perestroika under Gorbachev, who was one of the few Soviet officials to actually engage in public repentance for his own role in the Soviet regime over a fifty-year period. Through his work in the archives, and later as president of the Presidential Commission on Repression under Lenin and Stalin, Yakovlev authored several important volumes, including *A Century of Violence in Soviet Russia*, published in translation by Yale University Press in 2001.[13] Solzhenitsyn says that the Russian people are in debt to people like Volkogonov and Yakovlev for making so much of the material in the archives available for a serious coming-to-terms with the Communist past. He admires these men for their deep intellectual and moral seriousness and he expresses his—and society's—debt to them (*DDD*, 99).

Solzhenitsyn also adds that reports of censorship in Russia are greatly exaggerated. He mentions the fact that while it is harder than it had been in the past to gain access to archival material, the massive national archives of the Russian Federation (GARF is the acronym) are indeed available to researchers (*DDD*, 99). In this connection he mentions the seven-volume *History of Stalin's Gulag* with which he cooperated. He says that this volume is as comprehensive as could be expected. In his introduction to the work he called it "a major and decisive step in the systematic exploration of the history of communist repression in the Soviet Union," even as he called for further exploration of the repression of "the Lenin-Dzerzhinsky period"—the founding moment of Communist totalitarianism in the U.S.S.R. It was his belief that "readers will find these books satisfying and exciting."[14]

13 Alexander N. Yakovlev, *A Century of Violence*, translated by Anthony Austin (New York: Yale University Press, 2002).
14 *The History of Stalin's Gulag: Late 1920s–Early 1950s. Collected Documents in 7 volumes* (Moscow: Rosspen, 2004). Solzhenitsyn's Introduction appears in volume 1, pp. 25–26. This piece shows that Solzhenitsyn's partial "accommodation" with Putin entailed no abatement of his deep and abiding anti-totalitarianism.

Solzhenitsyn is thus absolutely supportive of the need to make archival materials available to researchers, while also stressing the great deal that has already been done. Those who talk about "the closing" of the archives rarely mention things like the availability of the national archives of the Russian Federation or the publishing achievement which was the seven-volume *History of Stalin's Gulag*. They were more interested in showing that nothing had really changed in post-Communist Russia. Again, Solzhenitsyn puts things in perspective.

Two Revolutions

Let us turn now to the important question of the February and October Revolutions. We know that much of Solzhenitsyn's mature work centered around the study of the Russian revolutions of 1917, or, more broadly, what he termed the unfolding "red wheel." Solzhenitsyn employs the image of the red wheel as a kind of accelerating train, as a kind of unfolding cosmic vortex. At the same time, he is a critic of all historical determinisms. He combines the two because he believes that because of decisions that were made—or not made—the Russian revolution took on the character of an inexorable force. To understand Solzhenitsyn, therefore, is to understand his principled opposition to all forms of historical determinism and, on the other hand, his view that the corruption, passivity and inaction of the Russian old regime, and the weakness and mistakes of the provisional government established in February 1917, contributed to making the Bolshevik Revolution inevitable. Over time, what was contingent became "necessary."

In response to a question suggesting that he blames everything on the provisional government, Solzhenitsyn notes that Lenin and Trotsky were exceptionally "nimble" and energetic politicians who managed, in a short period, to take advantage of the weakness of Kerensky's government (*DDD*, 99). They were vitally important "particular causes," to use the terminology of Tocqueville and Montesquieu. But the general cause was the "Red Wheel" itself, the inexorably unfolding revolutionary process.

For Solzhenitsyn, the *real* Russian Revolution of 1917 was the February Revolution, while the so-called October Revolution is a "myth" (it was a *coup d'état,* a conclusion he establishes in *The Red Wheel*). In the BBC interview with Solzhenitsyn in February 1979, he stated that it was only when he came to the West that he was able to confirm his belief that everything flowed from the *fact* of the February Revolution.[15] However, as he says in the *Der Spiegel* interview, "The reasons driving the revolution do indeed have their sources in Russia's pre-revolutionary condition, and I have never stated otherwise" (*DDD,* 100). The February Revolution had deep roots, and he insists that those roots in fundamental defects of the Russian old regime had been amply portrayed in *The Red Wheel*. The first among these is what Solzhenitsyn calls "the long-term mutual distrust between those in power and the educated society" (*DDD,* 100). Of course, Solzhenitsyn is not the first to observe that fundamental opposition. It is a major theme of the historiography of the final fifty years of the Russian old regime. It was, famously, taken up in the novels of Turgenev and Dostoevsky. *The Red Wheel,* however, shows with rare force, power, and literary talent the bitter distrust that rendered impossible any compromises, any "constructive solutions for the state" (*DDD,* 100), as Solzhenitsyn phrased it. The greatest responsibility falls on the authorities. "Who if not the captain is to blame for a shipwreck?" (*DDD,* 100). This, however, in no way entails that Lenin was merely an "accidental person" (*DDD,* 100). General causes are always accompanied by particular causes. Lenin was a particular cause whose ideological conviction, conspiratorial activities, and nimbleness as a revolutionary opportunist helped contribute in a powerful way to the disaster that was 1917.

Solzhenitsyn also states that there was "nothing natural" for Russia (*DDD,* 100) in the October Revolution. That is an observation pregnant with insight. The October Revolution, the *coup d'état* which, as Solzhenitsyn puts it, finally "broke Russia's back"

15 *East and West,* pp. 152–55.

(*DDD*, 100), did not arise naturally. The October Revolution unleashed Red terror: the leaders of the Bolshevik party were willing "to drown Russia in blood" (*DDD*, 100). One is reminded once again of Lenin's 1918 essay "How to Organize the Competition" (quoted in vol. 1 of *The Gulag Archipelago*) where the founder of the Soviet state pledged "to purge Russia of all kinds of harmful insects."[16] No responsible Russian patriotism can accept the October Revolution as a legitimate reflection of Russian national consciousness.

In the Russian old regime, the conflict between power and society combined with the corruption, inactivity and passivity of the leaders of the old order. The great exception of course was Pyotr Stolypin, the reformist Prime Minister of Russia from 1906 to 1911, who knew how to defeat revolution through reform. But with the single exception of Stolypin, the Russian old regime bears the primary responsibility for allowing the destruction of a political and social order that was not beyond repair. And once the progressives and socialists, the "nullities"[17] as Solzhenitsyn calls them, came to power in Russia in February 1917, and succeeded in weakening state power, then the most active, determined, and fanatical ideologues were bound to come to the fore. This is where Lenin's fanaticism became decisive.

Two Hundred Years Together

The interview now turns to a discussion of Solzhenitsyn's *Two Hundred Years Together*. This is a work that has yet to appear in English, although excerpts have appeared in *The Solzhenitsyn Reader*, co-edited by Edward E. Ericson, Jr. and myself. As we discussed at some length in chapter seven, this, perhaps, is Solzhenitsyn's most misunderstood work. *Two Hundred Years*

---

16 Quoted in Solzhenitsyn, *The Gulag Archipelago, 1918–1956*, Volume 1, translated by Thomas P. Whitney (New York: Harper & Row, 1974), p. 27.
17 *East and West*, p. 151.

Together arose out of material that Solzhenitsyn had gathered for the publication of *The Red Wheel*. Solzhenitsyn made clear in interviews that he was very careful not to include an excessive amount of material on the "Jewish question" in it, in large part because he did not want to contribute to the pernicious notion that the Russian Revolution was in any essential way a product of Jewish machinations or a Jewish "conspiracy." This is a notion near and dear to extreme nationalists and right-wing elements at the time of the Revolution and in Russia today. In *Russia in Collapse*, Solzhenitsyn bitingly remarks that they were singularly and stupidly preoccupied with Jews and Free Masons on whom they blamed all of Russia's problems.

The interviewers with *Der Spiegel* seem not to know the work very well. They comment that *Two Hundred Years Together* has been met by perplexity in the West, which is undoubtedly true. But they also seem to suggest that Solzhenitsyn believes that Jews have a unique responsibility for the Russian Revolutions of 1917. Solzhenitsyn emphatically denies that he engaged in or called for any scorekeeping of the moral responsibility of one people or another (*DDD*, 101). Above all the work is a call for self-reflection and self-examination on the part of both Russians and Russian Jews. He quotes from a central passage at the end of chapter fifteen of volume two of *Two Hundred Years Together*, one whose significance we have already examined at some length in chapter seven. He prefaces it by saying that you get the answer to the question about whether or not Jews carry more responsibility than others for the failure of the Soviet experiment from the book itself. Here is the passage: "Every people must answer morally for all of its past, including that past which is shameful. Answer by what means? By attempting to comprehend. How could such a thing have been allowed? Where in all this is our error, and could it happen again? It is in that spirit specifically that it would behoove the Jewish people to answer both for the revolutionary cutthroats and the ranks willing to serve them. Not to answer before other peoples, but to oneself, to one's consciousness, and before God." For their part Russians "must answer—for the pogroms, for the merciless arsonist peasants, for the crazed revolutionary soldiers, for the savage sailors" (quoted in *DDD*, 101).

Solzhenitsyn emphatically denies in chapter nine of volume one of *Two Hundred Years Together* that the Russian Revolution of 1905 was in any way a product of a Jewish "plot" or conspiracy.[18] He insists that Russians above all have responsibility for their own fate. But he makes clear, as Jewish scholars such as the great Russianist and political scientist Leonard Schapiro have done before him, that there was a major Jewish presence in the revolutionary movement in Russia, that that presence was augmented during and after the Bolshevik Revolution, and that Jews need to come to terms with that not inconsiderable involvement in the revolutionary movement.[19] They need to come to terms with the historical fact that much of the Jewish community gave support to the Bolsheviks in the period between 1917 and 1930, and that it was only during the 1930s and '40s that the Soviet regime under Joseph Stalin began to turn against its Jewish population. In this connection, as we have already pointed out in chapter seven, in volume II of the work Solzhenitsyn names names, provides a lot of numbers, and might appear to be engaged in "scorekeeping." But his main point is that there is plenty of evidence that *all* the constituent communities that made up the Soviet Union have much to repent for. However, just as Solzhenitsyn said earlier that "pressure from the outside" does not do a lot of good, he understands that his work at most can serve as a call to mutual repentance and mutual responsibility.

Responsibility is the key notion. Solzhenitsyn is a firm believer, less in collective guilt, although he thinks acknowledgement of guilt is part and parcel of the moral responsibility of people, but rather of collective responsibility. He says at the very end of

18 *The Solzhenitsyn Reader*, pp. 495–97.
19 Leonard Schapiro, "The Role of Jews in the Russian Revolutionary Movement" in *Russian Studies*, edited by Ellen Dahrendorf with an Introduction by Harry Willetts (New York: Viking, 1987), pp. 266–89.

chapter fifteen of volume two of *Two Hundred Years Together* that there cannot really be a people without responsibility. In the West, we are very used to liberal notions of *individual* responsibility. We think there is something deeply problematic about appeals to collective guilt or collective responsibility. Without in any way denying the fundamental drama of good and evil in every individual soul, Solzhenitsyn knows, additionally, that if there is going to be a meaningful notion of a *people*, there has to be an understanding and appreciation of collective responsibility.

Learning About the Past

In response to a question about whether or not Russians have learned the lessons of the two revolutions and their consequences, Solzhenitsyn is surprisingly positive (*DDD*, 1001–1102). He says it seems that the Russian public is starting to, and he gives some evidence to support this judgment. He refers to a state television program based on Varlam Shalamov's *Kolyma Tales*. He says that it was in no way watered down, that it conveyed the "terrible, cruel truth" (*DDD*, 102) about the gulag. He also refers to what he calls the "large-scale, heated and long-lasting discussions" (*DDD*, 102) on his own *Reflections on the February Revolution*. As we pointed out in chapter two, this was an essay that Solzhenitsyn originally wrote in the early 1980s. Its four parts were initially intended to be introductions to the four volumes of *March 1917*. Solzhenitsyn finally decided that to include these essays with each of the volumes of *March 1917* would have been excessively didactic and decided to publish it separately as an essay in 1983. He republished the essay in 1995 in the journal *Moskva*, but it did not get much attention at the time. But when it was published in 2007, on the ninetieth anniversary of the February Revolution, it received a great deal of attention. Solzhenitsyn was cheered by the attention given to it by critics who did not all share his understanding that the February Revolution was the fundamental revolution, many of whom remain committed to the standard liberal narrative of the

February Revolution which sees it as the "good" revolution of 1917. But the fact that there was for the first time since Solzhenitsyn's return to Russia in 1994 a serious public discussion of the nature of February 1917 was for Solzhenitsyn a welcome step forward.

Three Leaders

The interviewers now return to a question about Solzhenitsyn's judgment about the three principal political leaders of Russia in the years since 1985 (*DDD*, 102). In response to this question, Solzhenitsyn engages in a comparison of Vladimir Putin's governance with his predecessors, an issue he had already broached in his discussion of the various prizes offered to him. Solzhenitsyn is particularly critical of Gorbachev, partly because the late Soviet leader naïvely remained committed to the revolutionary principles of 1917. However misguidedly, he saw himself as a faithful "Leninist." Solzhenitsyn emphasizes that he was above all "politically inexperienced and naïve" (*DDD*, 102). But, he adds, Gorbachev gave the country *glasnost*, or "openness," with accompanying freedom of the press and freedom of speech (*DDD*, 102). And that was a precious contribution. So despite a generally negative evaluation of Gorbachev, Solzhenitsyn gives him credit for taking the first steps in tearing down the wall of totalitarian repression.

As we have seen, Solzhenitsyn is particularly critical of Yeltsin. As he says in *Russia in Collapse*, under the leadership of Yeltsin and Gaidar, the Prime Minister during the early 1990s, there was a fire sale of the national patrimony, the institutionalization of corruption, and above all, the betrayal of everything involved in the democratization of the country.[20] But under Putin, in contrast to Gorbachev and, especially, Yeltsin, the country saw what Solzhenitsyn calls "a gradual restoration" (*DDD*, 102). Those words might come as something of a shock

20 See *The Solzhenitsyn Reader*, pp. 464–84.

to Western readers who identify Putin with the establishment of an authoritarian political and social order in Russia. Solzhenitsyn, however, goes on to say that there is no democracy in Russia today. At the same time, he gives Putin credit for a gradual restoration. One has to ask, "A restoration of what?" I think Solzhenitsyn has in mind the restoration of the nation. For Solzhenitsyn the nation first has to exist, there have to be prospects for its future, before the building of democracy becomes a real possibility.

As we proceed we will see that Solzhenitsyn is critical of aspects of Putin's rule. I think that Solzhenitsyn would be more critical of Putin today, especially of his refusal to give up power. We know that Natalia Solzhenitsyn, in her 2008 *Russian Life* interview, put a lot of hope in the presidency of Dmitri Medvedev.[21] She would no doubt be disappointed that Medvedev, despite his constant call for modernization and liberalization, his attack on "legal nihilism," and his commitment to opening up the political process, turned out to be a politician who subordinated himself to the political ambitions of Vladimir Putin.

But here is what Solzhenitsyn has to say about the country that Putin inherited in 2000. "Putin inherited a ransacked and bewildered country, with a poor and demoralized people. And he started to do what was possible—a slow and gradual restoration." Solzhenitsyn adds that these efforts "were not noticed or appreciated immediately" (*DDD*, 102). And then he adds that in any case "one is hard-pressed to find examples in history when steps by one country to restore its strengths were met favorably by other governments" (*DDD*, 102). Solzhenitsyn is fully cognizant of the fact that Russia today is not a democracy in any meaningful sense of that word. On the other hand, he gives Putin credit for his role in gradually restoring the strength and self-respect of the Russian nation.

21 Interview with Natalia Solzhenitsyn, *Russian Life* (September–October 2008), p. 35.

Building Democracy From the Bottom Up

The interviewers note that Solzhenitsyn was always in favor of civic self-government, yet remain perplexed by this (*DDD*, 103). They say that Solzhenitsyn contrasted this model with Western democracy. Solzhenitsyn quarrels with this characterization. He says that he has "always insisted on the need for local self-government for Russia, but never opposed this model to Western democracy." On the contrary, Solzhenitsyn says that he tried to "convince my fellow citizens by citing the examples of highly effective self-governance systems in Switzerland and New England, both of which I saw first-hand" (*DDD*, 103).

This is an emphasis in Solzhenitsyn's work that is little appreciated by commentators in the West. One might say that most judgments about Solzhenitsyn are still stuck in the 1970s. There was a widespread failure on the part of commentators, journalists, and even academics to keep up with Solzhenitsyn's unfolding reflection in the years after 1980 or after his return to Russia in 1994 (other than to note his "indulgence" for Putin). In fact the key political theme in the last twenty-five or thirty years of his life was his support for local self-government. In *The Little Grain*, he writes about witnessing cantonal elections in Appenzell in Switzerland. He speaks admiringly about the Swiss tradition of self-government, the Helvetic Confederacy, going back to the Middle Ages.[22] In *Rebuilding Russia*, published in Russia in 1990 and in the United States in 1991, he writes with admiration about self-government of the Swiss or New England variety.[23] In his farewell remarks to the people of Cavendish, Vermont in 1994, he spoke about democratic self-government of the kind that he saw at work in

22 Soljénitsyne, *Le grain tombé entre les meules: Esquisses d'exil*, translated by Geneviève and José Johannet (Paris: Fayard, 1998), pp. 164–70.
23 Solzhenitsyn, *Rebuilding Russia: Reflections and Tentative Proposals*, translated by Alexis Klimoff (New York: Farrar, Straus and Giroux, 1991), pp. 82–88.

Vermont   as
precisely what was missing in Russia and what most needed to
be developed.[24]

A critic might ask whether Solzhenitsyn was naïve to think
that the Swiss or New England models can provide any guidance
for the development of political liberty in a huge nation-state such
as Russia that spans nine time zones. But in fact Solzhenitsyn
always coupled his call for the development of local self-government in Russia with the recognition that there had to be a strong
"vertical of power," as he called it. He knew there needed to be a
strong presidency and a strong central government, but that *self-
government* could only really be developed from the bottom up.
When Solzhenitsyn returned to Russia in 1994, he flew into
Vladivostok rather than flying directly into Moscow and he
stopped in many towns along the way before arriving in the
Russian capital. He did his best to stimulate the interest of the
local people in this theme of local self-government (he notes in the
introduction to *Russia in Collapse* that he was always the one to
raise the issue with his interlocutors).[25] In 1995 he presided over
a meeting of local officials dedicated to this theme. So this theme
of self-government and the revitalization and renewal of the nineteenth-century Russian *zemstvos* or provincial councils is vitally
important to Solzhenitsyn's political reflection.

A Meaningful Opposition

Solzhenitsyn might be accused of being too sanguine about political
developments in Russia on the eve of his death in 2008, but I think
it is a mistake to read Solzhenitsyn as simply a partisan of
Putinesque authoritarianism. Mrs. Solzhenitsyn, in an address to
the International Solzhenitsyn Colloquium at the University of

---

24 *The Solzhenitsyn Reader*, p. 607.
25 *The Solzhenitsyn Reader*, p. 470: "Indeed, almost no one talked of
self-government and how to set it up; it was not on their minds; usually I was the one raising that point."

Illinois, in June 2007, made clear that there were certain features of Putin's Russia that very much displeased her husband. Among these were the massive corruption, the failure to promote any kind of sustainable public repentance for the terrible crimes of the Communist period, and the slowness of movement toward democracy and democratization. It is a gross mistake to see Solzhenitsyn as somebody who finds in Putin his *beau ideal* of a statesman. As he says to the interviewers for *Der Spiegel*, he laments the absence of a real, meaningful opposition in Russia. Russia needs a "constructive, clear and large-scale opposition" (*DDD*, 103) if there is to be a real democracy. I should add that Natalia Solzhenitsyn stresses the same point in her *Russian Life* interview in 2008.[26] (I cite this interview again because in many ways it is an extrapolation of key themes in Solzhenitsyn's work itself.) In that interview, Mrs. Solzhenitsyn said it is really up to society to create a meaningful opposition. Perhaps we began to see that in the winter of 2011–2012, when tens of thousands of protestors gathered in Moscow and demanded political accountability and genuine democracy in Russia.

Solzhenitsyn also makes clear the main reason for the absence of a meaningful, that is, non-Communist, opposition in Russia. The lack of a real opposition has everything to do with the discredit borne by the so-called "democrats" (*DDD*, 103–104), the same individuals who are applauded in the West and who are asked to write op-eds for the *Wall Street Journal* and *The New York Times*. They are discredited precisely because they are associated with the criminal levels of corruption and the kleptocracy of the 1990s. People in the West are insufficiently aware of just how closely associated the so-called democratic camp was with the worst excesses and crimes of the 1990s. The shameful past of the democrats is a large part of the problem, according to Solzhenitsyn.

Parties and Popular Representation

The *Der Spiegel* interviewers now turn to a question about the

26 *Russian Life* (September–October 2008), p. 33.

abolition of direct elections for State Duma deputies. The abolition occurred under Putin. This so-called electoral reform means there is no direct election for parliamentary representatives at all. Instead, people vote for a slate belonging to a party, and then the representatives for the State Duma are picked by party leaders as a result of a percentage of votes that each parties wins. Solzhenitsyn is asked, "Is this not a step back?" (*DDD*, 104). In an earlier interview with *Der Spiegel*, Solzhenitsyn had criticized the fact that only half of the positions for the State Duma were elected by direct election. Here Solzhenitsyn replies that yes, this is a mistake. He begins by characterizing himself as "a convinced and consistent critic of party parliamentarianism." He is for the "non-partisan election of true people's representatives" and adds that he supports recall for those who work in an unsatisfactory manner. Solzhenitsyn also says that he sees "nothing organic in political parties" (*DDD*, 104).

In my book *Aleksandr Solzhenitsyn: The Ascent from Ideology*, I criticized Solzhenitsyn for not recognizing that liberty in the modern world depends on the functioning of a pluralistic party system and that the idea of a non-partisan representative regime is really beyond the possible.[27] Solzhenitsyn's views of parties are shaped partly by the fact that the Bolshevik party was a criminal conspiracy against human liberty and the public good, and partly from what he saw of the selfishness and short-sightedness of political parties in the West after he went into exile in 1974. Interestingly enough, in discussing political parties he approvingly cites Trotsky, whom in other respects he saw as a malevolent architect of twentieth-century totalitarianism (*DDD*, 104). Solzhenitsyn thus fails to distinguish adequately between constitutional parties and criminal conspiracies or totalitarian parties dedicated exclusively to ideological ends.

But the specific point that Solzhenitsyn makes in his response

27 Daniel J. Mahoney, *Aleksandr Solzhenitsyn: The Ascent from Ideology* (Lanham, MD: Rowman & Littlefield, 2001), pp. 106, 137, 150.

seems to me eminently defensible. Let me quote: "Voting for impersonal parties and their programs is a false substitute for the only true way to elect people's representatives: voting by an actual person, for an actual candidate. This is the whole point behind popular representation" (*DDD*, 104). The people need to vote for an actual person who needs to be held responsible for his or her actions. Solzhenitsyn sees something deeply problematic with the electoral system in contemporary Russia and, in his view, Putin was responsible for making that electoral system less representative and less democratic. This criticism once again belies the claim that Solzhenitsyn was an uncritical supporter of Putin's authoritarianism.

Making Room for Small Businesses

The interview also addressed the question of the enormous contrast between rich and poor in Russia. The *Der Spiegel* interviewers asked Solzhenitsyn what could be done to improve the situation (*DDD*, 104–5). We know from the public remarks that Solzhenitsyn issued in February 2007 at the time of the publication of his essay *Reflections on the February Revolution* that this was an abiding concern. At that time Solzhenitsyn made clear that he was deeply concerned by the gap between the rich and the poor in the country. In response to the question from the *Der Spiegel* interviewer, Solzhenitsyn says that this is an "extremely dangerous phenomenon" (*DDD*, 105) that needs the immediate attention of the state. But at the same time, Solzhenitsyn adds that it is a mistake to go after big businesses. Instead, what the Russian state needs to do is "give breathing room to medium and small businesses" (*DDD*, 105). These remarks reflect Solzhenitsyn's good sense and moderation. The important point is that he does not let his indignation about the dislocations of the Russian 1990s get in the way of articulating a sober path forward.

The great challenge facing Russia is to protect its citizens and small entrepreneurs from "arbitrary rule and from corruption" (*DDD*, 105). The country needs to invest its revenues from national resources into "national infrastructure, education, and healthcare" (*DDD*, 105). In addition, active efforts need to be made to shape the character of the Russian people. In other words, Solzhenitsyn continues to express his commitment to self-government. A people who are prepared to govern themselves are also a people who are prepared to be entrepreneurs, to compete responsibly within a lawful market order. A major misunderstanding about Solzhenitsyn is the notion that he is somehow anti-capitalist. In contrast, I am quite struck by how sympathetic he is to a market economy under the rule of law, to small and medium business, and to the idea of a thriving entrepreneurial class. He was a friend of the market economy but a critic of a doctrinaire "market ideology."

A "National Idea"?

The *Der Spiegel* interviewers inquire if Russia needs a "national idea" (*DDD*, 105). This was a much debated term in Russia from 1990 onward. With the death of Communism some argued Russia needed some kind of a national idea to give direction to the present and future. Solzhenitsyn is skeptical about the term, which he calls "unclear." He is also skeptical about the substitution of some new ideology for the inhuman ideology that governed the Soviet Union from 1917 to 1990. He says that the whole discussion of developing a national idea hastily began in post-Soviet Russia and that he did his best to "pour cold water on it" (*DDD*, 105). As he had made clear in his fall 1994 address to the Duma, it was sufficient for Russia to have one task, what he called "the preservation of a dying people" (*DDD*, 105). This idea of the preservation of a people, which he had already introduced in *Rebuilding Russia* in 1990, indicates that Solzhenitsyn was principally concerned with the existence and character of the Russian people. There is no doubt he would like Russia to develop into a democracy, as we have seen. And he was certainly a most articulate defender of self-government. But he knew that what comes first is the preservation of the nation. Whatever misgivings he had about the residual authoritarianism of Russia under Vladimir Putin, he believed that for the first time since the fall of Communism, Russia had a government that in some sense was concerned with the preservation of a dying people.

It might seem hyperbolic to refer to a "dying people." But if one reads 1998's *Russia in Collapse*, one sees just how prophetic Solzhenitsyn was. There he wrote that Russia was "dying" in a double sense. It was "dying" demographically and it was dying because the moral roots of freedom were absent. These passages express, therefore, an overriding concern of Solzhenitsyn's: the first priority is for there to be a people. There has to be a *demos*, a people, a nation, for there to be democracy. And too many in the West at the time took for granted the survival of the Russian people. What the 1990s in fact brought was a new time of troubles that came dangerously close to destroying Russia. This theme shows what a non-ideological thinker Solzhenitsyn is. What comes first is survival, and not some ideological program, whether that program be at the service of the market or of democracy.

Russia and the West

The *Der Spiegel* interviewer notes that "Russia often finds itself alone" (*DDD*, 105), and this occasions a series of reflections by Solzhenitsyn on his country's relationship to Europe and America. The Russian writer first speaks of the "clash of illusory hopes against reality" (*DDD*, 106), the overwhelmingly pro-Western sentiment of the Russian people at the time of the collapse of the Soviet regime which has been replaced by the growing perception that the West was not what he calls "a knight of democracy" (*DDD*, 106). The positive view of the West has been replaced with the "disappointed belief that pragmatism, often of a cynical and selfish character" (*DDD*, 106), lies at the heart of Western policies. Of course, at this juncture Solzhenitsyn is observing and reporting. His own views are somewhat more complex.

Let us go back to the very revealing interview that Paul Klebnikov conducted with him ("Zhirinovsky Is an Evil

Caricature of a Russian Patriot"), published in the May 9, 1994 issue of *Forbes* magazine.[28] The interview was conducted in Vermont, shortly before Solzhenitsyn's return to post-Communist Russia. In that interview Solzhenitsyn made clear his disappointment with the increasingly belligerent attitude of the United States and the Western democracies toward Russia, especially in the cases of the Ukraine and Serbia. He had always been an advocate of independence for the constituent republics of the former Soviet Union, but he also advocated a deliberative reconstitution of borders. He was a critic of what he called the "Leninist borders" that had arbitrarily been imposed during the Communist period. For example, there were many people in the Ukraine, Russian speakers, whose sympathies lay with Russia. He had in mind the Crimea, which was arbitrarily given to Russia by Khrushchev in 1954, as well as several Russian provinces that had been given to the Ukraine much earlier by Lenin, dating all the way back to 1919. As Solzhenitsyn observes, these provinces had not historically belonged to the Ukraine, and he believed that the people of eastern and southern territories of today's Ukraine ought to have a say in their governance and whether or not they were to be part of a new, independent Ukrainian state. So in the *Forbes* interview Solzhenitsyn spoke about what he called "the sudden and crude fragmentation of the intermingled Slavic peoples"[29] by arbitrarily determined borders that tore apart millions of family ties and friendships. He repeats this judgment almost word for word in the *Der Spiegel* interview.

In this connection, Solzhenitsyn was genuinely surprised by the vehemence of the American support for the Ukraine and the lack of sensitivity to the fate of twenty-five million Russians in what came to be called the "near abroad." He spoke about eight to ten purely Russian provinces in the Ukraine, but also northern Kazakhstan and some other neighboring republics, where these twenty-five million ethnic Russians immediately ended up as

28 Klebnikov interview.
29 *Ibid.*

undesirable aliens. These were places where they and their families had lived for up to three centuries, and they now faced persecution in their jobs and the suppression of their culture, education, and language. In this he saw Russia as a victim of thoughtless policies that created the largest diaspora in the world. He saw a Russia that was sick, weak, and prostrate and a Western public opinion that nonetheless treated Russia as an aggressor.

It is also the case that Solzhenitsyn disapproved of the Western policy of tipping the scales heavily against Serbia, as if she were to blame for everything in the conflict in the Balkans in the 1990s. He saw the problem in Yugoslavia as remarkably similar to the problem in the former USSR. There the Communist dictator Tito had laid out what Solzhenitsyn calls "arbitrary, ethnically nonsensical, and historically unjustifiable internal administrative boundaries."[30] And when the various constituent peoples of the former Yugoslavia declared their independence at the time of the fall of the Communist regime, when Yugoslavia began to fall apart, the leading powers of the West with "inexplicable haste and irresponsibility"[31] rushed to recognize these states with their artificial borders. So he held the Western powers, along with Tito, principally responsible for the bloody and exhausting war that followed.

He also spoke very critically about what he called intervention "for the sake of humanism."[32] He believed that this kind of humanitarian intervention was a very dangerous thing, based on a colossal misunderstanding of the situation. This judgment led to some of Solzhenitsyn's more acerbic comments—he denounced NATO bombing of Serbia in 1998, comparing NATO's policies to Hitler's assaults on some of the countries of East Central

---

30 *Ibid.*
31 *Ibid.*
32 *Ibid.*
33 Once again it was a matter of an intemperate tone more than an immoderate or aggressive take on the world. Solzhenitsyn was right in my view about the limits of humanitarian intervention, but wrong to invoke the murderous and lupine imperialism of Nazi Germany as a precedent for this event.

Europe.[33] No doubt those remarks were hyperbolic and lacked sufficient moral proportion. They risk giving the impression that Solzhenitsyn is acting like a traditional pan-Slavist who thinks Russia has a role in upholding the Serbs and in creating and sustaining an alliance with the South Slavs. But that would be a false inference. Solzhenitsyn means it when he says that he was an opponent of pan-Slavism. But he was deeply disturbed by a "humanitarian" intervention that led the United States to intervene in a one-sided way, showing a complete lack of appreciation for the genuine aspects of the problem.

In the *Der Spiegel* interview Solzhenitsyn speaks about the West's "panic" (*DDD*, 106) as Russia began to rebuild and to regain some of her strengths as an economy and state. Solzhenitsyn believes that the Western democracies, and particularly the United States, felt more comfortable and supportive of a prostrate or weak Russia of the kind that existed in the 1990s, than with a strong one. As Russia became a stronger state, economy, and society after 2000, this led to a fearful reaction on the part of the United States and the Western democracies. Solzhenitsyn roots that apprehension in the continuing identification by many in the West of Russia with the "ex-superpower," the Soviet Union. With considerable understatement, he says it is "too bad" (*DDD*, 106) that so many in the West associate Russia with the Soviet Union. It does not, however, cause him surprise. As he observes in the interview, this has been a longstanding theme of his, going back to the 1970s. This is not the first time he has had the question posed to him. In the *Forbes* interview Klebnikov says that a lot of people in the West think it was not Communism but traditional Russian imperialism that drove Stalin to grab Eastern Europe. Solzhenitsyn's response could not have been more emphatic: "Absolutely not! This was not Russian imperialism, which in the past only expanded its border somewhat. This was communist imperialism, which aimed to take over the whole world."[34]

In *The Little Grain* Solzhenitsyn placed great emphasis on an

34 Klebnikov interview.

official U.S. document from 1959, Law 86–90, which does not include Russia in the list of nations oppressed by Communism. On the contrary, Russian imperialism, not Communism, was held responsible for the conquest of some twenty countries, including China, Tibet, and some made-up place called Kazakia.[35] Solzhenitsyn added that one is amazed that this "silly law" is still on the books today.

If one reads Solzhenitsyn's treatment of Law 86–90 in *The Little Grain*, it becomes clear that this obscure law that so few Americans know about had a deep impact on him. It helped shape his impression that, in their heart of hearts, the majority of American policy makers and politicians were more anti-Russian than anti-Communist. Yet Solzhenitsyn thinks the position underlying Law 86–90, the position underlying the thinking of people like Henry Kissinger and Zbigniew Brzezinski, is as he tells Klebnikov "complete delirium."[36] He adds, "When was Russia ever in Africa? When did Russia ever want to snatch Angola or Cuba? When was she ever in Latin America?"[37] Historical Russia never tried to take over the world, whereas the Communists had precisely that aim. There was something limitless about Communist imperialism, while traditional Russian imperialism expanded its border unjustifiably as he categorically states about Poland, but nonetheless in an infinitely less significant way.

In the next part of the *Der Spiegel* interview Solzhenitsyn returns to a theme he had already introduced, namely the fact that "Russia is not a democratic country yet; it is just starting to build democracy" (*DDD*, 107). When one looks at Solzhenitsyn's own political reflection going back to the 1973 *Letter to the Soviet Leaders*, one can see that Solzhenitsyn always thought that the path down from the icy cliffs of totalitarianism would take a great deal of time and effort. Solzhenitsyn assumed some kind of authoritarian transition during which Russia moved away from

35 *Ibid.*
36 *Ibid.*
37 *Ibid.*

ideological despotism, rejected the censorship, political centralization, and oppression of totalitarianism, and began to build institutions of democratic self-government from the bottom up. Solzhenitsyn assumed a transition, not an immediate transformation; he knew it would be very difficult to establish democratic institutions and habits and impossible to do so quickly. Solzhenitsyn's comments here, therefore, are a counsel and encouragement to the Western world to be patient, to not expect an immediate transformation of mores and institutions. Such a transformation would be impossible in a normal country, but is especially unthinkable in a country that had lived through seventy years of soul-destroying ideological despotism.

Solzhenitsyn offers additional counsel to the West. He states that there is both ingratitude and a double standard when it comes to Western policies toward Russia. He reminds his readers that "Russia clearly and unambiguously stretched out its helping hand" (DDD, 107) to the West after 9/11. And he adds that the West will need Russian support in the twenty-first century. In so doing he refers to comments he made years earlier in his interview with Paul Klebnikov: "If we look far into the future, one can see a time in the twenty-first century when both Europe and USA will be in dire need of Russia as an ally" (DDD, 107). As Klebnikov noted in his introduction to the interview, this is a somewhat cryptic observation, with Solzhenitsyn saying that the U.S. will have need of Russia as an ally against a threat he did not name. Klebnikov asks, "What threat?", and he reports that on different occasions Solzhenitsyn has warned of an expansionist China, an insurgent Islam, and other dangers from the so-called Third World.[38] My guess is Solzhenitsyn had all of those real and continuing dangers in mind.

The interview now turns to a brief interchange about Solzhenitsyn's relation to Germany. Solzhenitsyn expresses great admiration for German culture, for German music (Solzhenitsyn says his life is unthinkable without Bach, Beethoven and

38 *Ibid.*

Schubert), and for a German philosopher and writer such as Schelling (*DDD*, 107). Then the conversation moves on to a discussion of literature.

The Future of Russian Literature

In that discussion Solzhenitsyn expresses his qualified hopes for Russian literature today. He knows that a time of crisis is not a particularly good time for any national literature. But he adds, in a very beautiful line, "I do believe that justice and conscience will not be cast to the four winds, but will remain in the foundations of Russian literature so that it may be of service in brightening our spirit and enhancing our comprehension" (*DDD*, 108). Solzhenitsyn himself, of course, is deeply rooted in that tradition of Russian literature. He believes that literature heightens one's appreciation of justice and conscience, that it speaks to the human soul, that it brightens the spirit and enhances our comprehension. Solzhenitsyn therefore has confidence that that tradition of Russian literature, that understanding of the ethical underpinnings of Russian literature, will persist in the future. It is also the case that he worked to sustain and encourage this understanding of Russian literature. In 1998 he established the Solzhenitsyn Prize which awarded $25,000 to an author or current of work that carries on the tradition of which Solzhenitsyn speaks. It has become the premier literary prize in Russia today. It is an example of Solzhenitsyn's effort to shape the future, to give support to those writers who under very difficult circumstances were doing their best to sustain the most humane traditions of Russian literature.

The Church in Russia Today

Much of the rest of the interview deals with the question of Orthodoxy in contemporary Russia. Like many in the West, the questioners for *Der Spiegel* fear the collaboration of religious authority and civic power in the new Russia, the development of a new Caeseropapism (*DDD*, 108). Solzhenitsyn does not deny that in the past there has been a kind of collusion of religious authority and state power. But he also argues that the Church is increasingly acting independently and that the civic authorities are learning to respect the independence and initiatives of the Church. He notes, for example, that the Orthodox Church is just beginning to formulate a social doctrine, and one that is independent of the state and in decisive respects light years ahead of the secular authorities in formulating ethical imperatives for Russia (*DDD*, 108). Solzhenitsyn also highlights something very important and not widely appreciated in the West, namely the crucial role of the Church in holding "round-the-clock prayers for the repose of the souls of victims of communist massacres" (*DDD*, 109). They have done that at Butovo, the site outside of Moscow, where tens of thousands of bodies were discovered in the 1990s, many of them clergy, or other religious believers, and also on the Solovetsky Islands, the first major gulag camp in the Arctic north, as well as in other places of mass burials.

A Man of Faith and Reason

The interview more or less ends with the *Der Spiegel* interviewer asking Solzhenitsyn about his views on religion. "What does faith mean for you?" (*DDD*, 109) the interviewer asks. Solzhenitsyn responds, "For me, faith is the foundation and support of one's life" (*DDD*, 109). It is a brief but revealing comment on Solzhenitsyn's part. An excursus on Solzhenitsyn's views on religion will be helpful here. Too many people in both Russia and the West treat Solzhenitsyn as if his fundamental ideas were simply derivative from Orthodoxy. My own view, a view I first articulated in my book *Aleksandr Solzhenitsyn: The Ascent From Ideology*, is that Solzhenitsyn independently arrived at certain philosophical conclusions that were close to and compatible with the Orthodox tradition, that Solzhenitsyn returned to Christianity in the 1950s and deepened his religious understanding and com-

39 Mahoney, *Aleksandr Solzhenitsyn: The Ascent from Ideology*, pp. 41–64.

mitments in the course of the 1960s and '70s.[39] Solzhenitsyn's Orthodoxy is not the *cause* of his reflection, but rather Solzhenitsyn's reflection led him to return to Orthodoxy. The first affirmation of that return is the beautiful prayer "Acathistus" which I have already cited. That return is then traced with luminous insight in the chapter on "The Ascent" from the fourth section of *The Gulag Archipelago*, "The Soul and Barbed Wire." It was the camp experience that above all crystallized Solzhenitsyn's religiosity. Those who see his thought as simply a reflection of the Orthodox tradition miss something essential in Solzhenitsyn's *intellectual* itinerary and self-understanding. He was groping in the camps, searching for answers, and he found that Christianity offered many of them.

One of the best discussions of the place of faith and reason in Solzhenitsyn's life and thought is found in the book *Soljénitsyne: un destin*,[40] *Solzhenitsyn: A Destiny*, by the French writer, Véronique Hallereau. Hallereau points out that Solzhenitsyn has a scientific and rational mind, and yet at the same time this great writer remains "open to mystery." As she puts it: "With Solzhenitsyn, faith and reason are not opposed. His heart is not torn between two contradictory tendencies in his being, rational lucidity and the anguished need to believe." Rather, his faith is a logical consequence of the limits of reason. It is never irrationality, but rather "supra-rationality," according to Hallereau. "Faith crowns the edifice of reason," she writes, "completing it while recognizing its limits."[41] That is very nicely put. Hallereau adds that Solzhenitsyn's faith had the same source as his art, his experience of the camps. It was in the camps that he felt the hand of God on him. It was the camp experience that led to his return to the Orthodox Christianity of his youth, because "this accorded most logically with what he knew and experienced."[42] And he above all

40 Véronique Hallereau, *Soljénitsyne, Un Destin: Portrait Littéraire* (Paris: Editions de l'Oeuvre, 2010).

41 *Ibid.*, p. 181.

42 *Ibid.*

came to experience a superior reality, Providence, the hand of God in human affairs. Hallereau points out that the name of Jesus Christ is seldom uttered by Solzhenitsyn.[43] The principal role is held by a personal God who assigned him a "mission" to tell the truth about the terrible experience of Russia in the twentieth century, a God who has guided him as he has paid tribute through his life and witness to the millions of victims of ideological despotism.

Providence, a "Supreme Complete Reality" who cares for man, is therefore central or foundational in Solzhenitsyn's reflection. One of the fullest discussions of Providence in Solzhenitsyn's work can be found in his February 1979 BBC interview with Janis Sapiets, an interview that I have already had occasion to discuss. Sapiets asks Solzhenitsyn, "What do you yourself rely on, Aleksandr Isayevich? What do you believe in? In Providence?" And Solzhenitsyn responds by saying, "I would not take the name of Providence in vain. When you pronounce that word, you enter a solemn sphere. I am convinced of His presence in every human life—in my own and in that of entire peoples. But we are so superficial that we can understand nothing in time. We discern and understand all the zigzags of our life very, very belatedly. I am convinced that, someday, we will also understand the purpose of 1917."[44] As we see, Solzhenitsyn believes that Providence plays a special role in the individual life of human beings, but also in the collective life of nations and peoples. This affirmation of Providence is *the* key to understanding Solzhenitsyn's religiosity.

Three Prayers

Solzhenitsyn composed three prayers that I know of. The first is the song of praise, "Acathistus," which is quoted in *The Gulag Archipelago*. "Oh great God! I believe now anew!" This is the great expression and marker of Solzhenitsyn's return to the faith

43 *Ibid.*, p. 182.
44 *East and West*, pp. 175–76.

of his childhood, a return mediated by reflection on his experience in the camps. The second prayer is a prayer he wrote shortly after the publication of *One Day in the Life of Ivan Denisovich*, when he had first experienced worldly fame, when he burst out on the scene as a great Russian and world writer. This beautiful prayer circulated in *samizdat* in the 1960s. I quote it *in toto*:

> How easy for me to live with you, Lord!
> How easy to believe in you!
> When my mind casts about
> or flags in bewilderment,
> when the cleverest among us
> cannot see past the present evening,
> not knowing what to do tomorrow—
> you send me the clarity to know
> that you exist
> and will take care
> that not all paths of goodness should be barred.
> At the crest of earthly fame
> I look back in wonderment
> at the journey beyond hope—to this place,
> from which I was able to send mankind
> a reflection of your rays.
> And however long the time
> that I must yet reflect them
> you will give to me.
> And whatever I fail to accomplish
> you surely have allotted unto others.[45]

Solzhenitsyn certainly had the conviction and confidence that God exists, that Providence had given him a mission and would continue to guide him. If one examines his great memoir *The Oak and the Calf* that chronicles his struggle with the Soviet state between 1960 and 1974, one sees just how central the idea of a

45 *The Solzhenitsyn Reader*, pp. 624–25.

providential "mission" is to Solzhenitsyn's self-understanding.

There is a third prayer, a "Prayer for Russia," that Solzhenitsyn wrote in 1997 and that he recited every day in the final period of his life. It is a moving prayer written at the time of Russia's worst disasters, during the "third time of troubles," when he came very close to despairing for the future of his country. In this prayer he asks that a just and merciful God help Russia fortify her spiritual sources, renew herself, and become whole and strong again.[46] In reading it, it would be a mistake to think that Solzhenitsyn is somehow subordinating religion to political or national purposes. He once again is acting on his understanding of Providence, his belief that Providence is active in the life of nations and peoples as well as the life of individuals.

An Encounter With the Polish Pope

It should also be pointed out that Solzhenitsyn was an admirer of the Polish pope, John Paul II. This admiration is particularly important for understanding just how non-sectarian Solzhenitsyn's Christianity was. He was an Orthodox Christian, but he shared none of Dostoevsky's disdain for the Poles or vehement hostility to Roman Catholicism. In the Sapiets BBC interview in 1979, when discussing hopeful currents in the contemporary world, including the presence of religion in the lives and minds of thoughtful young people, Solzhenitsyn comments about Pope John Paul II, the Roman Pontiff: "Words fail me. It's a gift from God!"[47] We know from other sources that Solzhenitsyn considered the election of the Polish pope to be one of the most important developments in world affairs since the First World War. That is a very strong claim, one that Solzhenitsyn made in the

---

46 *Ibid.*, p. 634.
47 *East and West*, pp. 175–76.
48 Cited in George Weigel, *The End and the Beginning: Pope John Paul II — The Victory of Freedom, the Last Years, the Legacy* (New York: Doubleday, 2010), p. 101.

presence of his then-secretary, Irina Alberti.[48] He also met with the pope on October 15, 1993, on the fifteenth anniversary of John Paul II's election as Roman Pontiff. He reports on the three-hour meeting he had with the pope in *The Little Grain*.[49] Solzhenitsyn and the pope expressed mutual respect and admiration for each other. Solzhenitsyn also spoke about his admiration for Catholic social teaching. There also was a brief exchange about Roman Catholic efforts to "take advantage" of Orthodox weakness in the border lands of the Soviet Union in the 1920s. Solzhenitsyn says that his reference to this topic made the pope uncomfortable. But on the whole, the meeting appears to have been a deeply respectful and constructive one.

One should add that when John Paul II died, Solzhenitsyn commented on the legacy of the pope. In April 2005, following the death of John Paul II, Solzhenitsyn paid his own personal tribute (I cite Joseph Pearce's 2011 revised edition of *Solzhenitsyn: A Soul in Exile*): "Pope John Paul II was a great man. In the centuries-long great line of Roman popes, he stands out markedly. He influenced the course of world history, and in his tireless pastoral visits across the world he carried the warmth of Christianity to all."[50] We thus see that Solzhenitsyn's admiration for John Paul II persisted during the full length of the twenty-seven year pontificate of the Polish pope.

Orthodoxy and the Neo-Pagan Temptation

I suggested earlier in this chapter that Solzhenitsyn's attitude towards Orthodoxy is a complex, dialectical one: Solzhenitsyn was an Orthodox Christian, but his deepest philosophical and political reflections did not flow from Orthodoxy so much as were

49 Soljéntsyne, *Esquissses d'exil: Le grain tombé entre les meules: 1979–1994*, translated by Françoise Lesourd (Paris: Fayard, 2003), pp. 649–50.

50 Quoted in Joseph Pearce, *Solzhenitsyn: A Soul in Exile*, revised and updated edition (San Francisco: Ignatius, 2011), p. 354.

congruent with Orthodoxy. I think it is important, though, to note that Solzhenitsyn did in fact grow closer to Orthodoxy in the last decades of his life, that he died a convinced Orthodox Christian, although one who did not deny the truth in other Christian affirmations, or, for that matter, in other non-Christian religious affirmations. Solzhenitsyn had a remarkably ecumenical understanding of religious truth, as some of the early chapters of *November 1916* indicate. At the end of chapter six of that work, he writes that "God's truth was like 'Mother truth' in the folk tale. Seven brothers rode out to look at her, viewed from seven sides and seven angles, and when they returned each of them had a different tale to tell."[51]

To further understand his relationship to Orthodoxy, I would like to highlight an important chapter in 1998's *Russia in Collapse* entitled "The Orthodox Church in This Time of Troubles." This chapter, the thirty-second in the volume, makes clear just how important Orthodoxy was to Solzhenitsyn's self-understanding. Among other things, the same Solzhenitsyn who had written a scathing letter to Patriarch Pimen in the early 1970s castigating the church's subordination to a vile atheistic totalitarian state, now wrote with sympathy for the difficulty the Church faces to find solid ground to stand on and to renew itself after seventy years of Communist totalitarianism. Solzhenitsyn notes that the persecution of the Orthodox Church, and the persecution of religion more broadly in the Soviet Union, far surpassed the persecutions of the early church during the Roman Empire. In this context, he identifies with the difficult task of strengthening and rebuilding Orthodoxy in Russia.

Here he also speaks about the rise of a "neo-pagan" consciousness in Russia.[52] That neo-pagan consciousness is partly the result of the atheistic indoctrination promoted by Communism, but it is also part and parcel of the modernization of Russia. As

51 *The Solzhenitsyn Reader*, p. 363.
52 I have drawn on the French edition of the work, *La Russie sous l'avalanche* (Paris: Fayard, 1998), p. 311.

Russia becomes a more"normal" society it perforce is influenced by the beliefs and values of what Solzhenitsyn elsewhere calls "current modernity."[53] Solzhenitsyn believes that Orthodoxy provides an essential spiritual foundation for resisting and moving beyond our "neo-pagan epic."[54] Any Russian nationalism that rejects what he calls "the gift of Orthodoxy"[55] will be cruel and crude, intolerant and excessively nationalistic. Orthodoxy will have an important elevating and humanizing influence. At the very end of the chapter Solzhenitsyn writes, "We Russians must hold firmly and with devotion to the spirit of Orthodoxy as one of the last gifts that we have not yet been made to lose."[56] The Russian cultural type—the heart, the mores, the spiritual meaning of what it means to be Russian—was decisively shaped by Orthodoxy. If, in the decades to come, Russia continues to lose more inhabitants and more territories, *even if it were to lose statehood*, the only thing that would remain, that would be truly imperishable, would be the Orthodox faith "with the high perception of the world that it instills."[57] Those critics such as Father Alexander Schmemann who worried that Solzhenitsyn's conception of religion was exceptionally nationalistic, who see him as Orthodox because Russian, fail to take seriously the depth of his critique of "pagan" nationalism. Solzhenitsyn the patriot is a critic of a nationalism devoid of a higher perspective, a nationalism that ignores spiritual imperatives. He is a critic of a nationalism that puts national self-assertion above a humble attitude toward God's heaven.

A Calm and Balanced Attitude Toward Death

The interview finally ends with a question about death (*DDD*, 109). It is not surprising that a question about religion would be

53 See Pearce, *Solzhenitsyn: A Soul in Exile,* p. 327.
54 *La Russie sous l'avalanche*, p. 311.
55 *Ibid.*, p. 314.
56 *Ibid.*
57 *Ibid.*

followed-up by a question about death. The *Der Spiegel* interviewers ask Solzhenitsyn if he is afraid of death and Solzhenitsyn says, "No, I am not afraid of death anymore. When I was young, the early death of my father cast a shadow over me—he died at the age of twenty-seven—and I was afraid to die before all my literary plans became true. But between thirty and forty years of age, my attitude to death became quite calm and balanced. I feel it is a natural but by no means the final, milestone of one's existence" (*DDD*, 109). In parting the *Der Spiegel* interviewers add, "Anyway, we wish you many years of creative life," and Solzhenitsyn rather strikingly responds, "No, no. Don't. It's enough" (*DDD*, 109). He had lived a full and richly satisfying life. In 2007 it is rather apparent that, given his physical health, he did not expect to live much longer. What Solzhenitsyn's answer indicates is that he not only preached a balanced approach to life and death, but he had attained and lived that balance. In his 1993 farewell address to the West at Liechtenstein, "We have ceased to see the Purpose," his reflection on politics and ethics at the end of the twentieth century, Solzhenitsyn speaks about the "crisis of modern progress."[58] He notes that it is up to us to stop seeing Progress as a "stream of unlimited blessings" but rather to view it as a gift from on high sent down for an "extremely intricate trial of our free will."[59] In that farewell Solzhenitsyn returned to many of the key themes he had already developed in his Harvard address of 1978.[60] In both speeches he spoke of the need for human beings to establish a real internal harmony between our spiritual and physical beings, as well as the need to have a clarity of spirit which rejects a relativistic flattening of the absolutely indispensable distinction between good and evil. Above all, Solzhenitsyn said, "We need to recover, not only a sense of the eternal questions that remain, but we need to overcome our cur-

58 *The Solzhenitsyn Reader*, pp. 594–95.
59 *Ibid.*, p. 596.
60 See my detailed discussion of the two addresses in Mahoney, *Aleksandr Solzhenitsyn: The Ascent from Ideology*, pp. 19–39.

rent helplessness of the spirit, our intellectual disarray" which is most apparent, Solzhenitsyn wrote, in the "loss of a clear and calm attitude towards death."[61] We moderns see death as the extinction of the entire universe at a stroke, precisely because we have succumbed to neo-paganism. We have lost confidence in the "unchanging Higher Power above us."[62] That Solzhenitsyn did not fear death, that he had a calm attitude toward death, was tied to his confidence in Providence, to the fact that he did not believe that death is the final reality.

Solzhenitsyn not only developed these themes in some of his important prose writings that I have already referred to, but he wrote a beautiful prose poem near the end of his life called "Remembrance of the Departed," in which he speaks about prayer for the souls of the departed.[63]

In a quite moving way he writes about how the departed are somehow still here, still among us, still with one foot in the temporal realm as it were, even if they have departed to a transcendent spiritual realm. We can almost touch them. We can certainly feel them—and yet they remain unknowable. This is further evidence, if any is needed, of Solzhenitsyn's belief that death is not the final word.

Solzhenitsyn knew when enough was enough, because life of earth does not exhaust our destiny. He knew there was a time where death was the appropriate final act in one's earthly life. Solzhenitsyn was ready to die. One is reminded of the remark of the ancients, Cicero and Plato, who affirmed that "to philosophize is to learn how to die." There is one reading of that remark which suggests that the philosopher alone truly knows what death is, that he will die and that's it. He alone has the courage to face the fact of human mortality. There is another understanding of that

---

61 *The Solzhenitsyn Reader*, p. 596.
62 *Ibid*.
63 "Remembrance of the Departed" in *The Solzhenitsyn Reader*, pp. 633–34. This was one of the last "miniatures" or prose poems written by Solzhenitsyn and among the most affecting.

line, however, that philosophical reflection can allow us to discern the immortal character of the human spirit, that it can allow us to appreciate both the natural and supernatural destinies of man. We come back to Véronique Hallereau's remark that Solzhenitsyn was a man of reason, a man of science, who also recognized the limits of reason, who also had a rich appreciation of the hand of God in human affairs, who lived and died confident in the truth of Providence.

"Really Existing Socialism" and the Archival Revolution[*]

Wooden Words

It is often said that the "archival revolution" of the last twenty years—the publication of Soviet party, governmental, and secret police archives both in Russia and the West—has fundamentally transformed our understanding of what the Soviets used to call "really existing socialism." The volumes in the Yale University Press "Annals of Communism" series (twenty-seven in all) give ample support to this thesis. That series includes indispensable volumes of Lenin's secret writings, along with the key documentation surrounding the Katyn Forest massacre of 1940 (in which over 20,000 Polish nationals were murdered on the order of Stalin and the Soviet politburo), and the Great Terror, which refers to Stalin's purge trials of the 1930s and the wider terror that accompanied it, and the war against the independent peasantry, which includes the collectivization and forced famines of the early 1930s.

Other volumes include the correspondence between Stalin and his deputy Vyaschestav Molotov, documentation on popular resistance to the Communist authorities during the post-Stalinist period, and a heart-rending volume on "children of the Gulag," as well as Anne Applebaum's deftly edited volume of classic *Gulag Voices: An Anthology* (Yale University Press, 2010). We

[*] This essay originally appeared in *Academic Questions* (Summer 2012), pp. 308–13. It is reprinted with the permission of Springer Science & Business Media.

see things from the Communist regime's point of view, a perspective that was just as ideologically driven as anti-Communists in the West always presumed. Even behind closed doors, the Soviet authorities spoke the *langue du bois*, the wooden language of ideology.

Red Holocaust

It is also generally assumed that the official documentation—the self-reporting of the Communist regime, so to speak—provides the key to understanding the number of people incarcerated as well as the number of victims of political repression in the Soviet Union between 1917 and 1953, when Stalin died. But there are reasons for caution. As the longtime president of Russia's Presidential Commission for the Rehabilitation of Victims of Political Repression Alexander N. Yakovlev argued in his authoritative *A Century of Violence in Soviet Russia* (Yale University Press, 2002), the self-reporting of active participants in the repression leaves out the victims of Leninist repression ("whom nobody counted") and generally downplays the numbers of those arrested or killed during collectivization and the famines that followed, as well as those whose arrests or deaths were not recorded by the Soviet regime even after Lenin's death in 1924.

Yakovlev's argument is supported by the painstaking research of Steven Rosefielde in *Red Holocaust* (Routledge, 2010). With the help of Soviet census data, Rosefielde, a distinguished authority in Soviet/Russian studies and comparative economic systems, highlights the "incompleteness of NKVD archival data on executions and excess mortality in Gulag camps, colonies and prisons." Rosefielde's book is particularly useful in pointing out the "ambiguities" that "remain regarding the incidence and scale" of what he calls Stalin's "Red Holocaust." Despite the limits of the archival data, Rosefielde concludes that the "archival revolution," read in light of the census data, supports a figure of at least twenty million people killed as a result of Soviet policy from 1929 through 1953.

Black Book

The best use of archival material I have come across is the work of Nicholas Werth, the distinguished French historian and Sovietologist who authored the definitive account of Soviet repression, "A State against Its People: Violence, Repression, and Terror in the Soviet Union," in *The Black Book of Communism: Crimes, Terror, and Repression* (Laffont 1997; Harvard University Press, 1999). *The Black Book* is the first comprehensive attempt to catalog and analyze the crimes of Communism in every country around the world. Werth pays attention to high politics and social history, to the ideological sources of Communist violence and mendacity, and to the specific social and political context that gave rise to Leninist-Stalinist repression. He explodes once and for all the myth that Lenin's rule was somehow more humane than Stalin's and that the heir betrayed the humanist goals of the founder.

Werth shows the links between Lenin's War Communism—the initial Soviet effort to eliminate private property and market exchange—and the more systematic assault on the independent Russian and Ukrainian peasantry that unfolded after 1929, as well as the roots of the Great Terror of the 1930s in that same assault. He does not hesitate to speak of a "war" conducted by the Soviet leaders against their own people, a war deeply rooted in the Communist project itself. His statistics are uniformly conservative, rooted in available archival material, and they thus almost certainly underestimate the extent of the violence that unfolded after 1917. He nonetheless arrives at a figure of twenty million victims of Communism in the years between 1917 and Stalin's death in 1953. Unlike Rosefielde's, Werth's numbers rely exclusively on archival documentation.

Werth's methodological restraint makes his narrative all the more compelling, since he can in no way be accused of exaggeration or rhetorical overreach. Werth was also one of the editors of the *History of Stalin's Gulag* (Moscow: Rosspen, 2004), an authoritative seven-volume collection of documents that is unrivalled in any language. Robert Conquest and Aleksandr Solzhenitsyn lent their considerable authority to this project by writing introductions to the collection.

English-language readers should consult Werth's archive-based account of the 10,000 "enemies of the people," mainly inhabitants of Moscow and Leningrad, who were abandoned on the remote island of Nazino in the Ob river in western Siberia in 1933 without food or shelter. Nazino quickly became in the title of Werth's book, *Cannibal Island: Death in a Siberian Gulag* (Princeton University Press, 2007). Werth expertly shows how this episode was an extreme manifestation of the larger Soviet war against real or imagined "enemies of the people." "In Nazino, a modernizing utopia of purifying and civilizing social engineering under complete control caused a whole set of archaisms to rise to the surface. In this sense, this episode mirrored the Stalinist vision—and its reality—as a whole." Those archaisms included cannibalism brought about by an unprecedented form of state control and social engineering.

Gulag Memoirs

One can thus speak of the *bon usage* of the archives. The opposite of the good use of the archives might be called an archival fetishism that ignores other indispensable modes of learning about Soviet—and Communist—reality. Anne Applebaum generally assumes that the archives provide *the* key for understanding the number of victims of the Leninist-Stalinist regime. I have already suggested the unwarranted character of that presupposition. But in her "Introduction" to *Gulag Voices*, Applebaum makes the case for Gulag memoirs as indispensable works of literature and moral and historical testimony. They "cannot be relied on for names, dates, and statistics" but "they are an invaluable source of other kinds of information." The Soviet archives "tell only the dry, official version of events," while "the best Gulag memoirs continue to provide insights into human nature which are as fresh and relevant as on the day they were written."

Applebaum's fine volume, which includes distinguished memoirists such as Dmitry Likhachev, Alexander Dolgun, Nina Gagen-Torn, Gustave Herling, and Lev Kopelev needs to be supplemented by Paul Hollander's *From the Gulag to the Killing Fields* (ISI Books, 2006), a remarkably capacious and cross-cultural collection of "personal accounts of political violence and repression in Communist states." The memoirs from Eastern Europe, China, Vietnam, Cuba and North Korea supplement accounts from the Soviet Union and show that Communist regimes have the same repressive "genetic code," as the great historian of Russia Martin Malia liked to put it, in radically different cultural contexts.

Testaments to Violence and Lies

The Applebaum and Hollander volumes generally include well-known testimonies to Communist violence and repression. In contrast, the seven memoirs collected by Aleksandr Solzhenitsyn in *Voices from the Gulag*, introduced and translated by Kenneth Lantz (Northwestern University Press, 2010), give voice to lesser-known witnesses—including a circus performer, a teenage boy, and a Red Army soldier. These are precisely the kinds of testimonies that came Solzhenitsyn's way after the quasi-miraculous publication of *One Day in the Life of Ivan Denisovich* in the Soviet Union in November 1962. These testimonies are unadorned and lack the literary power of the better known writings of Likhachev, Shalamov, and Solzhenitsyn himself. But they are precious and poignant witnesses to the assault of a brutal ideological regime on the bodies and souls of human beings and thus welcome additions to the Gulag literature.

Solzhenitsyn argued that violence and lies were the twin pillars of ideological despotism. *The Gulag Archipelago*, now available in a 510-page abridgement for Russian high school students that was prepared and introduced by Solzhenitsyn's widow Natalia (Moscow: Proveschchenie, 2010), is, as we have shown throughout this work, the most powerful and profound discussion of the meeting point of ideologically inspired violence and the "Lie" that human beings and society can be radically transformed according to a preconceived plan.

Jean Crépu and Nicolas Miletitch are the creators of a riveting 2008 film, *L'histoire secrète de l'Archipel du Goulag*, widely show on European television, which tells the story of the secret writing, hiding, and dissemination of the great work that definitively transformed what human beings think of Communism and all its works. Nicolas Miletitch conducted the last interview with Solzhenitsyn in Moscow in December 2007, an interview that is interspersed throughout their film. The aging writer, physically frail and seemingly wasting away, speaks with verve and a sparkle in his eyes about a work that clandestinely unfolded over ten years between 1958 and 1968 and that was typed and sent to the West with the help of Solzhenitsyn's secret army of "invisible allies." Miletitch's interview with Solzhenitsyn could not be more moving. The full text of the interview can be found in *Le choc Soljenitsyne*, a special issue of the French quarterly *Histoire et Liberté* (Entretien avec Alexandre Soljenitsyne," no. 37, Winter 2008–2009).

History and the Totalitarian Temptation

The task of reflecting on Communism is finally a moral and philosophical one. Peter Baehr has provided the best book on the political philosopher par excellence of totalitarianism, Hannah Arendt. In *Hannah Arendt, Totalitarianism, and the Social Sciences* (Stanford University Press, 2010), Baehr engages Arendt and other great analysts and critics of totalitarianism such as Raymond Aron and Jules Monnerot. Baehr's is a first-rate work of intellectual history, showing how great minds came to terms with the defining deformation of the twentieth century long before there were any archives to draw upon. F. Flagg Taylor IV has edited *The Great Lie* (ISI Books, 2011) an excellent anthology of "classic and recent appraisals of ideology and totalitarianism." Aron, Arendt, Solzhenitsyn, Kolakowski, Miłosz, Havel, Alain Besançon, and a host of lesser-known figures from the East and West all make appearances in a work that aims to uncover the "moral destruction" that was coextensive with twentieth-century totalitarianism. The final section on "Lessons" reminds us that the ravages of Communism were tied to a broader crisis of civilization, one that survives the fall of Communism and that may well give life to new forms of the totalitarian temptation in the future. As Taylor's anthology makes clear, it is incumbent on every thoughtful human being and citizen to come to terms with the meaning of Soviet totalitarianism. We make a fatal mistake when we treat it as a distant episode in an alien civilization rather than a characteristically modern attempt to embody utopia-in-power.

Appendix 2
THE GIFT OF INCARNATION
NATALIA SOLZHENITSYN

INTRODUCTION

BY DANIEL J. MAHONEY*

Russia is no longer the Soviet Union, but it has a long way to go to free itself once and for all from the residues of its Communist past. If there was one book responsible for the delegitimization of the Soviet enterprise in the first place, it was Aleksandr Solzhenitsyn's *The Gulag Archipelago*. That work—well-described by the author's widow Natalia Solzhenitsyn as different parts historical inquest, personal reminiscence, political treatise, and philosophical meditation (without being reducible to any one of these genres)—is, in the end, an "epic poem" chronicling the evils of ideology and the prospects for good and evil within the human soul. It is a *cathartic* work that conveys not only "pain and anger, but an upsurge of strength and light." It is also the most powerful critique ever written of the ideological impulse to remake men and society at a stroke, and it will remain politically relevant as long as human beings are tempted, as perhaps they

* This Introduction originally appeared in *The New Criterion*, September 2012, p. 4.

always will be, to put utopian schemes above a concrete engagement with politics and the human soul. While never losing sight of the prospects for the "ascent of the human spirit," even under totalitarian despotism, it shows that the grim movement from "Lenin's degrees to Stalin's edicts" was "the inevitable outcome of the System itself," an inhuman byproduct of the ideological war on human nature. The book provides an eternal indictment of Communism and all its works, even if it is much more than that.

An updated edition of *The Gulag Archipelago* was published in Russia in 2007 in an edition that contained detailed information on the 256 men and women who had clandestinely provided Solzhenitsyn with precious eyewitness accounts of the Soviet system of repression. After Solzhenitsyn's death in August 2008, Natalia Solzhenitsyn, who had also served as his editor and intellectual and spiritual companion, prepared an abridgement of the work (totaling about one quarter of its original 1800 pages) for adoption in Russian high schools. That abridgement, published in October 2010, now joins other works of Solzhenitsyn, such as *Matryona's Home* and *One Day in the Life of Ivan Denisovich*, as required reading in Russian high schools. Mrs. Solzhenitsyn has provided an incisive, elegantly written introduction to that new edition that describes the genesis of the book (it was written in utmost secrecy, mainly during the winters of 1965 and 1966) as well as the highlights of the work as a whole. While primarily speaking to young Russians, she makes clear the universal significance of this work. Its publication in an abridged version for young Russians makes ignorance of the Soviet tragedy more difficult, and a repeat of the past all but impossible. As Mrs. Solzhenitsyn makes clear, Solzhenitsyn has written more than an historical and political indictment, even if *The Gulag Archipelago* is the greatest critique of a political regime ever written. His is "an experiment in literary investigation" that brings "the living *presence* of the truth" to bear on the worst events of the twentieth century. Only art can fully convey the truth of the soul and expose ideology as the chimera that it is.

THE GIFT OF INCARNATION
BY NATALIA SOLZHENITSYN*

A strange-looking manuscript turned up at the offices of the Moscow journal *Novy Mir* in the fall of 1961. It was a single-spaced text with no margins, typed on both sides of the paper, bearing an odd title—*Shch-854*[1]—and no indication of the real author's name.

The editor of the journal's prose section, Anna Berzer, was quick to grasp the significance of the unusual submission, and passed it on to *Novy Mir's* editor-in-chief, Aleksandr Tvardovsky, with the remark that it was about "a prison camp though the eyes of a peasant, a very national kind of work." In the admiring words of Solzhenitsyn,

> She couldn't have found the way to Tvardovsky's heart more effectively than she did with these few words.... The fate of the muzhik [peasant] Ivan Denisovich could not have been a matter of indifference to the superior muzhik Tvardovsky and the supreme muzhik Nikita Khrushchev.... As Tvardovsky later told the story, that night he took the manuscript with him as he went to bed. But after two or three pages he decided that it couldn't be read lying down. He got up and dressed. While his household slept, he read through the night, with breaks for tea in the kitchen, reading the story through to the end, then re-reading it once more.... So the night passed, followed by the early hours

---

*   Natalia Solzhenitsyn's essay appears in translation in unabridged form for the first time in this volume. An abridged version appeared in the September 2012 issue of *The New Criterion*, pp. 5–12.

1   This prisoner identification number was the original title of the manuscript that in its published form was titled *One Day in the Life of Ivan Denisovich*.

that peasants consider morning.... [But] Tvardovsky had no intention of going back to bed.... He was on the phone asking his staff to find out the identity and whereabouts of the author, and was particularly pleased to learn that it was not all a hoax devised by some well-known writer ... and that the author was neither a professional *littérateur*, nor a Muscovite.[2]

That night was the starting point of Tvardovsky's seemingly unattainable quest to have the story of Ivan Denisovich's day appear in his journal.

> To publish, to publish! There is no other goal. To overcome all odds, to go to the very top... To prove, to convince, to make objections impossible.... It's been said that Russian literature is dead. Baloney! Here it is, right in this folder with ribbon ties. But who is he? No one has yet seen him.[3]

"He" turned out to be a schoolteacher who had been teaching physics and astronomy in Ryazan over the preceding five years. Before that he had taught mathematics in a rural school in the Vladimir district. And before that he had been in exile in Kazakhstan. (The sentence of exile was meant to be "perpetual," but in 1956, Khrushchev's "thaw" had succeeded in melting this "permafrost.") But we must proceed systematically.

Aleksandr Solzhenitsyn was born in 1918 in Kislovodsk. His parents, both of whom were of peasant stock and were the first in their families to gain an education, were married in August 1917

---

2 Aleksandr Solzhenitsyn, *Bodalsia telenok s dubom: Ocherki literaturnoi zhizhni* (Moscow: Soglasie, 1996), pp. 25–26. Translations are mine except as indicated.

3 Tvardovsky's words according to Viktor Nekrasov. See *Kontinent*, No. 18 (1978), p. 4.

at the front, where the writer's father was a second lieutenant in an artillery brigade. In 1914 he had left Moscow University in order to enlist in the military in WWI, putting in three and a half years of service and returning to the Kuban region in early 1918. He died as a result of a hunting accident six months before the birth of his son. The writer's mother raised the boy by herself in hardscrabble circumstances, living in drafty tumble-down shacks that had to be heated with coal and needed water to be carried in by bucket.

Sanya, as the boy was called at home, read a great deal and, strange to say, at the age of eight or nine decided that he had to become a writer, though of course he had no real understanding of what this might entail. His childhood and youth were spent in Rostov-on-Don. Upon graduating from a local secondary school, he enrolled in Rostov University, majoring in mathematics and physics, combining this with a correspondence course in literature at Moscow's Institute of History, Philosophy, and Literature. The outbreak of the war with Nazi Germany found him in Moscow at the beginning of a summer session at this institute. Joining the military as a private, he completed a short-term course in artillery school in December 1942, was promoted to lieutenant and placed in command of a sound-ranging battery. He served first on the northwest front, then on the Bryansk front, receiving the Patriotic War medal after the battle of Kursk and the Red Star medal after the capture of Rogachyov in Belorussia. Solzhenitsyn's battery participated in front-line action throughout the war, and he remained in command until February 1945 when he, now a captain, was arrested for intercepted correspondence with a friend from his school years. In their letters, the two officers had criticized Stalin for "betraying the cause of the Revolution" as well as for his treachery and cruelty, calling him *Pakhan*, a head of a criminal organization. The retribution was swift. The twenty-six-year-old Solzhenitsyn was sentenced to eight years of forced-labor camp with "perpetual exile" to follow after the end of that term.

Imbued as he was with memories of his earlier youth, with images of the war, with the impressions made by what he heard from his wartime friends, by the cruel reality of prisons and camps, he began to write, or more exactly to compose in his head, without leaving a record on paper. In response to the question how he became a writer, Solzhenitsyn said that in a serious sense this did not take place until he found himself in prison.

> I had tried my hand at literary writing even before the war, and had made determined efforts of this kind while I was a university student, but this could hardly be called serious writing because I lacked life experience. I began to write in earnest in prison, doing it in a conspiratorial fashion, concealing the very fact that I was writing—this was absolutely crucial. My method involved remembering the texts composed and learning them by heart. I started doing this with verse, then with prose as well.[4]

Solzhenitsyn spent part of his sentence in a so-called "sharashka," a prison research institute where prisoners with specialized training were put to work on projects bearing on radio and telephone communications. This experience gave birth to the novel *In the First Circle*.

From 1950 to 1953 Solzhenitsyn was imprisoned in the forced-labor camp of Ekibastuz in Kazakhstan. Prisoners here were stripped of their names and were addressed by the identifying number inscribed on patches sewn to their caps, chest, back, and knee. The writer was assigned to a masonry brigade, then to a foundry, and this is the camp described in *One Day in the Life of Ivan Denisovich*. Solzhenitsyn has recalled that

> On one long winter workday in camp, as I was lugging a handbarrow together with another man, I asked myself how one might portray the totality of our camp existence. In essence it should suffice to give a thorough

---

4 Aleksandr Solzhenitsyn, *Publitsistika*, 3 vols. (Iaroslavl: Verkhne–Volzhskoe kn. izd., 1995–1997), II, p. 417.

description of a single day, providing minute details and focusing on the most ordinary kind of worker; that would reflect the entirety of our experience. It wouldn't even be necessary to give examples of any particular horrors. It shouldn't be an extraordinary day at all, but rather a completely unremarkable one, the kind of day that will add up to years. That was my conception and it lay dormant in my mind for nine years.[5]

In 1952, a year before the formal end of Solzhenitsyn's labor camp sentence, he developed a cancerous tumor that was surgically removed in the camp's clinic, but the cancer had had time to spread. Exiled to the settlement of Kok-Terek (Dzhambul oblast) after his release from camp, Solzhenitsyn taught mathematics, physics, and astronomy in a local secondary school. And wrote. But the cancer continued spreading and Solzhenitsyn, now racked by pain, managed to obtain permission from the authorities to travel to the oncological clinic in Tashkent, where he arrived "virtually a dead man" as he later said. Despite a prognosis offering no hope of survival, he was restored to life with the help of massive doses of radiation therapy. (This experience of dying and recovery found later reflection in *The Cancer Ward*.) The treatment lasted several months and Solzhenitsyn came to look upon his well-nigh miraculous return to health as a "postponement" granted from on high.

In May 1959, when Solzhenitsyn was living in Ryazan, he finally sat down to write *Shch-854* (*One Day in the Life of Ivan Denisovich*). He wrote it and put it away. He risked offering it for publication only some two years later, after Khrushchev's vociferous attack on Stalin's "cult of personality" at the Twenty-Second Party Congress.[6] And Tvardovsky, once he had joined battle for

5 *Publitsistika*, III, p. 21.
6 The Twenty-Second Congress of the Soviet Communist Party took place in October 1961 and featured Nikita Khrushchev's second offi-

One Day, began gathering appraisals of the work from the most authoritative writers of the day, in order to pass their testimonials to the powers-that-be. Kornei Chukovsky titled his review "A Literary Miracle" and wrote that

> Shukov exemplifies the character traits of a simple Russian man: he is steadfast, resistant to evil, hardy, cunning but kind, and a jack-of-all-trades to boot.... This story marks the entry of a powerful, original, and mature new writer into our literature.... I shudder to think that such a wonderful tale might remain unpublished.[7]

And Samuil Marshak added this to his review: "Judged by the criteria of clarity and courage, the author can perhaps be compared to Archpriest Avvakum.... In his work the Russian people themselves have begun to speak."[8] Asked her opinion of the manuscript, Anna Akhmatova responded by emphasizing each syllable of her verdict: "Every single citizen of the two hundred million inhabitants of the Soviet Union has the duty to read this text and commit it to memory!"[9]

And so, a year after the uncivilized-looking typescript had turned up at *Novy Mir* and after eleven months of Tvardovsky's efforts, maneuvers, and alternating periods of hope and dejection, the story appeared in the November 1962 issue of the journal, which then had a circulation of a little over 100,000. It was

cial denunciation of the Stalinist legacy. (The first one had taken place at the Twentieth Party Congress in 1956.)

7 Chukovsky's appraisal is reproduced in full in Lidiia Chukovskaia, *Zapiski ob Anne Akhmatovoi*, vol. 2 (Paris: YMCA Press, 1980), pp. 608–9.

8 Marshak's review appeared in *Pravda* on January 30, 1964. The additional phrase is recorded in Vladimir Lakshin's memoirs, *Golosa i litsa* (Moscow: Geleos, 2004), p. 213.

9 This was Akhmatova's spoken response to Lidiia Chukovskaia's question. See *Zapiski ob Anne Akhmatovoi*, vol. 2, p. 431.

a miracle. As Solzhenitsyn put it in an interview twenty years after *One Day's* appearance in print, "the 1962 publication of my tale in the Soviet Union is akin to a phenomenon defying physical laws, something like objects falling upwards of their own accord or cold stones becoming red hot without any external stimulus."[10]

Novy Mir was inundated with phone calls that November. Readers were expressing gratitude or just weeping; some were trying to contact the author. Libraries were forced to institute sign-up lists, and Moscow's newspaper and magazine kiosks were mobbed. Memories of this phenomenon are still vivid, as the recollections of Academician Sergei Averintsev testify:

> The unforgettable appearance of that eleventh issue of *Novy Mir* for 1962 had the effect of a jolt delivered to our disheartened generation: wake up and look around—history has not yet come to a halt! Just walking through Moscow at the time was exciting, there were crowds of people at every newspaper kiosk, all asking for the same sold-out journal. I'll never forget a man who was unable to recall the journal's name and was asking for "the one, you know, the one where the whole truth is printed." And the saleslady understood what he meant—this had to be seen to be believed. It was no longer the history of literature, but the history of Russia.[11]

In that same November, Varlam Shalamov wrote Solzhenitsyn a letter that begins as follows:

> I have not slept for two nights; I kept reading and rereading your tale, and recalling the past.... Your tale is like a poem, everything in it is perfect, all its parts serve

10 *Publitsistika*, III, p. 25.
11 *Novy mir*, 1998, No. 12, p. 3.

the same goal. Every line, every episode, every character sketch is so laconic, so intelligent, so subtle, and so profound that in my opinion *Novy Mir* has not published anything as organically coherent and as powerful in the course of its entire existence as a journal.[12]

Khrushchev's "thaw" proved to be short-lived, however, and by the second half of the 1960s libraries were withdrawing their copies of *One Day* from circulation in accordance with secret instructions, and soon enough (January 1974) the Central Administration for the Protection of State Secrets in the Press issued an administrative order banning all works by Solzhenitsyn published in the Soviet Union. But by then *One Day* had of course been read by millions of our countrymen and had been published in dozens of languages all over the world.

What mattered above all was that the publication of *One Day* seemed to have broken a dam. The writer was stunned by the response.

> There were letters to me, hundreds of them! Endless packets of letters were being forwarded by *Novy Mir*, others were brought in daily by the Ryazan postal service-some of them had been sent simply to "Ryazan" with no indication of the street address.... It was an explosion of letters from the whole of Russia, one that could not possibly be contained in any single breast. It provided a vantage point for an overview of zek lives, a subject previously quite beyond reach. Biographies, events, and episodes kept unfolding before me one after the other.[13]

Given these circumstances, it is hardly surprising that

12 Varlam Shalamov, *Sobranie sochinenii*, 4 vols. (Moscow: Khudozhestvennaia literatura, Vagrius, 1998), IV, p. 434.
13 An unpublished piece from Solzhenitsyn's private archive.

Solzhenitsyn came to look upon the writing of *The Gulag Archipelago* as an ineluctable moral duty, and went on to become the acknowledged chronicler of a nation's misfortune.

But it was difficult to hit upon a method of shaping the huge mass of material that kept arriving in unplanned, unpredictable, and disorganized fashion. Every bit of information that had managed to survive needed to be accepted, and a way had to be found to determine the appropriate place for each episode.

> At one point in camp I had the job of breaking up cast iron, shattering heavy cast iron objects into smaller pieces that were then thrown into the smelter, producing iron objects with different properties. I jokingly refer to my materials as lumps of cast iron of a particularly valuable kind. Melting them down permitted them to reappear in a new form.[14]

The task then was to choose the form or mold into which this molten material would be "poured." Solzhenitsyn was a principled opponent of inventing literary structures for the sake of novelty alone. He believed that the appropriate form, compactness, and texture of a particular work would be suggested by the constituent material itself if one makes a determined effort to attune one's ear to its essence. That was exactly what happened in this case:

> I had never thought about the form that a "literary investigation" should take, but the material making up *The Gulag Archipelago* imposed it on me. A literary investigation involves the use of factual (non-transfigured) life data in such a way that discrete facts and fragments *connected to each other by the aesthetic means at the disposal of a writer* coalesce in presenting a case that

14 *Publitsistika*, II, p. 420.

is no less convincing than a scholarly investigation of the traditional type.[15]

But it was quite impossible to work on this explosive material in an open and orderly fashion. The very fact that work on a book of this type was in progress had to be concealed, and the writer never had all the materials he had collected on his worktable at the same time. Most of *Gulag* was written in the winters of 1965–1966 and 1966–1967 in a secret location Solzhenitsyn called his Hiding Place. He could identify this site without endangering faithful friends only in 1991, a quarter of a century later: it was a farmhouse near Tartu, Estonia, a roomy cottage with large windows and a supply of firewood that stood empty in the winter.

> I arrived in my beloved Tartu on a snowy and frost-covered morning when the medieval features of the university town were particularly prominent, and the whole city seemed to be a part of Europe, entirely beyond Soviet borders.... For the first time in my life I felt as if I were safely abroad, as though I had left the USSR and broken away from the accursed surveillance of the KGB. This feeling calmed me and helped me begin my work.[16]

In the first of these two winters the writer spent sixty-five days in the Hiding Place; in the following year he stayed for eighty-one days. The hundreds of preparatory fragments were here transformed into a fiery text, a typescript of more than one thousand pages.

> During those 146 days at the Hiding Place, I worked as I never have worked in my whole life. It even seemed as if it was no longer I who was writing; rather I was

15 *Publitsistika*, II, p. 422.
16 *Bodalsia telenok s dubom*, pp. 433–34.

swept along, my hand was being moved by an outside force and I was only the firing pin attached to a spring that had been compressed for half a century and was now uncoiling.... During the second winter, when the temperature outside dipped to thirty below, I caught a bad cold, with chills and gnawing body aches. But even though I ran a fever, I continued to split logs for firewood, stoke up the stove, and do part of my writing standing up (with my back pressed to the hot mirror-like tiles of the stove in lieu of mustard plasters), while the rest of the time I wrote lying in bed under a blanket. In this way I produced the only humorous chapter ("The Zeks as a Nation").... I allowed myself no links with the outside world ... what was happening out there could in no way concern me: I had merged with my cherished material, and my single goal was that this union should give birth to *The Gulag Archipelago*.... I was even prepared to accept death if need be upon my return to the outside world. Those weeks represent the highest point in my sense of victory and my sense of estrangement from the world.[17]

After another year of making additions and emendations to the text of *Gulag*, in May of 1968 the writer met with three assistants to edit and type out the final copy in a small summer cottage near Moscow. (There were no neighbors to hear the clatter of typewriters.) Here is how Solzhenitsyn recalled it:

The editing and typing of *Gulag* went on from dawn to nightfall.... On top of everything a typewriter started breaking down daily and I would either solder it myself or take it to be repaired. The most frightening part of the whole undertaking was that we had the only authoritative text as well as all the typed copies of *Gulag* there

17 *Bodalsia telenok s dubom*, pp. 435–36.

with us. If the KGB had suddenly swooped down, the many-throated groan, the dying whisper of millions, the never-expressed testaments of those who had perished would all be in their hands, and I would never be able to reconstruct it all.... They had been so lucky for so many decades-surely God would not let them succeed once again? Was justice never to be done in the Russian land?[18]

But finally the work was completed, the text was photographed, and the rolled-up film was inserted into a capsule. It would be easier to preserve that way, and—at some appropriate future time—to send it to an inaccessible and safe place. But on that same day we received the news that a chance of sending it abroad would present itself within days!

We had just sat back contentedly because we had polished off the job when a bell started pealing! On that very day and almost at the same hour! No human planning could have brought these events so close together. It was the bell of fate and history, pealing deafeningly— though as yet no one could hear it in the tender green woods of June.[19]

Alexander Andreyev, a resident of Paris and a grandson of the writer Leonid Andreev,[20] had come to Moscow with a UNESCO delegation for a weeklong visit, and Solzhenitsyn's friends knew the whole family well. Could he be approached? And would he agree? If the film were discovered at customs control, the book would perish, together with the author and Andreyev as well. But then, would another opportunity of this kind ever present itself? "On the plus side was the fact that these people were completely

18 *Bodalsia telenok s dubom*, p. 207.
19 *Bodalsia telenok s dubom*, p. 212.
20 Russian prose writer and playwright, 1871–1919.

untainted. They had no mercenary motives and their love for Russia was unfeigned."[21] How good it would have been to take a breather at this point, but duty to those who had perished left no room for relaxation. It was decided to go ahead with the attempt. "The heart had emerged from one anxiety only to plunge into another. No rest for the weary."[22] A gloomy and tension-filled week passed before they learned that the operation had been successful. Solzhenitsyn was jubilant:

> Freedom! Relief from pressure! The whole world was now mine to embrace. Who says that I am shackled hand and foot? That I am constrained in my writing? On the contrary, whichever way I turn, roads open up before me! Everything that has been weighing me down for years has been cast off, a gate has been flung open giving unimpeded access to the most important thing in my life—*The Red Wheel*.[23]

In October 1970 a radio broadcast from Stockholm brought explosive news—Solzhenitsyn had been awarded the Nobel Prize in literature *for the ethical force with which he has pursued the indispensable traditions of Russian Literature* (to quote the citation). "The Nobel prize tumbled on my head like a merry load of snow falling off a branch," was how Solzhenitsyn remembered it.[24] But one might wonder at the "merriness" here: it had now been five years that the writer's name had been banned from public mention, his personal papers had been impounded, not a single line of his writings could be published in the USSR. After *One Day*, only four of his stories had appeared in the Soviet press, while *In the First Circle*, *Cancer Ward*, the plays, and even the

21 *Bodalsia telenok s dubom*, p. 498.
22 *Bodalsia telenok s dubom*, p. 212.
23 *Bodalsia telenok s dubom*, p. 213.
24 *Bodalsia telenok s dubom*, p. 277.

poems in prose had all been confronted with an impenetrable wall blocking publication, even though the samizdat network had gratefully absorbed them all. And a year earlier Solzhenitsyn had been expelled from the Writer's Union. Yet despite all this, Solzhenitsyn felt exhilaration—he was on the point of finishing *August 1914*, the first "knot" of his long-cherished epic about the Russian Revolution.[25] He decided against going to Stockholm to claim the Nobel Prize, fearing that his return to Russia would be barred.

The writer viewed the fact that the Prize had in effect been awarded too soon as a piece of luck.

> I had received it without showing the world much of my writing, there were just *One Day*, *Cancer Ward* and the "lightened" version of *In the First Circle*. All the rest I had kept in reserve. Given my newly elevated position, I could now roll out book after book, as it were helped by gravity.... But my conscience ached badly concerning *Gulag*. I had earlier planned to publish it at Christmas 1971. But that date had come and gone.... I now had the Nobel, but why was I deferring the publication still more? My reasons could not have appeared viable to those who had been tipped off a sled into camp burial pits like a load of frozen logs. Could it still be untimely in 1971 to speak of what had happened in 1918, in 1930, in 1945? Was it still too soon to redeem their deaths by at least telling their stories?[26]

But then the Archipelago is merely the heir and child of the Revolution. And concerning the latter, we have even greater

25 The first edition of *August 1914* came out in Paris in 1971. A much-expanded second edition appeared in Vermont in 1983, and the revised third and final edition was published in Moscow in 2006.
26 *Bodalsia telenok s dubom*, p. 287. The Christmas mentioned here refers to the date according to the Julian calendar, i.e., to January 7, 1971.

distortions, lies, and cover-ups. Future generations would have even greater difficulty digging up the truth. To reveal the existence of *Gulag* is to put one's head on the executioner's block; this is a book the regime won't wink at. The author will pay for it, and there will be severe trouble for the *zek* witnesses as well. *After* the appearance of *Gulag*, the regime will certainly cut short all work on the epic of the Russian revolution, and that means only one thing: maximum efforts must be expended to complete as much as possible of the epic *before* that time.

> In the peaceful literary life of peaceful countries, the order of publication of an author's works is determined by his maturity and by the works' readiness for publication. But in our country this is not a literary problem at all; it becomes a case of tension-filled strategic planning. Books are seen as divisions or army corps: at times they must dig in, hold their fire and keep their heads down; at other times they must wait for darkness to cross bridges in total silence; at still other times, they must hide their preparations to the last possible minute so as to launch an attack from an unexpected direction and at an unexpected moment. In this scheme, the author becomes an army commander, moving some units up to the front, withdrawing others to a waiting area.[27]

In accord with that idea, Solzhenitsyn immersed himself in work on *November 1916*, all the while collecting materials for subsequent knots. He traveled to the Tambov area, looking for the thoroughly suppressed traces of the Antonov uprising.[28] *The Gulag Archipelago*, he now decided with finality, would appear in May 1975.

27 *Bodalsia telenok s dubom*, p. 288.
28 Large anti-Bolshevik peasant revolt, 1920–1921, led by Aleksandr Antonov. Solzhenitsyn originally planned to dedicate a "knot" in *The Red Wheel* epic to this phase of the Russian Civil War.

But events were fated to take a different course. In August 1973, after lengthy surveillance of one of Solzhenitsyn's assistants, a sequence of tragic circumstances led to the KGB's discovery and seizure of a draft typescript version of *Gulag*. The writer learned of this accidentally due to a fantastic instance of the "grapevine effect" that our huge cities sometimes demonstrate, and he immediately (on September 5) sent instructions to Paris to start the process of printing *Gulag*. The following text appeared on the very first page of the book:

> For years I have with reluctant heart withheld from publication this already completed book: my obligation to those still living outweighed my obligation to the dead. But now that State Security has seized the book anyway, I have no alternative but to publish it immediately.[29]

The book was typeset and printed in total secrecy by YMCA Press in Paris, the oldest Russian émigré publishing house, and on December 28, 1973, news agencies of the world announced that the first volume of *Gulag* had appeared in France. The first reaction of the powers-that-be in the Soviet Union was stunned silence, explainable in part by the New Year's holiday, but by the middle of January a noisy campaign of vilification had been set in motion in the media, with daily increases in the degree of "popular anger." Responses from Europe were not slow in coming as well: "A flaming question mark over the entire Soviet experiment from 1918 on." "At some future moment, perhaps, we shall look upon the appearance of *Gulag* as the sign marking the beginning of the collapse of the communist system." "Solzhenitsyn calls for repentance. This work could become a guidebook of national rebirth if only the Kremlin were capable of reading it."

29 "Author's Note" in Aleksandr I. Solzhenitsyn, *The Gulag Archipelago* 1917–1956: *An Experiment in Literary Investigation* [vol. 1], tr. Thomas P. Whitney (New York: Harper & Row), p. vi.

The abusive media campaign drew responses too: "Armed rebels can be suppressed by tanks, but how does one suppress a book?" "Death, Siberia, or psychiatric prison would only confirm just how right Solzhenitsyn is."

Western journalists in Moscow were eager to interview him. "In your opinion, what actions will the regime take against you?" His response:

> I have no way of predicting.... I have fulfilled my obligation to those who have perished, and that takes a heavy load off my mind and brings me calm. The truth revealed in *Gulag* was supposed to be utterly destroyed; it had been beaten down, drowned, set on fire, ground to a powder. But here it is, whole and alive, published in black and white, and no one can ever erase it again.[30]

Solzhenitsyn announced that he would not collect any royalties from the sale of *Gulag*; all proceeds would go toward the memorialization of those who perished and to help the families of political prisoners in the Soviet Union.

The regime was meanwhile frantically searching for a means of ridding itself of Solzhenitsyn. It did not dare to crush him in sight of a world that was already reading *Gulag*, and on February 12, 1974 he was arrested, taken to Lefortovo prison, and charged with "treason to the fatherland." On the next day he was officially informed that he was being stripped of Soviet citizenship, taken under guard to the airport, and expelled from the country.

So what kind of book is *The Gulag Archipelago*? What was the result of melting down those heavy cast-iron fragments?

"The Archipelago Rises from the Sea" is the title of a chapter about the legendary Solovki camp of the early Soviet period.[31] What are the contours of this risen Archipelago?

30 *Publitsistika*, II, p. 66.
31 Part III, ch. 2.

We follow the author as he steps into a vessel that will take us from island to island, at times squeezing through narrow passages, at times sailing rapidly down straight canals, at times battling the waves of the open sea. The force of his art is such that we are soon transformed from observers into participants of the journey: we shudder at the hiss of "You're under arrest!" we agonize throughout our first sleepless night in a prison cell, we are marched with rapidly beating hearts to our first interrogation, we flounder helplessly in the meat-grinder that is the investigation process, we steal a peek at the neighboring death-row cells, and, after the farce of a "trial" or even without it, we are cast out onto the islands of the Archipelago.

Or else we spend days on end in an overcrowded boxcar converted for transporting prisoners, tormented by thirst; we are robbed by professional criminals on transfer points; we freeze in the camps of Siberia or Kolyma performing "general duties" in our emaciated state. If we have strength enough, we look around us and listen to the stories of peasants and priests, intellectuals and factory workers, former Party functionaries and military men, informers and trusties, common criminals and juveniles, representatives of every religion and every nationality in the USSR. We also see the camp administration, the guards, "the kids with tommy-guns,"[32] and the special-regime camps for political prisoners with columns of *zeks* marching with their prisoner numbers on rags affixed to their clothes, surrounded by German shepherds straining on their leashes. We ourselves shall perhaps never risk trying to escape, but we experience passion, hope, and despair as we follow the attempts of those who have dared to do so. When the time comes for prisoner uprisings, we are convinced that we would have been with everyone when "behind the wire the ground is burning."[33] Those of us who survive camp are subject to exile, a fate that can be even more

32 Chapter heading, Part V, ch. 9.
33 Chapter heading, Part V, ch. 10. This chapter describes the atmosphere leading up to camp revolts.

difficult to bear than camp. Here we discover to our astonishment that millions of our compatriots had been uprooted from their places of habitation: the "peasant plague"[34] had destroyed the best, hardest-working independent peasants together with their families. Every twitch of the party line due to internal struggles resulted in the deportation of hundreds of thousands of entirely innocent towns-people, while during and after WWII entire ethnic groups were exiled.

But above and beyond this gigantic canvas, illustrated as it is with hundreds of concrete human destinies, Solzhenitsyn brings to light the history of our waves and streams of arrests—what he calls "the history of our sewage disposal system"[35]—tracing its evolution from Lenin's decrees to Stalin's edicts, and demonstrating with grim clarity that the accursed Archipelago was not at all produced by some sequence of errors or "violations of legality," but was the inevitable outcome of the System itself, because without its inhuman cruelty it would not have been able to hold on to power.

But if the above features summed up all that is significant about *The Gulag Archipelago*, the book would share the fate of historical treatises that become sources of information about past epochs or, at best, monuments to them. The three volumes of *The Gulag Archipelago*, however, "cannot be approached *just* as a work of literature, even though they are literature, and very great literature indeed.... The work is in a genre that is absolutely *sui generis*, without precise precedent in either Russian or Western literature," as one of the early critical comments puts it.[36] But what is it? An historical inquest? Personal reminiscences? A political treatise? A philosophical meditation? No, it is more like an amalgam combining each of these genres, with the resultant product being more significant than the sum of its constituent parts.

34 Chapter heading, Part VI, ch. 2.
35 Chapter heading, Part I, ch. 2.
36 Martin Malia, "A War on Two Fronts: Solzhenitsyn and the Gulag Archipelago," *Russian Review*, vol. 36, No. 1 (1977), p. 50.

Closest to the mark are those who have called *The Gulag Archipelago* an epic poem. What is the poem about? Solzhenitsyn has provided an answer:

> Let the reader who expects this book to be a political exposé slam it shut right now. If only it were so simple! If only it were true that there exist evil people insidiously committing evil deeds, whom it is necessary simply to separate out and destroy. But the line dividing good from evil cuts through the heart of every human being.... This line is not static within us; it sways to and fro over the years. Even in a heart imbued with evil, it allows a small bridgehead of good to remain. And it permits a small niche of evil to survive even in the kindest of hearts.[37]

The book is about the ascent of the human spirit, about its struggle with evil. That is the reason why, when readers reach the end of the work, they feel not only pain and anger, but an upsurge of strength and light.

Here is what a Western critic wrote about the publication of *The Gulag Archipelago*:

> [The book] is extraordinary in still another respect. *Gulag* has become an instant multinational and multilingual best-seller, with total sales running into the millions of copies—a record approached by no other writer, living or dead, in any language—and yet it never has been published in the author's native land.[38]

Gulag was translated into dozens of languages, published and

37 *The Gulag Archipelago*, Part I, ch. 4, and Part IV, ch. 1. (Cf. vol. 1, p. 168, and vol. 2, p. 615, in the English translation).
38 Martin Malia, "A War on Two Fronts," pp. 46–47.

republished numerous times, discussed in hundreds of articles, but just reading faint copies of the text in the USSR could land you in jail. Yet despite this risk, brave souls persisted in making more and more copies, using typewriters or photographic paper. One such person managed to make illicit Xerox copies of the Paris edition while a second made use of his carpentry shop to cut the pages to size and bind them together. One of the custom-made books produced in this manner was delivered to the author with the following note:

> I'm delighted to present to you the local publication of the Book. The print run will be 1200 copies, with 200 produced in the first printing. I firmly believe that God will not permit this undertaking to be cut short. The edition is intended less for Moscow snobs than for the provinces. We have already taken into consideration Yakutsk, Khabarovsk, Novosibirsk, Krasnoyarsk, Sverdlovsk, Saratov, Krasnodar, Tver and some smaller cities...[39]

As Solzhenitsyn has written, it was an extraordinary experience to receive this book when he was already abroad. It was, he said,

> an amazing publication, with deadly danger for its publishers. This is how Russian young men are ready to sacrifice themselves to assure the movement of *Gulag* into the depths of Russia. Just imagining it brings tears to my eyes...[40]

Sixteen years passed. Our country has changed. *The Gulag Archipelago* has been published in Russia. The charges of treason against the author have been withdrawn and he was able to return to the country of his birth. Much, though not everything, has been declassified. The words of Anne Applebaum, who spent many

39 *Bodalsia telenok s dubom*, p. 527.
40 *Ibid.*

months pursuing research in Russian archives are significant in this connection. Re-examining *The Gulag Archipelago* more than fifteen years after the Soviet Union collapsed and the files of the Soviet past were opened, Applebaum notes that various errors in Solzhenitsyn's work have come to light. "Nevertheless," she continues, "what is most extraordinary about re-reading *The Gulag Archipelago* ... is how much he does get right [given that] he did not have access to archival documents and government records. Solzhenitsyn's general outline of the history of the Gulag ... has been proven correct. His description of the moral issues faced by the prisoners has never been disputed. His sociology of camp life ... is unquestionably accurate. [The work's] truthfulness continues to give the book a freshness and an importance that will never be challenged."[41]

And yet, as Father Alexander Schmemann has written,

> what must be borne in mind is that however truthful and objective an "investigation"—any investigation— might be, none is capable of becoming a *living presence* of the truth if it lacks the power of incarnation. The whole point is that the gift of transfiguration and incarnation is granted only to a writer—indeed that is his calling, his purpose and his manner of serving humanity. It is in the process of transformation and incarnation, as the text fills out with flesh and blood, with new life and strength, that "art" takes up residence.[42]

Could the melancholy prophecy made by Lidiia Chukovskaia in a letter to Solzhenitsyn, written after she had read *The Gulag Archipelago*, come to pass?

41 Anne Applebaum, "Foreword" in Aleksandr I. Solzhenitsyn, *The Gulag Archipelago 1917–1956: An Experiment in Literary Investigation*, 3 vols. (New York: Harper Perennial, 2007–2009), p. xv. This foreword is included in each of the three volumes. Anne Applebaum is the Pulitzer Prize-winning author of *Gulag: A History* (2003).

42 *Vestnik RSKhD*, No. 108–110 (1973–1974), pp. 172–73.

[The book] is a miracle that resurrects the dead, that alters the very composition of one's blood, and creates new souls. But there is a problem: you have lived long enough to experience everything—war, prison, special-regime camps, fame, love, hate, and exile. There is only one thing you will not live long enough to experience: literary analysis. Delight and indignation are both obstacles to an evaluation of literary genius and to the understanding of its essence.... When will a critic be born who will be capable of explaining Solzhenitsyn's phrase, Solzhenitsyn's paragraph, Solzhenitsyn's chapter? Dealing with issues of vocabulary is the easy part, but what about his syntax? Or the concealed rhythm of his prose, in the absence of any visible one? Or the richness of his word choices? Or the novelty of the way he develops a thought? Who could undertake such a task or even begin it? In order to analyze [a text] one must become accustomed to it and stop being burnt—whereas we are chained to issues of meaning and information, and are continually seared with pain...[43]

And perhaps Russia's fifth Nobel laureate in literature, Joseph Brodsky, had reason to be pessimistic:

If the Soviet regime did not have its Homer, it received him in the person of Solzhenitsyn.... Perhaps two thousand years from now a reading of *Gulag* will provide the same kind of pleasure as a reading of *The Iliad* provides today. But if *Gulag* were not to be read today, it is quite possible that much sooner than in two thousand years no one will be around to read either book.[44]

43 *Novy mir*, 2008, No. 9, p.105. Chukovskaia wrote this letter after reading volume 3 of *Gulag*.
44 *Literaturnoe obozrenie*, 1999, No. 1, p. 5. The published English version of Brodsky's review of *Gulag*, vol. 2, in *Partisan Review*,

During his exile years in Vermont, Solzhenitsyn received letters from American college teachers to the effect that their students could not cope with the three-volume length of *The Gulag Archipelago*, and that it would be a good idea to produce an abridged English-language edition. The author resisted the idea, but in the end Professor Edward Ericson succeeded in convincing him, and presented a plan for a one-volume version. Aleksandr Isayevich gave his consent with a sigh and said to me, "I suppose it can't be helped. If they can't get through three volumes, let's go ahead with this.[45] But when the time comes for a Russian publication, surely no abridgement will be needed."

But two decades later, in the last years of Aleksandr Isaevich's life, we came around to acknowledging that in Russia, too, contemporary life makes it impossible—at least for students in secondary school, if not university—to read the full three-volume *Gulag Archipelago*. With more than a touch of regret, Aleksandr Isaevich entrusted me with the task of putting together a single-volume edition for high school use. The goal differed from the one pursued by Professor Ericson in the same way that the collective memory and "genetic experience" (more so than knowledge) of Russian secondary school students differs from that of their American counterparts.

I set myself the goal of decreasing the length as much as possible while preserving the overall structure of the book, so as not to reduce the text to a collection of episodes and other fragments and allowing it to remain an uninterrupted voyage to the islands of the Archipelago. I wanted the author to remain the pilot guiding us along the unsurpassed trajectory he had so carefully thought out.

vol. 49, No. 4 (1977), is shorter and does not contain the quoted passage.

45 The abridged version edited by Edward Ericson was published in the U.S. in 1985, then in Great Britain and other European countries; it is widely used in the West by teachers and students. (*Natalia Solzhenitsyn's note.*)

In the text that follows, all sixty-four chapters of the full *Gulag Archipelago* have been preserved, albeit in abridged form. (Only three of them have been condensed radically to several sentences beyond the title.) Some explanatory footnotes have been added, the glossaries of prison terms and Soviet abbreviations have been expanded, and an index with notes on the most important names has been appended.

During the final phases of the project I benefited from the important corrections, advice and suggestions received from Solzhenitsyn's long-time friend and collaborator, Elena Chukovskaia, as well as from the high school teachers of literature T. Ia. Eremina, E. S. Abeliuk, and S. V. Volkov. Heartfelt thanks to them and to my sons, whose unflagging support has meant a great deal to me in the course of this important and complex task.

Translated by Alexis Klimoff

Index